The Wo

THE CALIFORNIA WORLD HISTORY LIBRARY

Edited by Edmund Burke III, Kenneth Pomeranz, and Patricia Seed

The World Hunt

An Environmental History
of the Commodification of Animals

John F. Richards

INTRODUCTION BY

J. R. McNeill

UNIVERSITY OF CALIFORNIA PRESS

Berkeley   Los Angeles   London

University of California Press, one of the most distinguished
university presses in the United States, enriches lives around the
world by advancing scholarship in the humanities, social sciences,
and natural sciences. Its activities are supported by the UC Press
Foundation and by philanthropic contributions from individuals
and institutions. For more information, visit www.ucpress.edu.

University of California Press
Berkeley and Los Angeles, California

University of California Press, Ltd.
London, England

Library of Congress Cataloging-in-Publication Data

Richards, John F.
    The world hunt : an environmental history of the
commodification of animals / John F. Richards ; contributions by John R. McNeill.
        pages   cm—(California world history library)
    Includes bibliographical references and index.
    ISBN 978-0-520-28253-7 (paperback)
    ISBN 978-0-520-95847-0 (ebook)
    1. Human ecology—History.   2. Nature—Effect of human
beings on—History.   3. Hunting.   4. Animal welfare.
5. Wildlife conservation.   6. Wildlife management.
I. Richards, John F. Unending frontier.   II. Title.
    GF13.R54   2014
    333.95'4—dc23

                                        2013048538

Manufactured in the United States of America

23   22   21   20   19   18   17   16   15   14
10   9   8   7   6   5   4   3   2   1

In keeping with a commitment to support environmentally
responsible and sustainable printing practices, UC Press has
printed this book on Natures Natural, a fiber that contains 30%
post-consumer waste and meets the minimum requirements of
ANSI/NISO z39.48–1992 (R 1997) (*Permanence of Paper*).

CONTENTS

MAPS AND TABLES

MAPS

TABLES

FOREWORD

Edmund Burke III

John F. Richards was a remarkable scholar of South Asia whose many books and articles have permanently shaped the South Asian field. But for much of his career he was also a world historian and an environmental historian, concerned initially with locating the history of pre-1750 India in a world-historical context. In his final book, *The Unending Frontier: An Environmental History of the Early Modern World* (Berkeley: University of California Press, 2003), he turned his historical global imagination loose. The result was a remarkable synthetic portrait of the environmental transformations of the (often forgotten) early modern period.

Originally published as part 4 of *The Unending Frontier, The World Hunt* is a work of major importance and of a stunning historical imagination. It is especially relevant to our time, as growing awareness of species extinctions and climate change rises to the fore. A major focus of this book is the commercial hunting of particular species (fur-bearing animals, fish, whales, and walruses are the ones that Richards examined). Through its bold willingness to go where few historians had dared to go, "The World Hunt" helped launch the field of environmental history into new areas. The growing bibliography of truly exciting historical works in the study of animals and their always problematic relations with humans is one testimony of the correctness of Richards's instincts.

The field of environmental history started with a close examination of the transformation of regional or even local ecosystems and ecologies at the hand of humans. Only recently has the "think local, act global" imperative at the heart of environmentalist thinking really begun to catch on. The reader of this book will discover just how far a commitment to studying the environment in a global context can take you. *The World Hunt* makes for both superlative world history and environmental history. Its vivid prose and well-chosen subjects lead the reader to discover alternative ways of examining the history of the early modern empires.

A final aspect of *The World Hunt* is its deep engagement with the history of climate, a subject scarcely in its infancy when Richards was writing. He was persuaded that the fate of species, if not of empires, was shaped not only by the onslaught of human avidity for furs, skins, protein, and other animal by-products but also by global shifts in climate. For the early modern period, this was the Little Ice Age (1300–1850), a phase of prolonged cooling of the global temperature. Richards was among the first to notice its shaping impact on the northern temperate zone around the globe (and not just on north-western Europe). Writing in the 1990s, before the emergence of the new historical work on the Little Ice Age, he was already able to see its importance for the rise and decline of species. Thus *The World Hunt* marks one of the first successful efforts to follow the interaction of humans and global climate change in shaping the fates of particular species.

The World Hunt distills the essence of all good world-historical writing: a compelling story, a global frame, and a strong sense of the importance of details. A stunning work of synthesis, it fills in the large blank of the commercial interactions of humans and selected species that form a backdrop to the world we inhabit today.

INTRODUCTION

J. R. McNeill

The World Hunt, by John F. Richards, is an extract from a 682-page book called *The Unending Frontier,* a study of world environmental history in the early modern centuries (c. 1500 to 1800). The text remains the same as that which the University of California Press published in 2003. In *The World Hunt,* Richards explores the environmental, economic, and social dimensions of commercial exploitation of fur-bearing animals, of deer, and of whales and walruses.

Commercial hunting, fishing, and whaling have long histories. Ancient Sumer had fish markets. Hunting to supply Roman circuses and gladiatorial combats with exotic animals was a thoroughly commercial business. But in the fifteenth century, when Richards begins his story, the scale, scope, and pace of commercial hunting, fishing, and whaling began to surge as never before. That surge has continued since that time, pausing only when populations of targeted species grew scarce or something went out of fashion. In the late nineteenth century, for example, the numbers of right whales dwindled to the point where chasing them no longer rewarded the effort. And beaver hats, de rigueur for European gentlemen in the seventeenth and eighteenth centuries, became quaint in the nineteenth, at the same time when beaver populations shrank. But by and large, the pressures of commercial hunting, fishing, and whaling continued to increase over the centuries.

Human impact on wildlife has been one of the central concerns of the scholarly field of environmental history since its inception in the 1970s. That impact, of course, comes in several forms, and habitat destruction has often been more important than commercial hunting. Much of the environmental history work on hunting concerns big-game and aristocratic hunting in nineteenth- and twentieth-century Africa and India, not the business-oriented hunting that Richards describes.[1] But the subject of commercial fishing and whaling continues to dominate the environmental history of the seas, and commercial hunting for elephant tusks or rhino horns remains on the agenda for environmental historians. So Richards's subject in *The World Hunt* continues to resonate within the community of environmental historians.

It resonates for environmentalism too. Despite efforts in recent decades by wildlife conservationists and fisheries management experts, some of the species that Richards wrote about are very scarce today. Most species of commercially hunted whales remain endangered. Walruses are officially a "candidate species," not quite endangered enough to be designated as such, but probably well on their way. Overfishing around the world, not least of the North Atlantic cod on which Richards focused, has in recent decades joined the list of environmentalist concerns. And Richards's interest in climate change, which shows up in passing several times in *The World Hunt* (and was a larger theme in *The Unending Frontier*), strikes another contemporary chord.

JOHN F. RICHARDS (1938–2007)

Professor John Folsom Richards was born and raised in Exeter, New Hampshire, and could play the flinty and gruff New Englander when he wanted to. He sometimes reveled in contrarian argument. Inside, however, he was a gentle and generous soul, with a heart as soft as a warm marshmallow. He spent much of his time helping and encouraging other scholars.

Richards was the eldest of three children. A studious sort, he graduated as valedictorian from the University of New Hampshire in 1961, whereupon he instantly married Ann Berry, now Ann Richards. They remained together until his death.

In 1963, Richards enrolled in the PhD program at the University of California at Berkeley, where he studied South Asian history. His dissertation, completed in 1970 under the direction of Thomas Metcalf, concerned Mughal administration in a region of southern India called Golconda. It became his first book.[2] Richards took a post at the University of Wisconsin in 1968, where he joined a group of historians interested in comparative and world history, and in 1977 moved to Duke University.

Richards remained a historian of Mughal India, one of the few people in North America able to navigate the difficult Persian-language sources essential for that sort of work. But he kept adding new interests as the years went

1. See, e.g., John Mckenzie, *The Empire of Nature: Hunting, Conservation, and British Imperialism* (Manchester: Manchester University Press, 1988); Julie Hughes, *Animal Kingdoms: Hunting, the Environment, and Power in the Indian Princely States* (Cambridge, MA: Harvard University Press, 2013).

2. John F. Richards, *Mughal Administration in Golconda* (Oxford: Clarendon Press, 1975).

by. He made important contributions in South Asian and world monetary history, in the global economic history of the early modern centuries, in the history of the opium trade, in South Asian land use and ecological history, and, as this book attests, in global environmental history.[3]

Richards was also something of an academic entrepreneur. He was active in professional associations and helped to create the American Institute for Afghanistan Studies. He was one of the three editors for the *Cambridge History of India*. And he secured sizable grants to fund a team project on land use change in South and Southeast Asia, which in the early 1980s brought him into contact with prominent ecologists working on the global carbon cycle—unusual terrain for a historian.

In 1977, Richards taught a required class for PhD students at Duke on historical methods. I took it and hated it. Students had to choose one of a handful of then-current historical methodologies and write a paper deploying it. I got last choice and wrote a psychohistory of Winston Churchill, full of unfounded speculation (loosely based on the theories of an Austrian psychoanalyst named Wilhelm Reich) about the meaning of Churchill's early childhood, his fondness for champagne and cigars, and so forth. I thought my paper was nonsense and resented the assignment. At the time, I thought learning about various forms of history that I would never practice was a waste of my time. Richards probably thought no better of psychohistory than I did but insisted the exercise was good for me.

I never took another class with him. But two or three years later, one Friday night, rather late, I encountered him in the stacks of the Duke library. I was surprised to see a tenured professor there at that hour and more surprised still to see a few books about colonial Cuba under his arm. He was pleased (and probably surprised) to learn that I was writing a dissertation much of which concerned eighteenth-century Cuba. I was able to suggest a few further works he might consult as he researched the environmental changes associated with the sugar plantation system in the Caribbean. We chatted for an hour or more, and my impression of Richards improved by the minute.

For me this proved a decisive encounter. Many months later, with a completed PhD and no job (other than roofing), I was rescued by Richards. He arranged a research position for me with his ecologist friends. I began to work in environmental history for the first time, writing brief accounts of

3. John F. Richards, ed., *Precious Metals in the Medieval and Early Modern World* (Durham, NC: Carolina Academic Press, 1983); Richards, *The Imperial Monetary System of Mughal India* (Delhi: Oxford University Press, 1987); Richards and Richard P. Tucker, eds., *World Deforestation in the Twentieth Century* (Durham, NC: Duke University Press, 1988); Richards, *The Mughal Empire* (Cambridge: Cambridge University Press, 1993); Richards, ed., *Kingship and Authority in South Asia* (Delhi and New York: Oxford University Press, 1998); Richards, ed., *Land, Property and the Environment* (Oakland, CA: ICS Press, 2002); Richards, *The Unending Frontier* (Berkeley: University of California Press, 2003).

land use and land cover change in Latin American countries over the previous five hundred years—which the ecologists wanted for their work on the global carbon cycle. Had Richards not done this, I suspect I would have left the history profession and am sure I never would have migrated into environmental history. So I owe him debts I never repaid.

THE UNENDING FRONTIER AND *THE WORLD HUNT*

Richards was a pioneer in environmental history, which scarcely existed when he came to Duke. In the early 1980s, he began to teach an undergraduate course in world environmental history, one of the first such taught anywhere. That experience prepared him, and perhaps motivated him, to write *The Unending Frontier.* The big book contains four parts, the first of which Richards called "The Global Context" and concerns political, economic, and climatic history, emphasizing contrasts between the Dutch Republic and Mughal India. Parts 2 and 3 consist of regional case studies, six of which focus on Africa and Eurasia and four on the Americas. Part 4 is the world hunt.

The Unending Frontier is about the extension and intensification of human modification of the environment that resulted from larger and more efficient economic and political organization in early modern times. Most of it concerns European states, colonialism, and capitalism in action overseas. Richards originally intended to carry the story up to the present but allowed practical considerations to dissuade him. At one point he tried to squeeze the story into the core-periphery framework of Immanuel Wallerstein's world-systems theory, but in the end he abandoned that scheme.[4] *The Unending Frontier* earned favorable notices in more than a dozen scholarly journals. As with any work of global history, reviewers found a few small errors in Richards's handling of some of his many subjects. None of them affect the overall picture.[5]

"The World Hunt" is the most thematically coherent part of Richards's big book. Its four chapters, reprinted here, explore the impacts of commercial hunting, fishing, and whaling in North America, Siberia, and the North Atlantic Ocean. In every case, the heart of the matter is either the transformation of some animal part into a commodity or a radical increase in the scale of the market for pelts, skins, blubber, or tusks.

The history of the North American beaver fur trade forms the core of its first chapter. Richards delves into the characteristics of *Castor canadensis* (the North American beaver), the ways in which Amerindians trapped beavers,

---

4. See Immanuel Wallerstein, *The Modern World-System* (Berkeley: University of California Press, 2011), 4 vols. Wallerstein's first volume first appeared in 1974.

5. Perhaps the most notable was that Richards placed Basque fishers and whalers in Newfoundland waters in the 1490s, when they did not get there until the 1520s. See Peter Pope's review in *Comparative Studies of South Asia, Africa and the Middle East* 29, no. 2 (2009): 338–39.

and the effects of the vast and expanding European market for fur on the beaver, the land, Amerindians, and colonists. Beavers are, as Richards put it, "energetic engineers," building dams and maintaining ponds. Reducing their population, as the fur trade did, changed the hydrology and ecology of the northern half of North America. The trades in fox, raccoon, bear, and other furs had smaller consequences.

The first chapter also takes up a less familiar subject, deer hunting in North America. Deer hides found a robust market in Europe too, one that Amerindian and colonial hunters eagerly sought to supply. The Creek Indians in the American South proved especially responsive to the market incentives in the early eighteenth century and sent piles of deerskins to the ports of the Carolinas in exchange for cloth, guns, alcohol, and other goods. The impacts of the fur and hide trades on Amerindians, complex and controversial matters in the historical literature, concerned Richards as much as did the ecological consequences.

The second chapter of *The World Hunt* carries the story of the fur trade to Siberia. Here Russians, Cossacks, and the several indigenous peoples responded to market incentives and trapped all the sables, marten, foxes, beavers, otters (and other fur-bearing animals) they could. Sable fur—soft and silky—was the most valuable. At times, the fur trade as a whole provided imperial Russia with as much as 10 percent of its revenue. The market was not the only mechanism for stimulating the Siberian fur trade. The Russian state imposed a tribute requirement, payable only in furs, on the indigenous male population of Siberia. Richards follows the Siberian fur trade geographically, west to east, all the way to the shores of the Pacific and the hunt for the fur-bearing sea otter. As in the previous chapter, he explores both social and ecological impacts of the trade.

In the third chapter of *The World Hunt*, Richards leaves the land behind and wades into the North Atlantic. Here he focuses tightly on one species, the codfish (*Gadus morhua*), which had long attracted European fishers in the northeast Atlantic. By the early sixteenth century, they had crossed the ocean and discovered unimaginably rich stocks off Newfoundland and New England. In the next three centuries, as Richards explains, cod provided a significant portion of European food intake, especially in France, Spain, and Italy. While impacts on indigenous peoples are not a significant part of the cod fishery story, here, as in earlier chapters, Richards assesses the ecological consequences of the long-lasting quest for cod. The near total crash of cod populations in the 1980s and 1990s, from which the species has yet to recover, lent a particular immediacy to his analysis.

The final chapter of *The World Hunt* stays at sea but switches the focus to whales and walruses. Bowhead and right whales had bone and blubber that could fetch a good price. Walrus tusk, bone, and hide could too. So these species, widely scattered in the Arctic and North Atlantic, became commodities, and after 1500, when Europeans sailed increasingly confidently in these waters, the hunt was on. Here indigenous peoples return to the story, as Inuit (Eskimo), Chukchi, and other circumpolar peoples enthusiastically participated in whaling. But the larger part of commercial whaling, and walrus hunting, was conducted by Europeans, from Basques to Britons to Russians. Whaling especially was big business, expensive to undertake, full of risk, but highly profitable when all went well. European rulers often regarded their whaling fleets as valuable enough to merit naval protection.

HOW *THE WORLD HUNT* HOLDS UP TODAY

Since Richards wrote, more than a decade's worth of new scholarship has emerged on his subjects. By and large, it confirms his portraits and underscores his belief that the environmental history of these centuries is an important part of their overall history. Concerning the fur trade, John Bocktoce has carried Richards's story to Alaska (which Richards ignored) in the eighteenth and nineteenth centuries, emphasizing Inuit and Chukchi roles, consistent with one of Richards's themes, the centrality of indigenous peoples.[6] Anne Carlos and Frank Lewis did something similar for the eighteenth-century fur trade around Hudson Bay.[7] A popular history of the fur trade in North America, by Eric Jay Dolan, pays some attention to environmental themes.[8] James Daschuk wrote brilliantly about the beaver, the fur trade, indigenous peoples, and the environment on the Canadian prairies in the eighteenth and nineteenth centuries in his *Clearing the Plains*.[9] All these books, and others too, provide more detail but in effect support Richards's presentation of the environmental history of the fur trades.

On cod fisheries, new work also buttresses Richards's handling of the subject. Two books in particular take an explicitly environmental approach. One, Jeffrey Bolster's *The Mortal Sea*, deals with the fishery pursued from New England ports and won a Bancroft Prize as 2013's best book in U.S. history. The other, by George Rose, treats the Newfoundland fishery and is unde-

6. John Bockstoce, *Furs and Frontiers in the Far North* (New Haven: Yale University Press, 2009). Carolyn Podruchny produced a social history of fur traders in Canada c. 1680–1860: *Making the Voyageur World: Travelers and Traders in the North American Fur Trade* (Lincoln: University of Nebraska Press, 2006).

7. Ann M. Carlos and Frank D. Lewis, *Commerce by a Frozen Sea: Native Americans and the European Fur Trade* (Philadelphia: University of Pennsylvania Press, 2010).

8. Eric Jay Dolan, *Fur, Fortune, and Empire: The Epic History of the Fur Trade in America* (New York: W.W. Norton, 2010).

9. James Daschuk, *Clearing the Plains: Disease, Politics of Starvation, and the Loss of Aboriginal Life* (Regina: University of Regina Press, 2013). See also Daschuk, "Who Killed the Prairie Beaver? An Environmental Case for Eighteenth Century Migration in Western Canada," *Prairie Forum* 37 (2012): 151–72.

servedly obscure.[10] The history of North Atlantic fishing in general underwent a boom after Richards's book, thanks to an international research project called HMAP (History of Marine Animal Populations). HMAP dealt with
several world fisheries, but much of its work focused on the North Atlantic,
including the cod fishery. Its website (http://hmapcoml.org/) lists publications, as well as bibliographies and databases that are crucial to the historical study of fishing and whaling. One work in particular that takes an
explicitly environmental approach, although to herring rather than cod fisheries, is Bo Poulsen's *Dutch Herring: An Environmental History, c. 1600–1860,*
which sets a high standard for research on North Atlantic fishery history.[11]

The history of whaling has inspired a good deal of strong popular history.[12]
New work on the arctic and subarctic seas of the sort that Richards drew upon,
however, has been scarce since 2003.[13] In this case, his interpretations are
not so much confirmed by subsequent research as left unchallenged.

One area of research of importance to Richards's work that has witnessed
a tremendous outpouring since 2003 is the history of the Little Ice Age. (This
was the period, c. 1300–1850, when global average temperatures dipped by
about one degree centigrade. The coldest spells came in the seventeenth century.) In *The Unending Frontier,* Richards devoted an early chapter to the Little
Ice Age and wove the theme of climate change into most subsequent chapters, including those reproduced here. He relied, appropriately, on the work
of historians of climate, such as Jean Grove and Christian Pfister. Since then,
however, the scientific and scholarly concern about contemporary climate
change has led to intensified research on prior shifts in climate, including
the Little Ice Age. Both text-based historians and natural scientists using proxy
data (e.g., tree rings, oxygen isotopes trapped in ice, speleothems) have contributed to a deeper knowledge of the character and consequences of the
Little Ice Age.[14]

10. W. Jeffrey Bolster, *The Mortal Sea: Fishing the Atlantic in the Age of Sail* (Cambridge, MA:
Harvard University Press, 2012); George A. Rose, *Cod: The Ecological History of the North Atlantic
Fisheries* (St. Johns, Newfoundland: Breakwater Books, 2007). Many other works treat the cod
fisheries in larger contexts, notably Peter Pope, *Fish into Wine: The Newfoundland Plantation in
the Seventeenth Century* (Chapel Hill: University of North Carolina Press, 2004).

11. Bo Poulsen, *Dutch Herring: An Environmental History, c. 1600–1860* (Amsterdam: Aksant
Academic, 2008).

12. See, for example, Eric Jay Dolan, *Leviathan: The History of Whaling in America* (New York:
W. W. Norton, 2007); Callum Roberts, *The Unnatural History of the Sea* (Washington DC: Island
Press, 2009).

13. But see Jan Erik Ringstad, ed., *Whaling and History II: New Perspectives,* issue 31 of *Publikasjon*
(Sandefjord, Norway: Kommandør Chr. Christensens Hvalfangstmuseum, 2006).

14. See, for example, Sam White, *The Climate of Rebellion in the Early Modern Ottoman Empire*
(New York: Cambridge University Press, 2011); Lajos Racz, *The Steppe to Europe: An Environmental
History of Hungary in the Traditional Age* (Cambridge: White Horse Press, 2013); Wolfgang
Behringer, *A Cultural History of Climate* (London: Polity Press, 2009). While concerned only with

For the foreseeable future, the last word on the Little Ice Age will belong to Geoffrey Parker's *Global Crisis*, which both synthesizes available information on the climate and argues for powerful climatic effects on demography, economics, and politics around the world.[15] Numerous severe political disruptions in the mid-seventeenth century, from Spain to China and beyond, had strong links to repeated bouts of cold (and often dry) years. The thrust of Parker's work is that the Little Ice Age was even more important for the early modern centuries, especially the middle of the seventeenth century, than anyone, including Richards, had supposed. In *The World Hunt*, Richards makes reference to the Little Ice Age in discussing, for example, the migration of codfish (which are highly sensitive to water temperature) and the demand for fur pelts. But nowhere does he make claims for the significance of climatic turbulence as pervasively as Parker. The two books, published a decade apart, if read together would provide anyone with a good grounding in early modern world history.

Another area into which Richards delves in *The World Hunt* is what is now sometimes called animal history. Richards did not see his work as such, perhaps only because the field—if that is what it is—scarcely existed in 2003. But *The World Hunt* is about prey as much as it is about hunters. Beavers, sables, codfish, walruses, and bowhead and right whales share the stage with trappers, hunters, and fishers. A great deal of the literature in animal history concerns domesticated animals—livestock—which was not one of Richards's concerns. And most of it is a form of cultural history, dealing with human attitudes toward and treatment of animals.[16] That sort of animal history forms only a small part of *The World Hunt*. Richards is more attuned to the economic utility of rodents, deer, fish, and whales and the consequences, for ecosystems and social systems alike, of sharp reductions in their populations. But the fact remains, *The World Hunt* is about animals.

---

the onset of the Little Ice Age, Timothy Brook's *A Troubled Empire: China in the Yuan and Ming Dynasties* (Cambridge, MA: Harvard University Press, 2013) also puts great emphasis on climate shifts in explaining political history.

15. Geoffrey Parker, *Global Crisis: War, Climate Change and Catastrophe in the Seventeenth Century* (New Haven: Yale University Press, 2013).

16. For a sampling, see Peter Atkins, ed., *Animal Cities: Beastly Urban Histories* (Surrey, U.K.: Ashgate, 2012); Martha Few and Zeb Tortorici, eds., *Centering Animals in Latin American History* (Durham, NC: Duke University Press, 2013); Juliet Clutton-Brock, *Animals as Domesticates: A World View through History (The Animal Turn)* (East Lansing: Michigan State University Press, 2012); Linda Kalof, ed., *A Cultural History of Animals in Antiquity* (London: Bloomsbury Academic, 2011); Kalof, *Looking at Animals in Human History* (London: Reaktion Books, 2007); Karen Raber, *Animal Bodies, Renaissance Culture* (Philadelphia: University of Pennsylvania Press, 2013); Brett Walker, *The Lost Wolves of Japan* (Seattle: University of Washington Press, 2008); Alan Mikhail, *The Animal in Ottoman Egypt* (New York: Oxford University Press, 2013). In many ways, the dean of animal history is Harriet Ritvo. See her *Noble Cows and Hybrid Zebras: Essays on Animals and History* (Charlottesville: University of Virginia Press, 2010), among several works.

A final area in which historians have added heavily to a literature that Richards uses in *The World Hunt* is the implications of environmental changes for indigenous peoples. This is a theme of frequent interest throughout *The Unending Frontier.* In *The World Hunt* it is a central concern in the fur trade chapters, a minor one in the whaling chapter, and absent—understandably enough—from the chapter on Atlantic cod. Works already cited (in notes 5–8) give some idea of the interest that recent scholarship has taken in this theme with respect to the fur trade. More broadly, the impact on indigenous peoples of environmental change brought about by resource extraction has become a major focus for environmental historians. In some ways, it always has been: some of the foundational texts of the field took it up.[17] More recently, scholars have inquired into this subject in contexts as varied as Mexican oil extraction, New Mexico uranium mining, and African hydroelectric development.[18] This is one of the enduring themes in environmental history, and it features prominently in *The World Hunt.*

In the years to come, these and other themes that Richards emphasizes in *The World Hunt* will acquire yet further elaboration. New generations of scholars will find new things to say and new angles of vision. It will be interesting to see how they accord with Richards's outlook. But for the time being, at least, *The World Hunt* remains consistent with the prevailing wisdom of environmental historians—a wisdom that Richards helped to shape. At present there is no better way to explore the environmental dimensions of hunting, fishing, and whaling in the early modern centuries than to read this little book.

17. E.g., William Cronon, *Changes in the Land* (New York: Hill and Wang, 1983).

18. Among dozens of titles, see, e.g., Donald Fixico, *The Invasion of Indian Country in the Twentieth Century: American Capitalism and Tribal Natural Resources* (Boulder: University of Colorado Press, 2011); Myrna Santiago, *The Ecology of Oil: Environment, Labor, and the Mexican Revolution, 1900–1938* (New York: Cambridge University Press, 2005); Sherry L. Smith and Brian Frehner, eds., *Indians and Energy: Exploitation and Opportunity in the American Southwest* (Santa Fe, NM: School for Advanced Research Press, 2010); Heather Hoag, *Developing the Rivers of East and West Africa: An Environmental History* (London: Bloomsbury Academic, 2013).

Chapter 1

Furs and Deerskins
in Eastern North America

European maritime contact with the New World thrust commercialized human predation across the North Atlantic Ocean. Commercial hunting proved to be the most lucrative way to exploit the northernmost regions of the Americas. Much of the early impetus for maritime travel to North America came from the profits to be made from hunting, killing, processing, and shipping animal skins back to Europe. Europeans found several prey species—beavers, foxes, marten, and other furbearers, and deer—that yielded high-value commodities for the home market with its pent-up demand for fur. Windfall exploitation of abundant New World fur-bearing animals raised the European standard of living.

By the early sixteenth century, supplies of furs were dwindling across Europe and prices had risen sharply. The European beaver, for example, was nearly extinct in southern Europe and fast disappearing elsewhere. Even rabbit skins were hard to get and were expensive.[1] Sable and marten, the costliest furs, were prohibitive in price for all save the very few. In England, fashionable taste was shifting away from fur-lined gowns toward "fabrics of an almost unbelievable richness."[2] Nevertheless, cloth did not provide the warmth of fur in the increasingly cold winters. In 1604, a Venetian living in London commented, "The weather is bitterly cold and everyone is in furs although we are almost in July."[3]

Unlike sugar and tobacco, producing furs required no heavy investment in land conversion and cultivation. Peltries demanded only a modest invest-

1. Elspeth M. Veale, *The English Fur Trade in the Later Middle Ages* (Oxford: Clarendon Press, 1966), 172–76.
2. Ibid., 143.
3. Ibid., 141.

ment in relation to their potential return. The indigenous peoples of North America supplied the human energy and skill needed for the hunt and its aftermath. Successive Indian groups were a cheap, readily available labor force that engaged in ever more arduous labor in return for inexpensive trade goods. If necessary, Indian groups bartered for beaver and other furs from more remote Indians with access to better hunting grounds. European colonists, even fur traders, did very little actual hunting and trapping themselves. Traders, farmers, and artisans saw little appeal in the rigors of the hunt. Somewhat later, by the late seventeenth century and through the eighteenth century, the warmer southern region of North America developed a new export product. Overshadowed by the far better known trade in beaver, fox, and other furs, deerskins became a staple product of the American Southeast. Market demand by the early modern European leather industry soared as domestic supplies of deerskin dwindled. European traders turned to North America, where the most plentiful deer by that time were those in the southern colonies. The indigenous peoples in the American Southeast responded to new market stimuli and became primary producers of semi-processed deer hides in ever increasing numbers.

The territorial reach of the fur trade far exceeded the extent of European settlement and direct contact. Long before any direct trade with Europeans occurred, Indian groups in the interior traded furs for goods brought by Indian middlemen. Some Indian groups became middlemen who acquired fur for trade goods from interior Indian hunters and exchanged them for more trade goods, especially European weaponry, with Europeans. Conflicts over middleman status could and did lead to war and the expulsion of the losers from their territories. In this "protohistoric era" of indirect trade, Indians moved perceptibly toward commercial hunting.[4] Archaeological data confirm that even the Indians of the Canadian subarctic were acquiring and using European trade goods by the end of the seventeenth century. During the "historic era," that followed, European fur traders traveled to Indian settlements and began direct trading relations. As contact intensified, the arrival of other, competing European fur traders generated new pressures to kill and overkill more animals.

THE SIXTEENTH-CENTURY FUR TRADE

Early-sixteenth-century voyages to engage in North Atlantic cod fishing and whaling put European seamen in frequent contact with Indians along the northern coastline of North America. French, Basque, and Portuguese sailors exchanged gifts with the Micmacs of the Maritime Provinces and the

---

4. J. C. Yerbury, *The Subarctic Indians and the Fur Trade, 1680–1860* (Vancouver: University of British Columbia Press, 1986), 10–13.

Montagnais groups of southern Labrador.[5] Gift exchanges soon evolved into a trading pattern. The Indians wore and used furs and pelts that had substantial value in European eyes. Beaver, bear, lynx, fox, otter, marten, badger, muskrat, and mink pelts could be conditioned then cut and pieced together to make warm and decorative fur garments. The skins of shorthaired seals, moose, elks, and deer, if properly treated, made exceptionally strong and supple leather garments. The coastal Indians were willing to exchange furs for European manufactured goods.

In these early encounters, the most desirable objects offered to the Indians were iron knives, hatchets, and kettles; wool blankets and other European textiles; and glass beads for decoration. Marten skins, rare and expensive in Europe, were plentiful in New England and could be obtained very cheaply in exchange for axes, knives, and other trade goods.[6]

In the latter part of the century, profits from the casual trade encouraged merchant-adventurers to invest in fur trading rather than fishing or voyages to the New World. In 1583, French merchants in La Rochelle, Saint Malo, and Rouen financed five fur-trading voyages to North America. Two years later, ten ships made the crossing. One Stephen Bellinger, a trader from Rouen, "brought home . . . divers beastes skynnes as beavers, otters, martense, lucernes, seals, buff, dere, skynnes. All drest and paynted on the innter side with divers excellent colors."[7]

The eastern Algonkian Indians—Micmacs and Montagnais among others—living along the Gulf of Saint Lawrence and in Nova Scotia were involved in low-intensity fur trading throughout most of the sixteenth century.[8] These Algonkian-speaking hunters had recently driven the horticultural Iroquois out of the Saint Lawrence River valley in a conflict over control of the growing fur trade. The Montagnais became the dominant middlemen, or trading specialists, who extracted furs from hunters in the interior in the Saguenay River drainage system in exchange for trade goods. The Montagnais in turn supplied those Spanish, Basque, Dutch, and French trading vessels that sailed up the Gulf of Saint Lawrence as far as Tadoussac, an Indian trading center located where the Saguenay River enters the Saint Lawrence.

In the last half of the sixteenth century, a new, intense European demand for beaver pelts stimulated fur trading in the New World. Molded and shaped hats made of felt from the inner fur of the beaver became popular for higher-status men in the late 1500s in western Europe and remained in

5. Laurier Turgeon, "French Fishers, Fur Traders, and Amerindians during the Sixteenth Century: History and Archaeology," *William and Mary Quarterly*, 3d ser., 55, no. 4 (1998).

6. Paul C. Phillips, *The Fur Trade*, 1st ed. (Norman: University of Oklahoma Press, 1961), 1:16–17.

7. Ibid., 1:21. Quote is from Richard Hakluyt's *Discourse Concerning Western Planting*.

8. Kenneth M. Morrison, *The Embattled Northeast: The Elusive Ideal of Alliance in Abenaki-Euramerican Relations* (Berkeley and Los Angeles: University of California Press, 1984), 12–19.

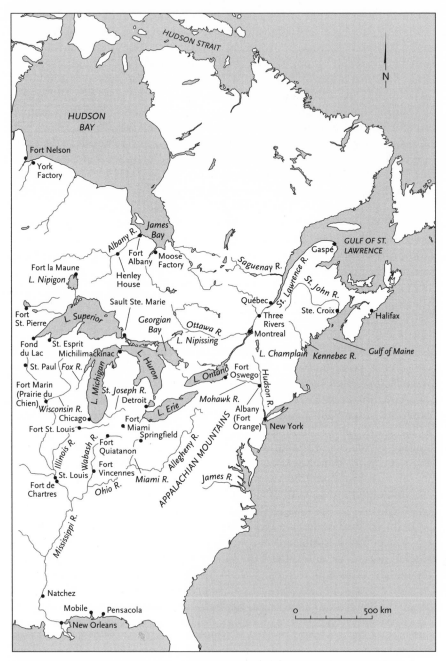

Map 1 North American fur trade routes. Adapted from W. T. Easterbrook and Hugh G. J. Aitken, *Canadian Economic History* (Toronto: Macmillan Co. of Canada, 1967), pp. 164–65.

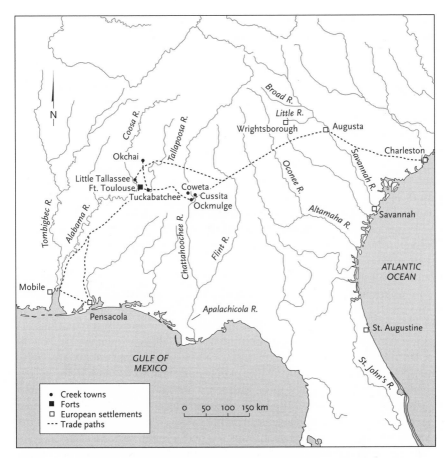

Map 2 Creek country and contiguous European settlements, 1772. Adapted from Kathryn E. Holland Braund, *Deerskins and Duffels: The Creek Indian Trade with Anglo-America, 1685–1815* (Lincoln: University of Nebraska Press, 1993), map 2, p. 91.

fashion throughout the early modern period. The North American beaver became the most valuable furbearer of the New World and prey to one of the longest sustained hunts for a single species in world history. Demand for beaver hats continued undiminished for three hundred years, until manufacturers perfected the cheaper and glossier silk hat in the 1840s. Thereafter, prices for high-quality beaver pelts declined steadily in the face of technological innovation in hat making.

Beaver pelts consist of coarse, two-inch-long outer, or guard, hairs that cover the inner, extremely fine down of the coat. The one-inch-long inner hairs have microscopic hooks at the ends that are ideal for the felting process. Skilled master hatters bought cleaned and graded beaver wool sheared from the skin. Journeymen boiled lesser quality wool with water and urine to enhance its felting qualities; the best quality needed no preparation. Next, the workers passed a large taut bow, similar to a violin bow, over the pile of wool. When vibrated, the bow's magnetic force aligned the hairs all in the same direction. Using heat and pressure, the hatter shaped the wool into batts of felt. Two large and two joining batts were pressed together to form a hat. After shaping or blocking, the hat underwent a finishing process that involved dyeing, stiffening, waterproofing, reblocking, ironing, trimming, and final shaping. The result was a durable, waterproof, warm hat with no discernible seams and a smooth nap that could be shaped and reshaped according to fashion, a hat that could be worn for years on end.[9]

Prices and profits on beaver pelts rose together. Most sought-after were beaver robes consisting of five to as many as eight pelts sewn together and worn for some time by their Indian owners. These "coat," or *castor gras,* beaver robes lost their guard hairs through friction and left the inner beaver wool pliant and workable as a result of its wearer's sweat and oils. Less valuable was the stiff "parchment," or *castor sec,* scraped skin that carried both guard hairs and inner wool. The latter required careful combing and separation from the skin before it could be used in felting.

During the sixteenth century, Dutch traders shipped the best-quality parchment skins via fifteen- to twenty-vessel fleets that left Amsterdam in the spring each year for the Russian port of Archangel on the White Sea; from there the skins traveled to Moscow. Furriers in Moscow held a trade secret. They combed out the inner wool from beaver skins while leaving the long guard hairs on the skin. Beaver pelts combed in this way fetched a higher price for use in trimming garments or even for wearing as a "natural" fur than uncombed beaver skins from North America. After the furs had been processed, the Dutch traders shipped two profitable goods with the return voyage each year.[10] Both combed beaver pelts and separated, high-quality beaver wool returned a profit despite the costs of shipping to Archangel and back. Paris, with its high concentration of skilled hatters, remained the primary market for processed beaver fur—at least until the flight of the Huguenots to London in 1685.

BEAVER AND OTHER FURBEARERS

The beaver is one of those wild animals whose singular appearance and work habits have become firmly engrained in United States and Canadian popu-

9. The manufacturing process is described by Hugh Grant, "Revenge of the Paris Hat: The European Craze for Wearing Headgear Had a Profound Effect on Canadian History," *The Beaver* 37 (1989).

10. E. Rich, "Russia and the Colonial Fur Trade," *Economic History Review,* 2d ser., 7 (1955).

lar culture (and indeed, world culture)—so much so that historians of the fur trade rarely think it necessary to describe its physical characteristics, life cycle, habitat, or industrious work ethic. This omission tends to minimize the extraordinary importance of the beaver in the shaping of the North American landscape and to elide the ecological significance of its market-driven near-extinction.

The densely furred, reddish brown to black North American beaver *(Castor canadensis)* is one of the largest rodents in the world. Adult beavers of both sexes are about the same size: from 600 to 800 millimeters in body length and twelve to twenty-five kilograms in weight. They have broad, flat, naked tails (100–130 millimeters wide) that add another 250–400 millimeters in length. They have unwebbed front feet with strong digging claws and webbed hind feet for swimming. Their strongly developed front teeth never stop growing but are worn down by incessant chewing and gnawing. Beavers are herbivores that feed on the cambium, bark, leaves, twigs, and roots of deciduous softwood trees—willow, aspen, poplar, birch, and alder—as well as on roots of aquatic plants such as water lilies. They are semiaquatic animals who prefer to live in burrows or lodges beside or in streams and small lakes near an abundant growth of their favored tree species. Strong swimmers, they reach a speed of six to seven kilometers per hour and routinely remain underwater for five minutes or more.

Beavers are social animals that live in family groups of four to as many as eight animals. Each group centers on a monogamous, mated breeding pair of adults who take care of young that are less than two years of age. Mating takes place once a year, about January or February, followed by a gestation period of 100 to 110 days. The litters, born April to June, usually number two to four kits that nurse for three months. Kits live with their parents until they reach sexual maturity, at which time their parents expel them from the colony to establish their own households nearby. Beavers in captivity can survive from thirty-five to fifty years, but the life span in the wild is probably shorter.[11] In short, beavers are both prolific and long-lived and have few dangerous predators.

These animals are energetic hydrologic engineers who work continuously to shape their home environment. Ponds afford them security and food storage for winter. They cut trees and bushes by gnawing and drag or float logs and poles for use in construction. Using earth, mud, stones, brush, and poles, beavers build dams to create or augment ponds and lakes, build submerged lodges on islands in the ponds or on the banks of rivers, and even dig waterways (beaver canals) that permit them to float logs readily from a

11. Ronald M. Nowak and Ernest P. Walker, *Walker's Mammals of the World,* 5th ed. (Baltimore: Johns Hopkins University Press, 1991), s.v. "Beaver."

distant source. Over years and decades, undisturbed beaver colonies continually augment and extend these works to an impressive scale.

In favorable habitats like northern hardwood forests, beavers can reach prodigious numbers. Reasonably credible estimates suggest that *Castor canadensis* numbered between 60 to 100 million animals before European settlement in North America. Some inkling of the cumulative impact of dense beaver populations on the North American landscape can be inferred from a mid-nineteenth-century study of an area where beavers were under minimal pressure from trappers.

Lewis Morgan, later to become prominent as an early ethnologist and anthropologist, began studying beavers in the mid-1850s. Morgan was involved in the construction of a railroad built to reach iron deposits in an uninhabited area in northern Michigan on the south shore of Lake Superior. The railroad cut through a "beaver district"; as a result of the railroad "opening this wilderness in advance of all settlement, the beavers were surprised, so to speak, in the midst of their works, which, at the same time, were rendered accessible for minute and deliberate investigation."[12] Morgan chose as his study area a mixed deciduous and coniferous rectangular tract measuring 9.6 by 12.9 kilometers. Within this 124-square-kilometer region traversed by two small rivers, the Carp and the Ely, Morgan found "sixty-three beaver dams, without reckoning the smallest, from those which are fifty feet [15 meters] in length, and forming ponds covering a quarter of an acre of land, to those which are three hundred and five hundred feet [91 to 150 meters] in length, with ponds covering from twenty to sixty acres [8.1 to 24.3 hectares] of land."[13] In this small region, beavers also built lodges on the banks of natural ponds and lakes. They constructed dozens of canals that enabled them to move timber and brush readily by water to their lodges. One of the longest canals, 153 meters in length, was designed to supply beaver burrows along its route and a lodge at the entrance to a natural pond.

Morgan also commented on the ubiquitous "beaver meadows" shown on the map of the study tract. These were low-lying areas adjacent to beaver ponds, where, in the wet seasons, standing water had killed off the tree growth and permitted a "rank, luxuriant grass" to flourish. The beaver meadows were "a series of hummocks formed of earth and a mass of coarse roots of grass rising about a foot high, while around each of them is a narrow strip of bare and sunken ground."[14] However, as Morgan was careful to emphasize, all these works required constant maintenance and repair by the at-

---

12. Lewis Henry Morgan, *The American Beaver: A Classic of Natural History and Ecology* (New York: Dover Publications, 1986), 8.

13. Ibid., 80.

14. Ibid., 203–4.

tentive beaver colonies that benefited from them. When hunting killed off beaver colonies in a region, the dams and canals deteriorated and rapidly altered those ecosystems associated with the beaver.

In addition to beaver pelts, European merchants encouraged Indian hunters to supply them with pelts from other furbearers. All were carnivores with smaller populations than those of the beaver and were more difficult to hunt. Their furs were not used for making hats but for garments or linings that offered warmth, comfort, and display in the traditional fashion. Second only to the beaver in annual numbers harvested was the raccoon *(Procyon lotor)*, whose fur was warm but considered less fashionable and valuable. Also targeted were highly valued pelts from the marten *(Martes americana)* and the fisher *(Martes pennanti)*, both close relatives of the Siberian sable. Along stream and riverbanks were found the mink *(Mustela vison)*, the river otter *(Lutra canadensis)*, and the less valuable muskrat *(Ondata zibethicus)*.

Furs from several species of fox found a market: red fox *(Vulpes vulpes)*, kit fox *(Vulpes macrotis)*, swift fox *(Vulpes velox)*, gray fox *(Urocyon cinereoargenteus)*, and in the far north, arctic fox *(Alopex lagopus)*. Pelts from two large cats, the lynx *(Felis lynx)* and the smaller and ubiquitous bobcat *(Felis rufus)*, sold readily in Europe. Killing the gray wolf *(Canis lupus)* and especially the rare wolverine *(Gulo gulo)* required both skill and perseverance on the part of the hunter. Long before contact with Europeans, Indian hunters pursued the black bear *(Ursus americanus)*, the largest, most dangerous, and most respected of their prey animals. Every year, several thousand black bear furs, along with those of a few brown bears *(Ursus arctos)* and even polar bears *(Ursus maritimus)*, reached Europe.

THE SEVENTEENTH-CENTURY SAINT LAWRENCE FUR TRADE

Pursuit of the beaver can best be described in terms of the river systems Europeans used to penetrate the interior. In the north, Indians employed light birch-bark canoes to transport packs of heavy furs along subsidiary streams to converge on a main river route that would take them to a European trading center. Use of the canoe permitted portaging around rapids and falls. To the north, the French followed the Saint Lawrence, Saguenay, and Ottawa River systems inland; further south, the Dutch relied on the Hudson River and its tributaries to gain access to Indian hunters and to transport their furs. The English moved up the Connecticut and Delaware Rivers to trade for furs. Toward the end of the century, the English, organized under a royal charter into a new company, sailed north into Hudson Bay and established trading posts in its vicinity.

The first organized French fur-trading expeditions in the early 1600s encountered eastern Algonkian Montagnais who offered them furs in return for trade goods. After Samuel de Champlain sailed up the Saint Lawrence River and founded Quebec in the narrows of the great river, the French could actively trade for furs with the Montagnais from a permanent base.

The intensified French trading presence in the seventeenth century had a perceptible impact on the eastern Algonkians and their habitat. Prior to contact with the French, they had hunted beaver for meat and for furs to wear as warm clothing, but apparently not with the intensity they displayed after exposure to market incentives. For the Algonkians—as for nearly all North American Indians—to hunt moose, bears, beavers, and other prey was a spiritual quest, a "holy occupation," during which "animals, in the Indian cosmology, consciously surrendered themselves to the needy hunter."[15] They did so, however, only if the hunter consulted his own "soul-spirit" for guidance in a dream before the hunt. If the dream were properly divined, the hunter's soul spirit, who had been in contact with the wildlife spirits, would lead the hunter to the game that had agreed to be slain.[16] Generally, the hunter felt a strong sense of kinship and even friendship with his game animals. He observed elaborate taboos and rules for deferential treatment of the slain animal's carcass. If he were careless in these observances, or if he killed too many animals, bad luck would follow. The animal spirits, angered and hostile, would punish the greedy or unobservant hunter by denying him willing prey.[17]

These cultural inhibitions that imposed dignity and restraint on Algonkian hunters faltered when juxtaposed with the seductive appeal exerted by commodities of the fur trade. Algonkian material culture became dependent on French trade goods. Iron tools and kettles replaced those of stone, wood, bark, and bone. Harquebuses and pistols replaced bows and arrows in hunting and warfare. European blankets, shirts, stockings, and other

---

15. Calvin Martin, *Keepers of the Game: Indian-Animal Relationships and the Fur Trade* (Berkeley and Los Angeles: University of California Press, 1978), 115. An intriguing theory, first advanced by Martin in the mid-1970s, is that this spiritual universe shattered in the sixteenth century. In advance of full-blown participation in the fur trade, the Algonkians went through a profound spiritual crisis. Confronted with catastrophic diseases brought by the Europeans, which their shamans or healers could not cure, they blamed the wildlife spirits for their affliction. This occurred partly, as Martin argues, because wild animals themselves were probably carriers of some of these diseases. Restraints based on mutual respect and deference dissolved. The Algonkians went to war with their animal tormentors. At this juncture, the fur traders offered material incentives and a rationale for the further killing and punishing of treacherous wildlife. With the rationale for their spiritual world ripped apart, the ideological assault mounted by Christian missionaries contributed further to the demoralization of the Algonkians. Since Martin published *Keepers of the Game*, other anthropologists have decisively rejected its validity and usefulness. See the rebuttal articles assembled in Shepard Krech III, *The Ecological Indian: Myth and History* (New York: W. W. Norton and Company, 1999).

16. C. Martin, *Keepers of the Game*, 123–25.

17. Ibid., 128–29.

items of clothing partially replaced beaver robes and deerskins. Flint and steel replaced the wooden drill for making fire. The practice of burying weapons and other possessions with dead warriors was a continuing drain on these goods.[18]

To obtain trade goods, the Algonkians traded beaver but also moose, lynx, otter, marten, badger, and muskrat hides. Avid consumers, the Indians hunted harder and killed more of these animals than they ever had before. In 1634, a French Jesuit, Father Paul Le Jeune, spent the winter with a band of Montagnais who were actively hunting beavers for the trade. Le Jeune observed that when the Montagnais found a beaver lodge, they "kill all, great and small, male and female." Le Jeune opined that they "will finally exterminate the species in this Region, as has happened among the Hurons, who have not a single Beaver."[19] Le Jeune further suggested that the Indians set up family-managed hunting territories for sustainable management, and that they restrict their kill to males of an appropriate size.[20]

The older practice of coalescing into groups of families for the winter and summer hunting seasons changed. Formerly, the head of the hunting bands had allotted territories each season to individual hunters. Instead, under the constraints of commercial hunting, individual families began to select sites for camping and to mark out their hunting territories. They asserted property rights in this territory by marking blazes on trees. Ownership of family territories was inherited by patrilineal descent. Growing scarcity of game encouraged this type of dispersal; so also did the French preference for dealing with individual hunters rather than groups.[21]

By mid–seventeenth century, beaver and other furbearers were severely depleted in the eastern Algonkian lands. Overhunting had serious consequences for the Algonkian food supply as moose, bears, beavers, and other larger fauna were killed off. Game birds such as geese and partridges came under heavy assault, especially from the growing use of guns for hunting. According to Nicolas Denys, Victor Hugo Paltsits, and William Francis Ganong:

> The musket is used by them more than all other weapons, in their hunting in spring, summer and autumn, both for animals and birds. With an arrow they killed only one Wild Goose; but with the shot of a gun they kill five or six of

18. Alfred Goldsworthy Bailey, *The Conflict of European and Eastern Algonkian Cultures, 1504–1700: A Study in Canadian Civilization*, 2d ed. (Toronto: University of Toronto Press, 1976).

19. Quoted in Krech, *The Ecological Indian*, 181.

20. Ibid., 182.

21. Bailey, *The Conflict of European and Eastern Algonkian Cultures*, 84–88; Janet E. Chute, "Frank G. Speck's Contributions to the Understanding of Mi'kmaq Land Use, Leadership, and Land Management," *Ethnohistory* 45, no. 3 (1999).

them. With the arrow it was necessary to approach the animal closely; with the gun they kill the animal from a distance with a bullet or two.[22]

The spiritual and material world of the Algonkian Indians offered impressive coherence, meaning, and well-being for its inhabitants. The fur trade, perhaps the single most important conduit for contact with the technically superior Europeans, devastated that world. Adaptation to demands of the market was simply one aspect of a larger cultural challenge.

Two common narcotics—one old and one new—stimulated Algonkian consumer demand and pushed them to hunt more voraciously. Smoking tobacco *(Nicotiana rustica,* the only crop grown by Algonkian men) was in active use and was traded widely before the French arrived. Having become acquainted with Brazilian tobacco on the Brazilian Atlantic Coast during the early sixteenth century apparently led to the French including it as part of the bundle of trade goods on offer to the Algonkians in New France. Tobacco from Brazil was made from the tropical tobacco plant *Nicotiana tabacum.* This was a larger tropical variety that dried to a more flavorful product than the indigenous variety. A large part of the Brazilian product's appeal lay in its additives: Portuguese growers added molasses and spices in a mix that sweetened and imparted a distinctive flavor to their product.

All Algonkian groups preferred Brazilian tobacco imported by the French to the native-grown and traded variety. Brazilian trade tobacco supplanted the indigenous product in leisure and recreational smoking, in use as a work drug to combat fatigue and hunger, and as a ceremonial drug in male councils. The indigenous variety retained its place in religious ceremonies. So pronounced had Algonkian taste become in this regard that the Hudson's Bay Company was forced to obtain Brazilian tobacco for its own fur purchases and to abandon attempts to introduce Chesapeake tobacco from the English colonies.[23]

Alcohol was far more damaging and costly. Very early on, the coastal Indians became addicted to wine and brandy offered by the French. Although frequently protested by the French missionaries and often banned, brandy remained a staple trade good offered for furs. Heavy alcohol consumption resulted in deeply felt depression and malaise in the Indian populations. Drunkenness prevailed during annual trading sessions. Many Algonkians died from alcohol poisoning or the effects of alcohol-induced diseases. Males killed each other in drunken quarrels and assaulted their parents and

22. Bailey, *The Conflict of European and Eastern Algonkian Cultures,* 52, citing Nicolas Denys, Victor Hugo Paltsits, and William Francis Ganong, *The Description and Natural History of the Coasts of North America (Acadia)* (Toronto: Champlain Society, 1908), 443.

23. Linda Wimmer, "African Producers, European Merchants, Indigenous Consumers: Brazilian Tobacco in the Canadian Fur Trade, 1550–1821" (Ph.D. diss., University of Minnesota, 1996), 202–14.

wives. Drunken women and men engaged in promiscuous and often public sex. After addicts sold all their furs for brandy, they and their families starved through the winters.[24]

Alcoholism and malnutrition reduced Algonkian resistance to infectious diseases. A major smallpox epidemic in 1639–1640 killed off thousands of Indians. A French Jesuit observer at Tadoussac in 1646 reported, "There were reckoned, formerly on the shores of this port, three hundred warriors or effective hunters, who made with their families about twelve or fifteen hundred souls[,] . . . humbled by diseases which have almost entire[ly] exterminated [them]. . . . Jesus Christ . . . seems to wish to repeople this tribe with a goodly number of Savages who land there from various places."[25] When beset by disease, the Indians often migrated to seek help from the French and further exposed themselves to infection.

Commodification in a new market setting was important, but it alone would not have wreaked such havoc. Disease, alcoholism, and war enveloped the fur trade in a miasmic cloak that corroded all aspects of Algonkian society and culture. The end result was a dependency that grew more pervasive and demeaning over time. By the latter 1600s, the eastern Algonkians were trading furs for biscuits, bread, peas, and prunes.[26] They had become dependent on European foodstuffs to make it through the long, boreal winter without starvation.

HURONS AND MOHAWKS

Important though the Montagnais and other eastern Algonkian Indians were for the French fur trade, the numbers of furs traded by them dwindled, and they soon were outstripped by the Hurons, the northernmost of the Iroquoian-speaking peoples, who established an alliance with the French in 1611. The Hurons, numbering about eighteen thousand persons in as many as twenty-five villages, the largest of them fortified, had concentrated their settlements at the southeastern corner of Georgian Bay of Lake Huron.[27] From this strategic site, located at the northern extremity of maize-growing climatic limits, the Hurons were well placed to control the major water routes that provided easy access to the hunting tribes of the north.

During the sixteenth century, the Hurons were a horticultural people who employed shifting cultivation to produce surpluses of maize every year. They enjoyed a higher standard of living than Indian groups to the north and

24. Bailey, *The Conflict of European and Eastern Algonkian Cultures*, 66–74.

25. Quoted in ibid., 83.

26. Ibid., 55–57.

27. Bruce G. Trigger, *The Children of Aataentsic I: A History of the Huron People to 1660* (Montreal: McGill-Queen's University Press, 1976).

west, who lived purely by hunting. They were skillful and assiduous traders and negotiators who bartered their maize surplus for furs and other luxury goods and who acted as middlemen for the trade between north and south. The Huron language had become a widely understood trading language employed in and around the Great Lakes region.

After Champlain established a French settlement at Quebec in 1608, he acted decisively to fend off an Iroquois threat to seize control of the fur trade of the Saint Lawrence River valley. Responding to overtures from the Hurons, Champlain led an allied Huron, Algonkian, and French force south along the Richelieu River to the southern end of Lake Champlain. There, in July 1609, his firearms were decisive in the Battle of Lake Champlain against a Mohawk war party. Next year, Champlain, at the head of another allied force, used his firepower to win a bloody battle with the Mohawks on the Richelieu River. After an intricate series of negotiations stretching over five years, in 1616 Champlain and the Hurons agreed on an alliance in the fur trade and united in opposition to the Iroquois. This alliance, which endured until the destruction of the Hurons at midcentury, permitted peaceful use of the Saint Lawrence River and made possible an annual fur-bartering expedition from Huronia to Quebec.

In the spring of each year, 200 to 250 Huron men loaded their furs on about sixty large canoes. The flotilla spent six weeks making its way down the Ottawa River to the Saint Lawrence to Quebec for an annual exchange of furs for goods with the French. Relationships between the Hurons and the French resembled more traditional exchange patterns between the Hurons and other Indian groups. There was no competition from other European fur traders. Before actually trading, both sides devoted several days to feasts, speeches, and the exchange of costly presents. The rituals reaffirmed the treaty of friendship between the Hurons and the French.

Each year, the Hurons sold twelve thousand to fifteen thousand beaver pelts, along with high-quality lynx, marten, otter, fox, and other furs. Lacking price information, they accepted the price for furs set by the French. If they perceived that the trade goods offered were too little, they phrased their request for more in terms of "an appeal for further proof of friendship" instead of haggling over individual furs. The French eagerly sought beaver since the price for a good quality beaver pelt in France rose from 2.5 livres in 1558 to 8.5 livres in 1611 and to 10 livres in 1618, where it remained for most of the century.[28] The Hurons were most anxious to obtain metalware—iron knives, axes, and awls—and glass beads. During this early period, the French refused to offer firearms. The Hurons did not demand or consume much alcohol.

28. Ibid., 1:364, 356.

When the exchanges were complete, the Hurons paddled back along the Saint Lawrence to the Ottawa River and home. A handful of French traders accompanied the Hurons on their return journey to spend the winter in one of their settlements and to help in defense against the Mohawks.

In the early years, the Hurons brought furs of beavers they had killed themselves, as well as those they had acquired by trading with other Indian groups. However, by 1630, they had hunted out the beaver on their own hunting grounds.[29] The Huron trading network extended as far north as James Bay, as far west as Lake Michigan, and to the southeast as far as Lake Erie and the territory of the Susquehannock Indians. Each year, several hundred Hurons traveled by canoe for weeks at a time to barter maize and trade goods with the Nipissings, Ottawas, Ojibwas, and neutral Indian groups in both the Lake Huron area and the Ottawa River valley. The finest pelts came from the Canadian Shield to the north. Algonkian-speaking hunting groups from the north spent the winter on Huron lands in order to have access to more reliable food supplies and a market for their furs.

By the 1620s, cargoes sent from New France to the metropolis exceeded twenty thousand pelts per year and reached a high point at thirty thousand beaver pelts in 1627.[30] Two-thirds of the French fur supply came from the Hurons; the French obtained the other one-third from the Montagnais and other coastal Algonkian speakers. The latter included the Abenakis of northern Maine.

The Hurons, unlike the Montagnais, Micmacs, and other Algonkian-speakers on the coast, seemingly retained their social organization and culture without overt damage. Their system of matrilocal residence apparently remained intact. With their new iron tools, they cleared more of the forest and produced more, rather than less, maize for themselves and for trade. Craft expression flourished in traditional pottery and tobacco-pipe making but also in a new form of ornamental metalworking.

The Hurons drank a little alcohol in the course of the welcoming ceremonies at Quebec but did not bring supplies back with them, nor did they suffer from alcoholism. The leading scholar of the Hurons comments:

> The Huron's lack of interest in alcohol correlates with their unbroken self-esteem. In their relations with the French, the Huron were still their own masters. Their role in the fur trade was built on earlier trade relations and the cultural fluorescence that this trade made possible was a realization of tendencies that had been inherent in their traditional culture, rather than a disruptive or degrading process. All of these developments contributed to a sense of achievement and well being. The Huron had no reason to resent the French or to feel

29. Ibid., 1:350.
30. Ibid., 1:356.

inferior to them. On the contrary, they seem to have felt more justified than ever in regarding other peoples as being inferior to themselves.[31]

The Hurons were also assisted in their rejection of alcohol by the Jesuits, who, before 1649, did as much as they could to prevent the French from offering brandy as a trade good.

Unfortunately for the Hurons, this happy condition did not last. Before 1634, the Hurons seem not to have been afflicted with European diseases, nor were they prone to infectious disease. However, between 1634 and 1640, they were assaulted by several severe epidemics. Prolonged encounters with influenza and other unknown diseases killed some Hurons and weakened many more in the years 1634 to 1637. The greatest blow came from smallpox—carried by a group of Saint Lawrence Indians who had visited the New England Abenakis—which hit the Hurons in 1639. Before the disease waned, approximately half the population, or nine thousand Hurons, had died. Despite these tragic losses, those Hurons who survived traded vigorously to keep up the level of their annual fur deliveries to the French. The average number of furs shipped from New France rose perceptibly in the 1640s to thirty thousand or more pelts each year.[32]

In the end, conflict over the fur trade destroyed and dispersed the Hurons. By the first decade of the seventeenth century, the Mohawks and the other Iroquois nations, traditional enemies of the Hurons, had developed an "economic lifeline" to the Dutch in the Hudson River valley.[33] Control over access to Albany ensured that nearly all pelts traded with the Dutch— whether hunted by the Mohawks themselves or pillaged from others— brought cloth, guns, wampum (shell beads strung by New England Indians), and metalware to the Mohawk consumer. As these goods replaced traditional handicrafts, the Iroquois became dependent on these imports.

Most damaging was the Iroquois demand for brandy. Unlike the Hurons, Mohawk men drank enthusiastically to excess, with devastating results. To some extent, drinking replaced long-practiced vision quests and trancelike states as a means to spiritual fulfillment. However, both group "brandy feasts" and individual drinking released pent-up aggressions in a context that excused drink-inspired violent behavior.[34]

31. Ibid., 1:433.

32. Ibid., 2:589–99, 603.

33. Daniel K. Richter and the Institute of Early American History and Culture, *The Ordeal of the Longhouse: The Peoples of the Iroquois League in the Era of European Colonization* (Chapel Hill: University of North Carolina Press, for the Institute of Early American History and Culture, Williamsburg, Va., 1992), 75.

34. Ibid., 86; Maia Conrad, "Disorderly Drinking," *American Indian Quarterly* 23 (summer 1999): 1–11.

The more aggressive Mohawks resorted to warfare to supplement their own hunting. They met their growing desire for European trade goods by raiding both the Huron and the Algonkian Indians to the north. In this new style of raiding, they seized furs and trade goods, as well as captives who could be assimilated into their own society as slaves or dependents. The latter device helped to remedy their own losses from smallpox, which were similar in magnitude to those of the Hurons.[35] As a result of Dutch firearm sales, the Mohawks were better armed than the Hurons.

For most of each year in the 1640s, the Mohawks kept as many as ten raiding parties active along the Saint Lawrence. A peace negotiated by the French with the Mohawks in 1645 soon broke down. Between 1646 and 1650, the Mohawks (joined by the Senecas) attacked and destroyed Huron settlements with the aim of destroying the confederacy. By 1649, the terror-stricken Hurons, weakened by their inability to grow food because of raids, burnt their own villages and dispersed as refugees either to Quebec or west to Lake Superior and Lake Michigan.

NEW ENGLAND AND NEW YORK IN THE SEVENTEENTH CENTURY

Along the New England coast, the early English colonists, like the French, seized upon furs as a cash crop to pay off their investors. The Pilgrim community at Plymouth made substantial profits from furs traded locally and by means of trading missions sent to barter with the Abenakis on the Kennebec River in Maine. The discovery that they could barter wampum—beaded in belts worn by high-status Indian sachems and other leaders—and trade the wampum for furs enhanced their profits. In 1632, they shipped 3,361 pounds of beaver pelts (equal to 2,305 prime beaver pelts) to England for sale.[36] As early as 1627, the first English colonists, funded by Bristol merchants, had peopled a fishing settlement at the mouth of the Pemaquid River and were trading for furs with the Abenakis.[37]

The Connecticut River proved to be the most durable and profitable area for the English fur trade. Between the spring of 1633 and the spring of 1634, a massive smallpox epidemic killed thousands of Indians between Maine and southern Connecticut. Of an estimated twelve thousand Indians then living in the Connecticut River valley, as many as three-quarters may have died. The survivors were disorganized and unlikely to offer any serious resistance

35. Trigger, *The Children of Aataentsic I*, 2:627.

36. For an overview of Indian-European interaction, see Neal Salisbury, *Manitou and Providence: Indians, Europeans, and the Making of New England, 1500–1643* (New York: Oxford University Press, 1982).

37. Neill De Paoli, "Beaver, Blankets, Liquor, and Politics: Pemaquid's Fur Trade, 1614–1760," *Maine Historical Society Quarterly* 33, nos. 3–4 (1993–1994): 172.

to settlers from the Massachusetts Bay Colony.[38] In the wake of these losses, the fur trade virtually halted.

In 1635, William Pynchon, given a license by the Massachusetts Bay Colony, moved into this vacuum and established a fur-trading post upriver, beyond the fall, or tidal, line adjacent to Agawam, a settlement inhabited by Indians of that name. At Agawam, renamed Springfield, Pynchon and his son extracted furs from upland western and northern New England and sent them on to European markets.

For four decades, William Pynchon was the most visible and successful fur trader in New England. The Pynchons themselves, or their approved English subtraders, offered wampum and trade goods to local Indian hunters— Agawams, Woronocos, Norwottucks, and Pocumtucks—and to those who became middlemen for more distant producers. Pynchon, by offering higher prices, also enticed Mohican Iroquois to bring their furs to Springfield, in preference to the Dutch post at Albany. At this early phase of the English colonist–Indian encounter, Pynchon and the inhabitants of Springfield seem to have negotiated with each other fairly and in a general spirit of goodwill and respect. Pynchon, whose linguistic and diplomatic abilities figure prominently, did not assume that "God's Grace and the King's charter" automatically gave the Puritans "full and final legal authority over the heathen Indians."[39] The Indians made good use of English trade goods; and the Puritans sold their furs to London. Both sides needed what the other offered and both sides benefited from the exchange.[40]

Springfield's role as a fur entrepôt was brief, lasting less than thirty years, and its total contribution not all that impressive by comparison with that of Quebec. Shipments in the 1630s and 1640s may have been higher, but the annual average for the decade 1651 to 1661 was 1,625 pounds, or 1,114 beaver pelts. In the 1660s, beaver supplies dropped substantially to an average of 487 pounds, or only 334 pelts, per year.[41] By the 1680s, the Connecticut River valley fur trade had dwindled into insignificance largely because of reduced beaver populations in the New England hunting grounds.

The most prolific and durable route to furs lay below New England, in the Hudson River valley. After the results of the 1609 voyage of Henry Hudson became known, Dutch merchants from Amsterdam fitted out two ships, under Hendrick Christiansen and Adrian Block, respectively, and sent them on repeated voyages to trade for furs and to explore the Hudson River and the

38. Peter A. Thomas, *In the Maelstrom of Change: The Indian Trade and Cultural Process in the Middle Connecticut River Valley, 1635–1665* (New York: Garland, 1990), 54–55.

39. Marty O'Shea, "Springfield's Puritans and Indians," *Historical Journal of Massachusetts* 26, no. 1 (1998): 46–47.

40. Ibid.

41. P. A. Thomas, "In the Maelstrom of Change," 287, fig. 7. Detailed account books for the years before 1651 have not survived.

coastline of Connecticut and New York. In 1614, the merchants organized themselves as the Company of New Netherland, with exclusive trading rights granted by the States General. The trading company built two trading posts: one on Manhattan Island and the other upriver on the Hudson, called Fort Orange, near the future site of Albany.[42] Access to supplies of wampum, made from the periwinkle shells found by the Montauks on Long Island, proved to be a trading asset for the Dutch. These early ventures were promising enough for the Dutch West India Company, chartered in 1621, to win approval from the States General to take over the Hudson River fur trade and trading posts as a small part of wide mandate for trade.

During their first year of operation, in 1624, Dutch West India Company traders shipped 7,246 beaver skins, 850 otter skins, and other miscellaneous furs from Manhattan Island to Amsterdam. For the next forty years, the Dutch sustained a profitable trade in beaver and other furs. They drew from a wide catchment area that extended to the Delaware River valley to the south, and into the Iroquois country of what is now interior New York State, and beyond. The Dutch managed to trade successfully with both the Mohawks and their avowed enemies, the Mohicans, throughout this period. Until the destruction of the Hurons, Dutch output was only a fraction of the French trade, amounting to several thousand beaver pelts a year, but considerably greater than that of the English. With the Mohawks as trading partners, the Dutch boosted their trade to a peak of 46,000 furs in 1657.[43] This was the highest shipment before the English conquest and annexation of New Netherland in 1664.

After the conquest of New York removed the Netherlands as a colonial contender, the English developed a vigorous fur-trading system competitive with that of the French. Colonial merchants continued to buy, bundle, and ship beaver and other furs from ports in New England and the Atlantic Coast states. In spite of continuing observations about depleted animal populations, Indians found sufficient furbearers to support an ongoing export fur industry in these regions.

With the Dutch removed from the scene, the British controlled Albany, the leading fur entrepôt for New York and New England, and its outlet to the sea, Manhattan, at the mouth of the Hudson River. Surviving Dutch fur merchants and new English traders located at Albany relied on the Mohawk Indians to deliver large numbers of beaver and other furs to them every year. James, duke of York, who held the patent for the newly conquered colony from Charles II on annual payment of forty beaver skins, permitted direct shipment of furs to Holland, where prices were generally better than in En-

42. Phillips, *The Fur Trade*, 1:149.

43. Allen W. Trelease, *Indian Affairs in Colonial New York: The Seventeenth Century* (Ithaca, N.Y.: Cornell University Press, 1960), 131.

gland. Albany merchants actually held formal rights to a monopoly of the fur trade confirmed by a charter granted by the governor of New York in 1686— a charter that was frequently evaded but which symbolized the predominance of Albany during the seventeenth century.[44]

The Mohawks and other Iroquois remained the dominant trading partners of the Albany merchants. The Iroquois domain in the seventeenth century stretched from the Mohawk River valley to the Buffalo area. To extend their hunting territories, the Mohawks attacked the Indians of southern Ontario and those to the south of Lake Erie. They also moved south into the valley of the Delaware River, attacked Indian groups living there, and took beaver pelts as tribute to trade at Albany.

The Iroquois, as did most other Indians, preferred English trade goods to those of the French. English strouds, or woolen blankets, were not only cheaper, but also warmer and more serviceable than those made by the French. English rum was cheaper and stronger than French brandy. These preferences strengthened the Five Nations in their hostility to the French and their military challenge to the French role in the northern fur trade (see below).

FRENCH AND OTTAWAS IN THE GREAT LAKES REGION

Flowing from Lake Ontario, the Saint Lawrence River offered a direct water route to the interconnected waterways of the Great Lakes and the Mississippi River valley. From the 1650s through the 1680s, several French explorers ventured deep into the interior as far west as Lake Superior and the valley of the Mississippi. Some of these men traveled without official authorization; most went with the encouragement of the French colonial authorities. Among those reporting and publicizing their discoveries were Jesuit missionaries who, by the 1640s, had reached the strategic juncture of Lake Huron and Lake Superior at Sault Sainte Marie and, by the 1670s, had mapped all the Great Lakes.[45]

To gain uninterrupted access to furs produced by the Great Lakes Indians, the French first had to develop an alliance with the Ottawas, whom Champlain initially had encountered in 1615. At their villages on the shores and islands of Lake Huron, the Ottawas were gatekeepers of interlake canoe transport and central actors in the wider Indian system of waterborne trade and diplomacy. The Ottawas held their strategic positions partly by their much-respected military prowess and belligerence but primarily because of their mastery of deepwater canoeing and navigation on the Great Lakes.

44. Phillips, *The Fur Trade*, 1:250.
45. Ibid., 1:220–21.

During the early seventeenth century, the approximately five thousand Ottawas divided into four named totemic groups.[46] To the east, fifteen hundred Kiskakons, descended from the black bear, spent the warmer southern months at the mouth of Nattawaga River on the southern shore of Georgian Bay. The Kiskakons were closely tied to and allied with the Iroquoian Tionnontates, or Petuns, whose villages lay to the south in the interior. The most ardent warriors of the Ottawas, the Kiskakons watched and defended the overland trails by which raiding parties from the Ottawas' inveterate enemies, the Five Nations Iroquois, would approach the lake.[47] On the southwestern coast of Lake Huron on the shores of Thunder Bay, seven hundred Nassaukuetons, descendants of Michachou, the great hare, scanned the water approaches from Lake Erie in the south. In the north, nearly two thousand Kamigas, descendants of the white sucker fish, from their villages at Michilimackinac on the coasts and islands of the Straits of Mackinac, controlled the route between Lake Michigan and Lake Huron. Finally, one thousand Sinagos, claiming descent from the gray squirrel, lived in summer fishing villages on the eastern end of Manitoulin, the immense island in northern Lake Huron. The Sinagos kept watch over the river routes flowing from Lake Nipissing into Lake Huron. They were also the guardians of the spiritual center of Ottawa culture and society on Manitoulin.[48] Manitoulin Island was the site for annual Ottawa councils that drew together the entire Ottawa nation.

Part of the Ottawa homeland lay in the boreal forest zone, with its truncated frost-free season, and part in the southern broadleaf forest zone that permitted reliable agriculture. The Ottawas followed a seasonal cycle of migration between summer settlements—used for fishing, trade, meetings, and ceremonies—and dispersed, small winter camps for hunting and trapping. In the summer, the Ottawas grew limited crops of beans and hardy "flint corn" but did not rely on these crops for the bulk of their food. They gathered berries and fruits and tapped maple trees for sap to make sugar.

Fishing supplied the most reliable portion of the Ottawa diet. Fishing in Lake Huron's rough waters was dangerous work that demanded great skill, courage, and canoes designed and built for open waters. The Ottawas cast

46. William James Newbigging, "The History of the French-Ottawa Alliance, 1613–1763" (Ph.D. diss., University of Toronto, 1995), 49. Newbigging gives the population estimates from Reuben Gold Thwaites, ed., *The Jesuit Relations and Allied Documents: Travels and Explorations of the Jesuit Missionaries in New France, 1610–1791* (Cleveland: Burrows Brothers, 1896–1901).

47. Ibid., 44. The Ottawas formed one branch of the Anishinabeg peoples, Central Algonkian speakers, who carried out this migration. The closely related Ojibwas occupied the Canadian forest north of Lakes Huron and Superior, and the Potawatomis went west to the broad-leaved Carolinian forest of southern Lake Michigan.

48. Ibid., 90–94.

and recovered gill nets weighted with sinkers and marked by floating buoys. They also used dip nets where fish came close to the surface.[49] When spring and fall spawning seasons brought masses of large lake fish into shallow waters, the Ottawas gathered a bountiful harvest. During the two-month spring spawning season, they caught lake sturgeons *(Acipenser fulvescens)*, channel catfish *(Ictalurus punctatus)*, white suckers *(Castotomus commersoni)*, and walleyes *(Stizostedion vitreum)*. In the shorter, two-week fall spawning season, they took lake trout *(Salvelinus namaycush)*, the smaller cisco or lake herrings *(Coregonus artedii)*, and above all, whitefish *(Coregonus clupeaformis)*. Women cleaned and smoked most of the catches for later consumption.

More than any other Great Lakes Indian nation, the Ottawas were superb long-distance paddlers and canoe handlers. Their experience fishing prepared them for traversing open waters across Huron and the other lakes with a boldness, speed, and endurance that few Indians could match. Building new lake canoes each year was one of the most important symbolic and economic acts of Ottawa society. In late winter, work parties of Ottawa women carefully cut and rolled wide sections of bark from white birches. From black spruce trees, they stripped thin, flexible roots for lashing and gum for sealing the canoes. Men found white cedar windfalls to split into narrow segments used for the canoe ribs, gunwales, and sheathing. Working together, both men and women constructed new canoes with high sterns and bows designed to survive open lake waters. When complete and watertight, the women applied dyes and designs to the canoes that denoted the four clan totems, as well as designs denoting either the sun or the spirit of water, called Michipichy.[50]

Ottawa males were determined hunters. During the long winter season, Ottawa hunters traveled hundreds of miles on foot and in their canoes up rivers in search of game. After extended fasting and dreaming ceremonies, they set off in the autumn on the dangerous task of hunting black bears, which, if successful, resulted in a great community feast and celebration. More prosaically, they stalked deer, moose, caribou, and elks for meat and for their hides, which they used for clothing. They shot ducks, cranes, geese, passenger pigeons, and other fowl with bows. They netted turtles and hunted wild turkeys for meat. They hunted wolves, mink, otters, marten, and muskrats for flesh and fur. In particular, Ottawa hunters devoted much time and energy to hunting beavers for meat and fur. During the winter months, after they had experienced favorable dream portents, groups of Ottawa hunters set out to find beaver ponds and inhabited lodges. They smashed holes in the dams to drain off the pond water under the ice, then broke into the lodges and netted and killed fleeing beavers. The Ottawas, in other

49. Ibid., 76.
50. Ibid., 64–70.

words, avidly hunted beaver and other furbearers long before the Europeans demanded beaver pelts.

The Ottawas were dominant figures in an intricate trading network that tied together Indians throughout the Great Lakes region. Various products circulated in what seems to have been largely an exchange of presents of accepted traditional value rather than a price-setting market. Much of the actual exchange of goods seems to have occurred in the presence of, and with the encouragement of, the Ottawas. They also seem to have carried exchange goods to the extremities of the system.

The more numerous Ojibwas, allied to the Ottawas by language and descent, fished and hunted along rivers to the north but were not cultivators. Instead, they and other northern Indians obtained maize, corn, beans, squash, and tobacco raised by Indians under more favorable climatic conditions to the south. The Ojibwas sent their furs and skins to those Indian groups to the south who were less devoted and energetic hunters. There were also specialized products. Ottawa women wove durable, colorful, and well-designed reed mats that were much in demand throughout the region.[51]

From their first acceptance of an iron-bladed ax from Champlain in 1615, the Ottawas entered willingly into a mutually advantageous trading relationship and a solidifying political and military alliance with the French. In return for furs, the French offered valuable iron implements and tools, blankets, and other trade goods, but above all else, muskets. The Ottawas were willing to trade their own furs and those obtained in their trade network for French goods. There is considerable evidence that, throughout this period, the Ottawas prevented the Ojibwas and other tribes from attempting to travel themselves to the French posts on the Saint Lawrence and, instead, acted as middlemen and exchanged trade goods with them.

For several decades, the Ottawas, along with Tionnontate Indians, sent joint flotillas of canoes laden with furs on the long, endurance-testing water route from Manitoulin Island to the French River, then inland to Lake Nipissing and, via portage, to the Matawwa River and then to the Ottawa River, where they traded their furs for trade goods via Huron intermediaries.[52] Trading in this fashion brought highly valued goods and, in this early stage, left Ottawa society and culture intact and vital.

However, in the aftermath of the midcentury destruction of the Iroquois and the Hurons, the Ottawas made direct contact with the French. The Ottawa-French relationship moved quickly toward a full-blown alliance. Removal of the Huron buffer brought new Iroquois attacks from the east that drove the Kiskakon Ottawas from Nottawasaga Bay, along with may of their

51. Ibid., 79.
52. There is no direct evidence that the Ottawa actually entered the Saint Lawrence or traded directly with the French before 1649. Personal communication from Bruce Trigger.

Tionnontate allies, to take refuge with the Sinago Ottawas on Manitoulin Island. Despite this reverse, the Ottawas vigorously defended their remaining territory against repeated Iroquois attacks throughout the 1650s and resumed their fur-trading journeys to Montreal.

In 1654, Ottawas and Tionnontates who came to Montreal with furs agreed to take back with them two young venturesome French traders, Médard Chouart des Groseilliers and Pierre-Esprit Radisson. Two years later, Groseilliers and Radisson returned to Montreal with sixty canoes full of prime furs worth a hundred thousand livres. In 1665, Nicholas Perrot made his headquarters at Sault Sainte Marie and began buying furs from the Great Lakes Indians. In 1670, Perrot returned to Montreal accompanied by nine hundred Ottawas in canoes loaded with furs. During the 1660s, several Jesuit missionaries accompanied the Ottawa fur flotillas back to Lake Huron and established Saint Ignace, a permanent mission station at Michilimackinac.[53]

THE IMPERIAL CONFLICT

Two British interventions in the latter half of the seventeenth century—the creation of direct sea links between Hudson Bay and England and the conquest of the Dutch Hudson River territory—neatly encircled the French fur-trading system of the Saint Lawrence River valley. From 1664 to 1763, the British and French struggled for imperial dominance in North America. This conflict found its most direct expression in ferocious competition for the fur trade. The great prize was access to the Indians and the still-plentiful furbearers of the Great Lakes and upper Mississippi territories. This greater European imperial struggle swept all northeastern Indian groups into its sphere. Every Indian group in the region was forced to align itself with one or the other colonial regime and, periodically, to die in its wars.

Between 1689 and 1763, Britain and France fought each other in four separate European wars that spilled over into North America: the War of the League of Augsburg (King William's War), 1689–1697; the War of Spanish Succession, 1702–1713; the War of Austrian Succession, 1739–1748; and the Seven Years' War, 1754–1763. Between 1689 and 1763, these European conflicts thrust North American colonists and Indians alike into hostilities for one year in every two. At the end of the War of Spanish Succession, the Treaty of Utrecht removed France from Newfoundland, Acadia, and the subarctic territories of northern Canada. The Treaty of Louisburg in 1763 marked the final defeat of the French and left most of North America, save for Louisiana, to British colonial rule. The Indians mobilized by each side did much of the fighting and suffered most of the losses in these conflicts.

In addition to these larger wars, Indians engaged in internecine warfare

53. Newbigging, "The History of the French-Ottawa Alliance," 159–65.

at a frequency and intensity seemingly beyond what they had known prior to the French intervention. Seeking security in a time when little was to be had, defeated Indian groups engaged in kaleidoscopic relocations and removals in reaction to adversity and threatened extinction. Rather than offer greater opportunities for advantage and maneuver, the two European contenders for territory and trade, in the end, diverted Indian energies into diplomacy and war. This, in turn, reduced whatever economic benefits they had previously enjoyed by supplying furs for the European market.

The French responded to British encirclement by linear extension of the Saint Lawrence system deep into the interior of North America.[54] Men like Jean Talon, intendant general of New France for eight years under Colbert, and his successor, Louis de Baude, comte de Frontenac (governor from 1672 to 1682 and 1689 to 1698), saw the potential richness of the fur territories to the west and acted vigorously to encourage and promote the expansion of French trade. Talon argued, rightly, that the western lakes and rivers afforded water routes that permitted easy access to and control of these new fur territories.[55]

The French imperial vision coincided with the interests of the Ottawas in the Great Lakes region. During the 1670s, the Ottawas pressed the French to establish a trading settlement at Michilimackinac. If the French would do so, the Ottawas could obtain guns and other trade goods without making the exhausting trip to Montreal every summer, and they could control the distribution of guns among the Great Lakes Indians. Finally, in 1683, shaking free of Colbert's restraints, Frontenac, the governor of New France, sent Daniel Grasolon Duluth with fifteen French-manned canoes to set up a trading post on the Straits of Mackinac. This action cemented the Ottawa-French alliance that survived intact until 1763.

From this base, the French sent more fur traders and began to build a network of trading posts throughout the Great Lakes region. Nicholas Perrot and Louis Jolliet founded a trading post at present-day Green Bay to trade on the Wisconsin River. In the 1680s, Duluth journeyed to the headwaters of the Mississippi and thereafter established successful fur-trading posts on Lake Superior, near the mouth of the Kaministiguia River, on Lake Nipigon, and on the Albany River.

French discovery of the Mississippi set the outer bounds of the western fur trade. In 1673, Louis Jolliet and Father Marquette portaged between the Fox and Wisconsin Rivers and followed the Wisconsin to the upper Mississippi River. Jolliet and Marquette traveled down the Mississippi, past its confluence with the Missouri and the Ohio, to the vicinity of the Arkansas River intersection before returning. In the 1680s, Robert Cavalier de La Salle, an active

54. Phillips, *The Fur Trade*, 1:220.
55. Ibid., 1:222.

fur trader and confidant of Frontenac, devised a grand scheme to reach the mouth of the Mississippi and to claim the Mississippi River valley for a French empire in the west. La Salle and his companion Henri de Tonty canoed down the Illinois River to its junction with the Mississippi and continued downstream to finally reach the Gulf of Mexico. On April 9, 1682, La Salle formally claimed the entire Mississippi Basin for the king of France.

THE FRENCH-IROQUOIS WARS

During the late seventeenth century, however, the Iroquois, not the British, were the major enemy of New France. It was the Iroquois Confederacy that directly and aggressively threatened the growing network of French settlements and New France's Indian allies. The French and Iroquois, each aiming to dominate the lands and peoples of the Great Lakes interior, clashed in raids and counterraids that rose in intensity and scale to reach the level of all-out war.[56] The French fought to control the western fur trade. The Iroquois, encouraged, supported, and supplied by the British at Albany, fought to prevent French intrusion into hunting lands they considered their own and to keep the French from arming and dominating non-Iroquois that the Iroquois had marked for future conquest and assimilation as war captives. They also fought to have access to the fur trade of the interior and the flow of trade goods imported to pay for those furs—especially guns, which were increasingly important for Iroquois military operations. Obtaining control over the fur trade was part of a complicated mixture of motives that shaped Iroquois diplomacy and war, but it was not their only goal.[57]

During the 1670s and 1680s, the Five Nations Iroquois became progressively more upset by French incursions into lands located around Lake Ontario and Lake Erie that the Iroquois used as their primary hunting grounds. They feared that French forts built in this region would encourage their Indian allies—enemies to the Iroquois—to freely hunt in these tracts and deplete their food and fur resources.[58] Simultaneously, they suffered dismaying population losses in at least five major epidemics. To recover these losses, they would have to follow their usual practice of going to war and taking captives who could be assimilated into their society.[59]

56. W. J. Eccles, "The Fur Trade and Eighteenth-Century Imperialism," *William and Mary Quarterly*, 3d ser., 40 (1983): 342–44.

57. José António Brandão, *Your Fyre Shall Burn No More: Iroquois Policy towards New France and Its Native Allies to 1701* (Lincoln: University of Nebraska Press, 1997); Francis Jennings, *The Ambiguous Iroquois Empire: The Covenant Chain Confederation of Indian Tribes with English Colonies, from Its Beginnings to the Lancaster Treaty of 1744*, 1st ed. (New York: W. W. Norton, 1984).

58. Brandão, *Your Fyre Shall Burn No More*, 117–22.

59. Ibid., 115, table B1.

In the 1680s, the French became increasingly perturbed over attempts by English and Dutch traders accompanied by Iroquois to open direct access to the western fur trade.[60] Governor Denonville, acting under direct orders from Louis XIV to bring the Iroquois under French royal authority, attacked the Senecas in the summer of 1687. The Iroquois responded with an attack on Niagara and a massacre at La Chine, a French settlement near Montreal. This war soon merged into the War of the League of Augsburg, which broke out in 1689.

Between 1687 and 1697, "the Iroquois launched thirty-three raids against the French alone, sent armies of a thousand men or more against the colony three times, and captured or killed close to six hundred people."[61] They mounted an additional sixteen assaults against the Indian allies of the French. This was an enormous effort for a force of slightly over 2,000 Iroquois warriors.[62] The French settlers, aided by 1,500 regular troops sent from France, mounted thirty-three raids of their own with the assistance of their Indian allies. The Iroquois suffered greater losses—between 2,158 and 2,351 persons killed, captured, or lost, most of them male warriors. The Iroquois followed their customary practice of assimilating some Indian, but generally not French, captives into their society and reemployed them as warriors. Despite this, the number of Iroquois warriors probably fell by half during the decade.[63]

When, in 1697, the war ended in Europe, the Iroquois, deprived of further English support, reluctantly entered into peace negotiations with the French that were to last four years. Finally, in August 1701, Louis-Hector de Callières, governor-general of New France, convened a grand assembly of 1,300 Indians at Montreal to confirm a comprehensive treaty. In addition to the representatives of the Five Nations Iroquois, those of twenty-eight Indian tribes allied with the French were also present.

The French recognized that the Iroquois could be a useful buffer between themselves and the British colonies if neutralized. The Iroquois, exhausted by the war, no longer hoped to drive out the French and had discovered that the British were unreliable in their support. The Iroquois negotiators recognized that they would be able to play the French off against the British in the future. Therefore, the Iroquois willingly agreed to a clause in the peace treaty by which they declared that, in any future war between the French and the British, they, the Iroquois, would remain neutral. At one stroke, the greatest single threat to French western expansion and the fur trade vanished.[64]

60. Phillips, *The Fur Trade*, 1:260–61.
61. Brandão, *Your Fyre Shall Burn No More*, 125.
62. Ibid., 157.
63. Ibid., 126.
64. Eccles, "The Fur Trade and Eighteenth-Century Imperialism," 344.

THE FRENCH WESTERN FUR TRADE

Each imperial contender adopted a distinctive approach to extending its share of the fur trade. The French colonial state actively organized a state monopoly system that sent individual traders in canoes out to a system of trading posts for direct purchases of furs from their Indian producers. The British regime left its traders free to organize a purchasing system that relied heavily on Indian hunters and middlemen. Wide-ranging Iroquois warriors acquired furs by direct hunting, trade, and frequently, plunder, and brought the proceeds directly to Albany to exchange for trading goods. The French approach encouraged continuing westward exploration and territorial claims in new fur-producing regions. The British approach conserved energy for settlement and development of territories already held.

By the late seventeenth century, French interests dictated a vigorous westward expansion of the fur trade. Montreal, rather than Quebec, became the dominant trading center. The movement west of surviving Hurons and other defeated enemies of the Mohawks extended the reach of the fur trade. Merchants in New France sent skilled woodsmen, the French, and mixed French-Indian *coureurs de bois* to trade with these new sources of furs. The *coureurs de bois* canoed long distances up the river system to trade directly with the Ottawas and other new middlemen around the Great Lakes.[65]

French monopoly control provided stable capitalization, trade goods, quality control, and the processing and shipping services necessary to send furs to metropolitan markets. The actual collection of furs from the Indians was the task of licensed individual fur traders, who were given a high degree of freedom to barter and trade where it was most profitable.

As they fought the Iroquois, the French tightened their grip on the Great Lakes fur trade by a long drawn-out process of trial and error. They planted dozens of colonial settlements throughout the region. Invariably the sites were at strategic locations along water transport routes. Some French settlements were solely mission stations, some were fur-trading posts; many combined both functions. French forts and garrisons protected the largest trading settlements.

Acting from long experience, French fur traders established intimate, generally amicable, and profitable relationships with one Indian group after another. As Perrot did with the Ottawas, the French traders lived with and adopted the dress, food, and habits of their hosts and often took Indian wives. They learned to speak their hosts' language acceptably. These intimate ties certainly facilitated the exchange of furs for trade goods and benefited both parties. French fur traders pressed eagerly westward to the Great Lakes,

65. Phillips, *The Fur Trade,* 1:203.

south to the Mississippi River valley, and finally north to the Hudson Bay drainage system.

For the six decades remaining to French imperial rule in North America, the *coureurs de bois* enlisted Indian hunters and traders; exchanged guns, woolens, alcohol, tools, implements, and other trade goods for furs and skins; and packed and carried their stocks back to Montreal. The eighteenth-century western French fur trade settled into a pattern that relied on nineteen major fur-trading entrepôts in the Great Lakes region and four in Louisiana territory. Together these twenty-three posts sent an annual flow of furs east. These were carried by canoe to Montreal to be bulked and shipped across the Atlantic to La Rochelle in France.

Operating under strict official regulation, traders at these posts could purchase 5,685 100-pound packs of furs each year (568,500 pounds).[66] Detroit was the largest supplier of furs, sending a total of 900 packs (15.8 percent) of all allocations. Next was Michilimackinac, the famed fur-trading center that mediated traffic between Lake Huron and Lake Michigan, which sent 650 packs (11.4 percent). Then followed Baie des Puants (Green Bay), located on the Fox River where it runs into an arm of Lake Michigan, which sent 550 packs (9.7 percent) of the annual allocation.

Fur traders from Montreal formed into small companies, often in partnership with post commanders, and purchased either monopoly leases (farms) for these posts or licenses to import a fixed amount of trade goods to the post. The Crown reserved trading at six of the easternmost posts—La Belle Rivière, Niagara, Frontenac, Rouille, La Présentation, and Domaine du Roi—for salaried royal agents. Altogether, the royal monopoly purchased 845 packs of furs, or 14.9 percent of the annual total.

Judging by output, French westward expansion was a success. The intake of beaver furs rose decisively from the modest 15,000 to 20,000 pelts of the annual shipments in the first half of the seventeenth century. During the 1680s, fur traders delivered an average of 73,000 beaver furs (weighing 100,850 livres) each year at Montreal's official warehouses.[67] In the 1690s, beaver fur deliveries spiraled upward to the point of glut during the Iroquois-French wars. For the entire seventeenth century, data for eighteen selected years put the annual average intake of beaver furs at 75,000 pelts (104,173 livres). Although subject to considerable fluctuations, totals continued to rise in the eighteenth century. Between 1700 and the final French defeat in

66. Richard C. Harris and Geoffrey J. Matthews, *Historical Atlas of Canada* (Toronto: University of Toronto Press, 1987), vol. 1, pl. 40.

67. Calculated from Harold Adams Innis, *Fur Trade in Canada: An Introduction to Canadian Economic History* (Toronto: University of Toronto Press, 1956), 149–52, appendix A. Each beaver fur weighed on average 680 grams. Beaver furs were recorded by weight, so the number of furs is an approximate number.

1763, traders sent, on average, 122,000 beaver furs (weighing 169,381 livres) each year to Montreal.[68]

Although beaver was the fur most in demand in European markets, furs and skins from other animals actually made up the greater part of exports sent from New France. Between 1728 and 1755, the value of fur shipments sent to La Rochelle from Quebec averaged 875,000 or so livres tournois per year. Beaver furs contributed 43 percent to this total, other furs 41 percent, and deer and elk skins and hides 17 percent.[69] Relative proportions are similar when calculating the numbers of animals slaughtered. Over the same period, in a single year, hunters killed on average around 286,000 animals to meet this annual export demand. Beaver populations clearly bore the greatest hunting pressure: the 114,000 beaver skins exported represented 38.8 percent of the total kill. Hunters pursued other furbearers with far less intensity. Only raccoons, at 25.6 percent, approached the beaver total, followed by marten at 11.1 percent, bears at 4.4 percent, river otters at 2.6 percent, and four types of foxes at 1.7 percent. Deer represented just under 7 percent, with an average of around 20,000 skins taken per year.[70]

THE EXPANDING ENGLISH FUR TRADE IN THE EIGHTEENTH CENTURY

Toward the end of the seventeenth century, both British and French fur traders were looking to the prolific fur-bearing animals of the far north, the Canadian subarctic. The colder regions of the subarctic—the boreal forest and tundra wetlands—produced the thickest and most valuable beaver pelts and other furs.

In the 1660s, two French fur traders had ventured north of Lake Superior overland to Hudson Bay. Pierre Radisson and Jean-Baptiste de Groseilliers tried to interest French merchants and officials in establishing a maritime route to Hudson Bay. Rebuffed by the French, they eventually were patronized by King Charles I of England. An exploratory voyage in 1668 was the stimulus for the founding of the Hudson's Bay Company in 1670. Chartered by the king, the joint-stock company received sole right to trade in Hudson Bay and its hinterland. The first Hudson's Bay Company expedition sailed in

68. Ibid. Based on data for twenty-nine of the sixty-three years in question.

69. Thomas Wien, "Castor, peaux, et pelleteries dans le commerce canadien des fourrures, 1720–1790," in *"Le Castor Fait Tout": Selected Papers of the Fifth North American Fur Trade Conference, 1985,* edited by Bruce G. Trigger, Toby Morantz, and Louise Dechene (Montreal: Lake St. Louis Historical Society, 1987). Average value and percentages calculated from data on p. 92, table 4. Data for ten years only. The numbers are certainly not reliable to the last pelt or hide but are probably reasonably close to the actual count. A ±10 percent margin of error seems a reasonable assumption. Numbers given in the text are rounded.

70. Ibid., 89, appendix A, table 2.

1671, found three sites for future trading posts on rivers flowing into the bay, and returned with three thousand pounds of beaver skins.[71]

The English had opened up a new, direct maritime route into Hudson Bay that, by making expensive canoe travel by European traders unnecessary, reduced costs substantially. The French responded by forming a rival trading company for Hudson Bay and sending ships to trade. Over the next decades, varying levels of threat and force marked the conflict over control of trade and the region. Control of the posts commanding the major rivers entering into the bay changed hands on numerous occasions. Not until the Treaty of Utrecht in 1713 expelled the French from Hudson Bay did the British gain clear and unchallenged supremacy over the northern water route. Despite the difficulties of French competition, the Hudson's Bay Company had been generally successful in sending back cargoes of furs and was extremely profitable.

After Utrecht, the Hudson's Bay Company traders operated from four posts surrounding James Bay—Forts Richmond, Eastmain, Moose, and Albany—and three posts on the southwestern shore of Hudson Bay: Forts Severn, York, and Churchill. From the posts, they developed durable trading partnerships with the Algonkian-speaking Crees and Siouan-speaking Assiniboines of the boreal forest regions, who served as middlemen for more distant tribes. From its earliest years of operation, York Factory attracted furs from Plains Indians like the Mandans, Bloods, Blackfoot, and Sioux, some of whom made a thousand-mile round-trip to the factory. By 1720, when the Plains Indians were adapting to horses, they were less inclined to make the difficult canoe trip to Hudson Bay, and the Crees and Assiniboines dominated the trade. Newly established in 1717, Fort Churchill became the westernmost Hudson Bay trading establishment. Here, despite stiff Cree resistance, English traders slowly built up direct trade with the Chipewyans and other Athabascan-speaking subarctic Indians.[72]

The seven trading posts bordering the James and Hudson Bays were located in low-lying boreal forest, muskeg, or tundra, which had little in the way of game or furbearers. Only great flights of geese twice a year, partridges, and rabbits could be looked to for a food supply. The Cree Indians visited the area yearly for goose hunting but did not live there. Productive agriculture posed real difficulties that far north. To provision the posts, the Hudson's Bay Company hired bands of Cree Indians to hunt year-round. What came to be called "Home Guard Cree," as distinct from the middleman

71. Phillips, *The Fur Trade*, 1:270.

72. Arthur J. Ray and Donald B. Freeman, *"Give Us Good Measure": An Economic Analysis of Relations between the Indians and the Hudson's Bay Company before 1763* (Toronto: University of Toronto Press, 1978), 45–51; Yerbury, *The Subarctic Indians and the Fur Trade*, 16–50.

fur-trading groups, settled down near the posts. They were paid with trade goods, including arms and munitions, and guaranteed food security in wintertime. These contract hunters ranged widely to obtain moose, caribou, deer, and geese to supply the posts. This put increased hunting pressure on these animals throughout radial hinterlands of extraordinary area.

Hudson's Bay Company traders regularly collected and shipped large numbers of beaver pelts and other furs from this new resource. In addition to beaver, Indians traded marten, wolverine, wolf, red fox, bear, wildcat, and muskrat pelts—all luxuriant, cold-weather furs fetching good prices. Marten, for which the company paid a price that was kept at one-third the price of prime beaver furs, were taken in numbers that at times approached those of beavers. Albany Fort, for example, averaged 6,600 marten and 10,500 beaver pelts per year between 1750 and 1763.[73] Beaver retained its value, however, and between 1700 and 1763 the fort shipped nearly a million beaver pelts, an average of over 15,000 per year.

By midcentury, the beaver catch had begun to drop as beaver populations were hunted out. Albany Fort averaged 19,000 beaver pelts a year in the first two decades of the century, which dropped to an average of 15,600 pelts annually between 1720 and 1749, followed by declining average annual yields of 10,700 for the period 1750 to 1763.[74] Simulations of prices and the annual Fort Albany yield and dynamics of the beaver population in the fort's hinterland corroborate the notion of depletion.[75]

Nevertheless, in spite of these trends, the Hudson's Bay Company traders bought, baled, and shipped sufficient numbers of high-quality northern furs to average 8,205 pounds sterling each year in customs valuations in London. Subarctic furs accounted for just under one-third (32.7 percent) of all North American colonial fur imports into England in the period 1700 to 1775.[76]

To the south of the French corridor, the English fur trade flourished in the six decades before the French defeat in 1763. From Charleston to Boston, ports along the Atlantic seaboard served as entrepôts for the fur trade. Even the Carolinas and Virginia sent a few thousand beaver furs each year to London (see below). Philadelphia drew furs from hunters in the Delaware River valley and in Pennsylvania. Boston was a catchment for furs taken by the Abenakis and other Indians to the Northeast. The leading fur

73. Calculated from Ann M. Carlos and Frank D. Lewis, "Indians, the Beaver, and the Bay: The Economics of Depletion in the Lands of the Hudson's Bay Company, 1700–1763," *Journal of Economic History* 53 (1993): 477, table 2.

74. Ibid., 474–75, table 1. York Fort, the highest-yielding post, had its best returns during 1720 to 1740, with an annual average of 33,616 pelts. For the period 1750 to 1763, this average slipped to just under 18,000 pelts per year.

75. Ibid., 480, fig. 3.

76. Data from John Lawson, *A New Voyage to Carolina* (Chapel Hill: University of North Carolina Press, 1967), 108–9, appendix E.

exporter in the British colonies, however, was Manhattan, the officially designated entrepôt for furs collected at the head of the Hudson River in Albany and Schenectady. From 1700 to 1775, New York's production was double that of New England, its nearest competitor. New York averaged 4,156 pounds sterling in furs sent each year to Britain, 16.6 percent of the annual average sent by the colonies for the period.[77]

As before, the Mohawks and other Iroquois were the primary trading partners for the English and Dutch traders of the interior. Some, but probably not a majority, of the furs collected in New York were the product of direct hunting by Iroquois warriors. A considerable portion of the furs bought by upstate traders was actually contraband smuggled by Christian Iroquois settled in New France near Montreal.[78] These Indians traded for western Indian furs before they reached Montreal and brought them down Lake Champlain to get better prices and better quality English trade goods at Schenectady and Albany. The French authorities turned a blind eye to this illegal commerce because, by this means, French fur traders obtained English strouds, kettles, firearms, and other goods to be sent west for exchange with Indian suppliers there.

Another growing portion of furs came from western Indians who traveled to Lake Ontario to exchange their furs directly with English traders. In 1724, New York's Governor Burnet built a fort at Oswego where the Oswego River (then the Onondaga River) empties into Lake Ontario. From Oswego, a water route led to Schenectady, interrupted only by a 4.8-kilometer portage between the Mohawk River and Wood Creek. Large numbers of Albany traders began journeying every year to buy furs from the Ottawas, Miami, Ojibwas, and other Great Lakes Indians who had been dissuaded by the lengthier journey to the Hudson River.[79]

CREEK DEER HUNTERS

The warmer southern regions of North America did not produce furbearers with coats as lustrous, thick, and longhaired as those in the colder north. Early British settlers found beaver dams throughout Virginia and the Carolinas. During the seventeenth and eighteenth centuries, coastal Atlantic Indian tribes such as the Tuscaroras and Westos hunted beavers and supplied pelts for export. Generally, however, the numbers were small and the pelts less valuable. Virginia, for example, sent only two thousand beaver pelts each

77. Calculated from Carlos and Lewis, "Indians, the Beaver, and the Bay," 477, table 2.
78. Jean Lunn, "The Illegal Fur Trade Out of New France, 1713–1760," *Canadian Historical Association Report of the Annual Meeting* (1939).
79. Richter and the Institute of Early American History and Culture, *The Ordeal of the Longhouse,* 248–52.

year to London between 1699 and 1714, and Charleston exported only about six hundred pelts per year.[80] Instead, colonists discovered that the immense herds of white-tailed deer in the south could be made profitable.[81]

In Virginia, the Carolinas, Georgia, and Florida, the deer population was enormous during the seventeenth century. All observers contemporary to the time commented on the extraordinary abundance of deer, elks, and even wild bison that slowly had returned to the Southeast. Such was the abundance and ease of the New World that deer could be freely taken by anyone without punishment or permission. Deer taken from the interior and at higher elevations were larger, fatter, and more desirable than those found in the heat of the coastal plain.[82] Postcontact Indian depopulation permitted deer and other wildlife numbers to escalate. For two centuries, successive waves of disease thinned the numbers of the indigenous horticulturists and hunters of the North American Southeast.[83] Few natural predators, apart from wolves and panthers, threatened the deer herds in a landscape seemingly made for browsing creatures.

The contrast with the Old World deer population is striking. American deerskins began arriving in England just as domestic herds of deer declined. Those deer herds that remained in England were semidomesticated. They survived only because an aristocratic hunting culture stringently enforced game laws and set aside land for protected deer parks and forest reserves. Even with these protections, widespread poaching and illegal sale of deer meat and deer hides continued to deplete the deer population. However, these were capricious and covert sources for the leather industry. Over time, deer parks and reserved forests gave way to the needs of the rural iron industry and agricultural expansion.[84]

The British leather industry turned to New World deerskins to manufacture durable, popular men's leather breeches, gloves, bookbindings, and other applications that demanded strong, supple, lightweight leather. Supplies of cattle hides from Europe were also constricted by an epidemic disease wasting cattle herds between 1710 and 1714 and recurring thereafter.

---

80. Timothy Silver, *A New Face on the Countryside: Indians, Colonists, and Slaves in South Atlantic Forests, 1500–1800* (Cambridge: Cambridge University Press, 1990), 98.

81. For an overview of the deerskin hunt, see Krech, *The Ecological Indian*, 151–71.

82. Lawson, *A New Voyage to Carolina*, 126–27.

83. For lists of episodes of epidemic and pandemic disease among the American Indians, see Henry F. Dobyns, William R. Swagerty, and the Newberry Library Center for the History of the American Indian, *Their Number Become Thinned: Native American Population Dynamics in Eastern North America* (Knoxville: University of Tennessee Press, 1983), 7–32. The first major pandemic of smallpox in 1520–1524 caused the greatest loss of life and disruption of Indian societies across the New World.

84. Roger B. Manning, *Hunters and Poachers: A Social and Cultural History of Unlawful Hunting in England, 1485–1640* (Oxford: Clarendon Press; New York: Oxford University Press, 1993).

Spared this disease, England banned import of hides and cattle from Europe. American deerskins increasingly made up shortages in raw materials for the domestic English industry.[85]

As was the case earlier with northern furbearers, Indians offered a cheap, easily mobilized source of labor to hunt and process deerskins. In the colonial South, Indians, who had long depended on deer for much of their meat and clothing requirements, began to kill and process deerskins for export. Almost all Indians in this region became producers for the deerskin market. Market demand originating in Charleston and other coastal port cities rapidly diffused throughout an extensive region and among many different groups of Indians. Along the coast, the Saponi peoples in the Roanoke River area of Virginia and the diverse Catawba groups in the Carolina Piedmont soon became active hunters.[86] By the turn of the century, Choctaws from the lower Mississippi region were in direct contact with English and French traders.

Production of hides for the deerskin trade depended on a relatively small population of Indian hunters and processors spread over a vast area stretching from the Atlantic Coast inland for a thousand miles to the lower Mississippi River valley. By 1700, the remnants of many groups of Indian tribes had coalesced into various "nations," or groups defined by shared kinship, cultural, linguistic, and political ties. The fast-declining Indian population of the southeastern United States—living in the area between Virginia and Florida, and between the Atlantic Coast and eastern Texas—is estimated to have numbered 130,600 at the turn of the century.[87]

The Creeks, who ranged widely over the best hunting grounds in the Southeast and who generally were conceded to be the finest hunters, numbered approximately 4,000 warriors among a total population of 14,000 to 20,000 in the 1770s.[88] Although the Creeks adapted quickly and successfully to the new incentives of the deerskin trade, they, like other Indian hunters in the Southeast, faced a basic contradiction.[89] Economic and political forces made it imperative that they deliver a maximal number of deerskins every

85. Kathryn E. Holland Braund, *Deerskins and Duffels: The Creek Indian Trade with Anglo-America, 1685–1815* (Lincoln: University of Nebraska Press, 1993), 42.

86. James Hart Merrell and Institute of Early American History and Culture, *The Indians' New World: Catawbas and Their Neighbors from European Contact through the Era of Removal* (Chapel Hill: University of North Carolina Press, for the Institute of Early American History and Culture, Williamsburg, Va., 1989).

87. Peter H. Wood, "The Changing Population of the Colonial South: An Overview by Race and Region, 1685–1790," in *Powhatan's Mantle: Indians in the Colonial Southeast*, edited by Gregory A. Waselkov, M. Thomas Hatley, and Peter H. Wood (Lincoln: University of Nebraska Press, 1989), 38–39, table 1.

88. Braund, *Deerskins and Duffels*, 9.

89. Hudson, "Why the Southeastern Indians Slaughtered Deer," 157–76. The Choctaw followed a path similar to that of the Creeks. See Richard White, *The Roots of Dependency: Subsistence,*

year. They became market hunters linked into the world market who used muskets to avidly pursue as many deer (and bear) as possible during their annual fall and winter season. Guns could be obtained only by offering deerskins to French, English, or Spanish traders. For the Creeks and other Indian groups who survived, muskets were essential for self-defense against Indians employed by the English as slavers in earlier years and in intra-Indian warfare throughout the eighteenth century.

Simultaneously, Creeks and other Indians believed that they existed in a special relationship to the deer, bears, and other animals they pursued. These animals had to be treated with respect or the consequences would be severe. Many taboos and rules regulated Creek behavior toward game animals, both before they were taken and after death. If hunters killed deer carelessly or disrespectfully, serious harm, including withdrawal of the herds and the onset of disease for humans, might be the result. Therefore, Creek hunters employed ancient ceremonies for purification by sweating and steaming and by singing, dancing, and dreaming as preparation for the hunt. Various potions were ingested; others were rubbed on the skin. The hunters carried charms like the physic-nut in buckskin pouches to aid their efforts. To the best of their ability, the hunters tried to treat their prey with respect and honor. They obeyed taboos against taking the skins of sick or dying deer.

Mutual respect also implied some restraint—that the hunters would kill deer sufficient for their needs, but no more. The imperatives of production for a world market made restraint difficult. Conforming to these pressures, each Creek warrior hunted with great ferocity and determination until his domestic needs and his market role were fulfilled.

Each hunter and his wife and children in a nuclear family formed a production unit. In October, the hunters and their families traveled on horseback to dispersed hunting camps and remained there until the end of February each year. The Creek warriors hunted with muskets, on foot in groups of men from the same clan. They depended on their knowledge of deer habits and habitats to stalk their prey day after day in a familiar hunting range. As one English observer commented, "Their manner of rambling through the woods to kill deer, is a very laborious exercise, as they frequently walk twenty-five to thirty miles through rough and smooth grounds, and fasting, before they return to camp loaded."[90] This sustained effort resulted in fifty to as many as seventy-five deer slain each season by each hunter.

In a good year, Creek hunters might harvest two hundred thousand to three hundred thousand deerskins, of which perhaps half were sold to

Environment, and Social Change among the Choctaws, Pawnees, and Navajos (Lincoln: University of Nebraska Press, 1983), 1–146.

90. Braund, *Deerskins and Duffels,* 67, quoting James Adair, *Adair's History of the American Indians* (Johnson City: Watauga Press, 1930; reprint, New York: Argonaut Press, 1966), 432.

traders. Damaged hides and home consumption of deerskin dictated that perhaps half of the skins taken were not traded but consumed at home.[91] Dried and smoked deer meat was the main source of year-round protein for the Creeks and their families.

Creek women, who formed the other side of the production unit, processed the skins for sale and for domestic use. Semiprocessed skins for the trade were cleaned of flesh and fur, stretched, sun dried, and smoked in an abbreviated treatment. Each finished export hide weighed between one and two pounds. Skins for domestic use went through additional steps such as soaking in a solution of water and deer brains, pounding, stretching, drying, smoking, and dyeing to become a soft, pliable, lightweight leather. Traditional female skills in leather working necessarily survived the transition to commercial production. So also did traditional skills in subsistence agriculture and pottery making.

The Creeks became enthusiastic consumers of the trade goods offered in payment for deerskins by English and French traders. William Bartram commented, "[They] wage eternal war against deer and bear, to procure food and cloathing [sic], and other necessaries and conveniences; which is indeed carried to an unreasonable and perhaps criminal excess, since the white people have dazzled their senses with foreign superfluities."[92] As did other Indians in the Southeast, the Creeks obtained smoothbore muskets (Birmingham muskets), powder, and shot; metal tools such as axes, knives, hatchets, needles, scissors, and especially iron kettles; red, blue, white, or striped heavy woolen blankets (duffles); lighter weight strouds, which were cheaper woolen cloths in scarlet or blue used for men's leggings and breechcloths and women's skirts; decorative glass beads and face paint; and finally, rum. The Creeks negotiated price lists for all these items with the British and French colonies that remained relatively stable throughout the century. Muskets, at six deerskins per gun, and duffel blankets, at four to six deerskins each, were the most expensive items.[93]

The new consumerism meant that most native manufactures fell away and the society depended on imported goods. Creek hunters lost older bow- and arrow-making skills and did not learn the technology of fabricating muskets—although they could make repairs. Traders extended credit to Creek hunters in the form of trade goods in the spring of each year. Debts were to be paid a year hence, when hides were brought back to the village. Trade goods were expensive by any measure, and debts mounted as the season's catch often failed to pay off previous credit extended by the trader. To maintain their standard of living, the Creeks continually warred against the

91. Braund, *Deerskins and Duffels,* 71.
92. Quoted in ibid., 121.
93. Ibid., 121–38.

Choctaws, the Florida tribes, and the Cherokees. Creek leaders engaged in ongoing negotiations with the English and French governments and with traders to improve the terms of trade.

Creek society adapted willingly and easily to the new economic regime. The Creeks maintained their social cohesion and sense of identity and acted decisively to control their destiny in the eighteenth century. For much of the century, deerskin production, however arduous, was seen as beneficial to the Creek. The relatively unchanged nature of women's roles played a critical part in Creek stability. Greater inequities in personal property were noticeable, but communal property in land persisted. The matrilineal kin system maintained its strength. Younger men, emboldened by rum, defied their elders and engaged in horse thievery or clashed with both white and red neighbors.

Still, chiefs and elder males maintained their effective influence and power. Even frequent bouts of drunkenness by groups of men and women, with their consequent loss of social constraints, did not rip apart the society—dismaying as these often violent displays were to outsiders. Creek society, with its air of hospitality, generosity, and corporate responsibility for each individual, retained much that European observers found appealing.

EIGHTEENTH-CENTURY DEERSKIN TRADE TRAJECTORY

New World deerskin production began to be substantial by 1700. Charleston, South Carolina, first settled under royal charter in 1670, took an early lead in this trade. By 1700, Charleston's five thousand inhabitants were well acquainted with the interior and its Indian residents. The colonists had settled on deerskins as the only commercially viable staples that could be exported (apart from Indian slaves). Between 1699 and 1704, Charleston shipped an annual average of 49,000 heavy deer pelts to London. By the late 1750s, Charleston's exports of pelts had more than doubled, to over 137,000 hides exported each year.[94] The founding of Augusta in 1735, and the subsequent organization of well-capitalized trading companies operating in Creek, Chicksaw, and Choctaw territory, stimulated Indian production. In the 1750s, Savannah shipped 100,000 or more hides per year.[95] The French entrepôts at Mobile and New Orleans sent an average of 50,000 pelts per year to the port of La Rochelle between 1720 and 1780.[96] In 1764, John Stuart, the

94. Converse D. Clowse, *Measuring Charleston's Overseas Commerce, 1717–1767: Statistics from the Port's Naval Lists* (Washington, D.C.: University Press of America, 1981), 54–55, table B-11.

95. Braund, *Deerskins and Duffels*, 98, n. 89.

96. Daniel H. Usner and Institute of Early American History and Culture, *Indians, Settlers, and Slaves in a Frontier Exchange Economy: The Lower Mississippi Valley before 1783* (Chapel Hill: University of North Carolina Press, for the Institute of Early American History and Culture, Williamsburg, Va., 1992), 246.

British colonial officer charged with administering the newly defined Southeastern Indian territories controlled by the British, estimated that the nearly
fourteen thousand Indian adult male hunters ("guns") under his control
could produce up to 800,000 pounds of deerskins per year. This figure con-
verts to 457,000 hides per year at an average weight of 1.75 pounds per
dressed pelt.[97]

From these and other figures, we can suggest that the eighteenth-century
export of deerskins from Virginia, the Carolinas, Georgia, Florida, and
Louisiana conformed to the classic pattern of market-driven raw materials
exploitation. At a conservative estimate, pelts shipped by British, French, and
Spanish traders each year rose from 50,000 at the turn of the century, to
150,000 in the 1730s, to peak at 250,000 to 300,000 per year in the 1760s and
early 1770s. In the 1780s, after the American Revolution, production dwindled to 175,000 with the depletion of deer herds and the expansion of colonial settlement and agriculture. By the turn of the century, the deerskin
trade had begun to collapse entirely.[98]

British customs records for imported hides and skins from the Americans
have a similar trajectory. The three-year average for 1699–1701 for skins and
hides was 23,000 pounds sterling; for 1722–1724, 34,000 pounds sterling; for
1752–1754, 46,000 pounds sterling; and for 1772–1775, 111,000 pounds sterling.[99]

For Indian market hunters, the American Revolution of 1776–1783 was a
turning point that dissolved the prewar institutions of the deerskin trade.
The British market for skins, which had provided credit and trade goods, disappeared. War left the Creeks and other Indian hunters short of guns, ammunition, and clothing. The Creek leader Alexander McGillivray devised
new trade ties and a new trade path to exiled loyalist merchants in Spanish-
held Florida. Panton, Leslie, and Company shipped about 125,000 skins per
year from Pensacola to Britain in the 1780s and 1790s. In 1783 and 1790, the
new American regime negotiated treaties that confirmed Creek hunting
rights in return for their conceding large hunting grounds for settlement.
Slowly, however, the trade began to reopen, with a few American traders operating from Augusta. In 1796, the United States government set up official
deerskin trading posts along the Creek border and offered an alternative
outlet for Creek deerskins in return for the usual trade goods.

Well before the century's end, the hunting economy of the Creeks, as well

97. Braund, *Deerskins and Duffels,* 70.

98. Ibid., 72.

99. Ralph Davis, "English Foreign Trade, 1700–1774," in *The Growth of English Overseas Trade
in the Seventeenth and Eighteenth Centuries,* edited by Walter E. Minchinton (London: Methuen,
1969). These figures were for all of British North America, Spanish America, the West Indies,
and West Africa. The bulk of the imports represented in these figures consisted of American
deerskins. Imports from the Americas far exceeded those from any other world region.

as that of the Choctaws and Chickasaws in the lower Mississippi, had begun to collapse, and Indian hunters faced a "severe socioeconomic crisis."[100] The catch declined as deer were either hunted out or pushed out by the livestock of encroaching settlers. Deer were localized in their habitats and did not readily move to new locations when their existing ranges were threatened. The Creek nation began building up substantial debt as the payment for skins never fully repaid the advances they received for trade goods. At the same time, the prices of trade goods rose and the value of deerskins dropped nearly 50 percent.

By this time, the American government was convinced that the day of the Indian commercial hunter had ended. The Creeks, Choctaws, Cherokees, and other Indians in the Southeast would have to accept civilization and become agriculturists like the white settlers. In 1805, the Creeks ceded 2 million acres of land and permitted construction of a federal road on their lands in return for a yearly annuity to be paid the chiefs.

Gradually, a split in the Creek nation developed between the traditionalists and those warriors, often mixed blood, who opted for livestock and settled agriculture. A visit by the charismatic Shawnee warrior Tecumseh in 1811 led to the Creek civil war of 1813–1814, American intervention, and a final massacre and defeat at Tohopeka. With the subsequent treaty, the United States seized 30 million acres of Creek lands for settlement and reduced the remaining Creeks to being American dependents. Creeks still hunted deer for a limited market, but both the deer and the commercial hunt essentially were finished.[101]

IMPACT OF THE FUR TRADE ON INDIANS

Easily one of the most complicated and unresolved historiographical issues in North American history concerns the effects of the fur trade on those Indian groups caught up in it.[102] Every year, Europeans enlisted tens of thousands of Indians to serve as hunters, processors, carriers, and traders of huge numbers of furs and skins for export from North America. Three intertwined questions lie at the heart of the matter: First, did involvement in the fur trade lead invariably to Indian weakness, dependence, and varying de-

100. Usner and Institute of Early American History and Culture, *Indians, Settlers, and Slaves in a Frontier Exchange Economy,* 285.

101. Braund, *Deerskins and Duffels,* 164–88.

102. For a discussion of the broader interpretation of Indian responses to European intervention in their world, see Trigger, "Early Native North American Responses to European Contact: Romantic versus Rationalistic Interpretations," *Journal of American History* 77, no. 4 (1991): 1195–1215. Trigger assesses the claims of cultural relativists versus rationalists in this article. He argues that a "cognitive reorganization" accompanied greater familiarity with Europeans and their ways that resulted in a rationalizing behavior on the part of Indians.

grees of cultural disintegration and despair? Second, did Indians change their cultural beliefs, institutions, and behavior in dramatic ways in response to the stimuli of price-driven markets and the availability of new, industrially produced commodities? And third, as a corollary to the second question, did the stimuli and pressures of the fur trade cause Indians to abandon ecologically sound hunting practices and beliefs in an indiscriminate slaughter of newly valuable prey animals? All these issues resonate directly with our most sensitive ideological and moral concerns in the twenty-first century. All scholars and writers on the history of the fur trade offer more-or-less explicit answers to these questions.

One general point seems indisputable. By the early nineteenth century, after more than two centuries of fur trading, all Indian groups in the eastern half of North America were enmeshed to varying degrees in a dependent relationship with European regimes and settler societies. All had suffered population declines, severe cultural shocks, and loss of previously vital institutions and skills. For example, even formerly powerful and impressive groups such as the Five Nations Iroquois had fallen into political and material dependency as early as the 1730s.[103] The Iroquois no longer negotiated with European authorities and traders from a position of relative strength and equality but from one of inferiority and weakness. They needed the cloth, guns, implements, alcohol, and tobacco purveyed by fur traders far more than the European society at large needed their furs. The Iroquois had lost the skills to make the craft objects that had previously sustained them.

Much of this decline can be traced to the onslaught of disease among unprotected populations. Certainly, hammer blows from introduced European diseases buffeted the Iroquois, as they did every Indian society in North America. Whether epidemics preceded direct contact is open to argument, but there is no question as to the numerous deaths and cultural and social disruption caused by new diseases in the seventeenth and eighteenth centuries. For example, the first smallpox epidemic, in 1616, sharply reduced populations of Indians along the northeast Atlantic Coast.[104] Only the fact that Indian groups were widely dispersed and thinly settled throughout the landscape and had limited contacts with Europeans saved them from greater suffering and losses. However, confident societies and cultures can and do shake off disease and, even after suffering heavy mortality, recover their numbers and reassert their identity.

European colonization of North America subjected the Indians to a new relationship with alien invaders who became increasingly more powerful

103. Richter and the Institute of Early American History and Culture, *The Ordeal of the Longhouse,* 268.

104. Dean R. Snow and Kim M. Lanphear, "European Contact and Indian Depopulation in the Northeast: The Timing of the First Epidemics," *Ethnohistory* 35, no. 1 (1988).

and uncompromising and more brutal in their demands. The fur trade was only one, albeit an extremely important, aspect of this unequal relationship. Indians' involvement as economic actors in the fur market was probably not a sufficient cause of Indian decline and dependence. No reasonable scholars deny the intrinsic appeal of metal blades and tools as replacements for those of stone, or woolen cloth as a replacement for or, more often, supplement to deerskin and fur clothing and blankets. In its initial phases, the exchange of furs for trade goods was not inequitable. When Indians swapped furs stripped and processed from animals that they had killed in the hunt for metal tools, cloth, guns, powder, and shot, the transaction enabled them to dispose of surplus goods in exchange for the means to live better and more comfortably.[105]

For two centuries, Indians were conservative consumers who restrained their wants in both variety and quantity. Trade goods focused on a very narrow basket of commodities that Indians emphatically told traders they wanted: muskets, balls, powder, brass kettles, knives, hatchets, needles, scissors, flints, woolen cloth and linen shirts for women and men, vermilion and verdigris for body painting, glass beads, mirrors, burning glasses for starting fires, steel and brass wire, glass bottles, clay pipes, tobacco, and rum or brandy. No item was acceptable that did not conform to a nicely calibrated consumer preference expressed by the Indians for specific decoration, material, and quality.

Eventually each of these items either wore out or was used up and had to be replaced by entering the market again. Archaeological evidence suggests that Indians consumed considerable amounts of trade goods as burial items placed with the deceased. But there is little evidence that any group amassed large quantities of trade goods as household possessions. Nor were Indians especially price sensitive. Numerous anecdotes record Indian hunters responding to higher fur prices by simply bringing in fewer furs to trade rather than acquiring more trade goods. If Indians were cautious consumers, slow to find new wants and desires, then it is difficult to see how commodification alone could have destroyed Indian cultures and institutions or have sent them into a frenzy of market-driven slaughter of game animals.

Only alcohol, among the standard trade goods, caused some Indians to consume to excess. Although old to Eurasia, fermenting and distilling alcohol was a new, complex technology for North American Indians. Alcohol's addictive and consciousness-transforming qualities, with its tendency to encourage violence, hit Indian societies with explosive force. Unlike Eurasian societies, Indians had no time to evolve those social rituals and cultural attitudes that erected defenses against the worst aspects of the drug before they had access to it in quantity. Alcohol consumption rent the stability and har-

---

105. Trigger, "Early Native North American Responses to European Contact," 1207.

mony of Indian communities.[106] Alcohol use was clearly destructive and probably acted as a depressant on people who already had much to be depressed about.

There is some evidence that European brandy and rum occupied a larger share in the trade goods offered to Indians as they became accustomed to it. For example, eau-de-vie and wine represented only 4 to 5 percent of the trade goods offered by French traders from Montreal during the seventeenth century. Much of this was consumed in the ceremonials of trade meetings and sociability rather than carried back to home villages for consumption. In general, the French, inhibited by Jesuit intervention, were less prone to offer alcohol than were the English or Dutch. The eighteenth century, however, saw rapid growth in Indian consumption of alcohol in exchange for furs.[107]

When they obtained rum or brandy from traders or, more frequently, as gifts on ceremonial occasions, younger male Indians tended toward immediate binge drinking that ended badly, in assaults and homicides.[108] Often, Indian hunters traded quantities of their season's furs for large amounts of rum, brandy, or whiskey at the expense of badly needed trade goods. Considerable anecdotal evidence suggests that on occasion Indian alcohol purchases so reduced the quantities of other trade goods obtained that hardship and suffering resulted in the following season. As mentioned above, some groups, like the Hurons, managed to contain and neutralize alcohol and minimize its abusive effects.

Since Indians never learned to ferment or distill their own alcohol, their desire for rum or brandy stimulated additional hunting for furs beyond that needed to acquire other trade goods. However, that desire had practical limits imposed by seasonal migrations. Indians did not store and transport bulky and heavy jugs of rum or brandy for regular consumption. Instead, they drank publicly, in groups, shortly after obtaining the intoxicant. This practice limited their consumption to the more spectacular forms of alcohol use reported by European observers.

Alexander Henry, a British fur trader, canoed west beyond Lake Superior to the Lake of the Woods in 1775. He reported an encounter with a band of Ojibwa Indians who had offered him and his men a warm welcome:

> From this village we received ceremonious presents. The mode with the Indians is, first, to collect all the provisions they can spare, and place them in a heap; after which they send for the trader, and address him in a formal speech.

---

106. For a systematic discussion of this issue, see Peter Mancall, *Deadly Medicine: Indians and Alcohol in Early America* (Ithaca, N.Y.: Cornell University Press, 1995).

107. Louise Dechêne, *Habitants et marchands de Montréal au XVIIe siècle: Essai* (Montréal: Boréal, 1988), 158.

108. Conrad, "Disorderly Drinking," 2.

They tell him, that the Indians are happy in seeing him return into their country; that they have been long in expectation of his arrival; that their wives have deprived themselves of their provisions, in order to afford him a supply; that they are in great want, being destitute of every thing, and particularly of ammunition and clothing; and what they long for, is a taste of his rum, which they uniformly denominate milk.

The present in return consisted in one keg of gunpowder of sixty pounds weight; a bag of shot, and another of powder, of eighty pounds each; a few smaller articles, and a keg of rum. The last appeared to be the chief treasure, though on the former depended the greater part of their winter's subsistence. In a short time, the men began to drink, while the women brought me a further and very valuable present, of twenty bags of rice. This I returned with goods and rum, and at the same time offered more, for an additional quantity of rice. A trade was opened, the women bartering rice, while the men were drinking. Before morning, I had purchased a hundred bags, of nearly a bushel measurement each. Without a large quantity of rice, the voyage could not have been prosecuted to its completion. The canoes, as I have already observed are not large enough to carry provisions. . . .

When morning arrived, all the village was inebriated; and the danger of misunderstanding was increased by the facility with which the women abandoned themselves to my Canadians. In consequence, I lost no time in leaving the place.[109]

Henry's description of this encounter clearly delineates the intensity of Indian desire for rum and its importance in the ceremonial exchanges of the fur trade. The passage suggests, however, that the Ojibwas contained alcohol use within certain manageable bounds for the time that the entire village, male and female, required to consume the keg of brandy. Sexual license occurred, but Henry does not mention any violence.

In the end, however, no matter how resolutely Indians regulated their consumer behavior, when they became commercial hunters they entered an inherently unstable and unsustainable realm. One after another, Indian ethnic groups drawn into trading furs for goods suffered the fate of all human groups who gain a livelihood by extraction of natural resources for the world economy. In responding to market signals, the Indians necessarily changed their patterns of hunting in order to obtain the specialized products most in demand. When European traders asked for beaver, marten, otter, and other luxuriant furs, Indian hunters pursued those furbearers longer and harder than they had before. When traders sought deerskins, Indians hunted deer. Each hunting group altered the diversity and resilience of its seasonal round of hunting, fishing, gathering, and horticulture in order to put more effort into hunting preferred species. Invariably, market demands translated into

109. Bruce M. White, "The Woman Who Married a Beaver: Trade Patterns and Gender Roles in the Ojibwa Fur Trade," *Ethnohistory* 46, no. 1 (1999): 114.

heavier hunting of preferred prey species that caused slow or fast depletion of their numbers.

It is likely that the Hurons, Iroquois, and other groups that depended more on horticulture had less to risk if they systematically depleted their own hunting grounds. This would be true also of former hunters who had settled down to become mission Indians. Hunting-and-gathering Indians, like the Crees and Montagnais, were less apt to hunt their prey into extinction. For example, the Montagnais in the eighteenth century protested that Hurons and Abenakis associated with French merchants from Quebec or Trois-Rivières were killing off their game.[110] The protests imply that the Montagnais, even had they tried to apply restraint themselves, could not have saved their hunting grounds and prey from market forces imposed by other Indian hunters.

Kinship and gender relations shifted in important ways. Men spent more time away, hunting nearly year-round. Pressures on women for speeded-up production of furs and skins grew. The group also made a new effort each season to carry these goods to traders—whether Indian or European—who could offer trade goods. Under some circumstances, Indians could also obtain trade goods by supplying provisions to itinerant European traders or to fur-trading posts. When the food they supplied involved the products of horticulture or gathering, women played a key role in the trade, as in the example of Ojibwa women trading wild rice for powder, shot, and rum given above.

Whether Indians before European contact were "conservationists" who killed only what they could use, or if in fact they frequently killed a greater number of prey animals than they actually consumed, is a thorny question. Indian attitudes and practices varied among ethnic groups and within each group according to the prey animal sought and to the circumstance. There is a recurring pattern, however, of a steadfast belief in the abundance of nature and its capacity to regenerate what they had consumed, whether wasteful or not. Some evidence exists from the postcontact period that, when Indians hunted animals with no market value, such as caribou, they routinely killed more animals than they really needed and consumed only the choicest parts of the carcasses.[111] To categorize the precontact Indian as a noble "ecologist and conservationist" reflects more on our contemporary fears and concerns for environmental issues than anything else.

The cumulative record of the fur trades in North America is clear and unambiguous. Once Indians were touched by the stimulus of market demand, any restraints they had previously maintained eroded rapidly. Pursuit of the

110. Personal communication from Denys Delâge.

111. Krech, *The Ecological Indian*, 186. See also Jeanne Kay, "Wisconsin Indian Hunting Patterns, 1634–1836," *Annals of the Association of American Geographers* 69, no. 3 (1979).

material rewards offered by the fur traders forced Indians to hunt preferred species steadily, despite declining numbers. As animals thinned out, the hunters pushed themselves to the limits of their skill and energy to sustain their yields. Whether or not the Indians had entered the market relationship as sensitive conservationists is irrelevant. What they became were commercial hunters caught up in the all-consuming market.

Could Indians have simply reduced their commercial hunting as furbearer populations declined? Could they have returned, with somewhat better metal tools and implements, to older forms of production and consumption? Why did so many Indian groups like the Five Nations and the Ottawas seek new hunting grounds or try to obtain furs by trade or coercion from more remote Indian groups when their own hunting lands were depleted? Raising these questions overlooks the critical role played by another complex technology introduced by the Europeans—that of firearms. In contrast to historians of New Zealand and Africa who assign central importance to the adoption of firearms, North American historians have tended to minimize their impact. Contrary to often-expressed opinion, matchlock and, later, flintlock muskets were superior tools for hunting and war that Indians enthusiastically adopted and used. With all their admitted deficiencies, even the earliest harquebuses were potent tools that offered accuracy and killing power beyond that of bows and arrows. No better testimonial to this is the speed with which Indian hunters abandoned their bows in favor of muskets for the hunt and for war. By mid– to late seventeenth century, wide adoption of the flint-striking mechanism and weight reduction put an even more imposing weapon into the hands of the Indian hunter and warrior.[112]

In diplomatic negotiations and in trade, the Indians always looked to obtain muskets, powder, and shot—as did the Ojibwas in the example given above. Unfortunately, Indians did not seek out and develop iron-working and toolmaking skills that would have permitted them to repair or even make their own firearms. They remained dependent on the exchange of furs for guns and on European blacksmiths and gunsmiths for repairs.

Muskets made war more deadly in the seventeenth and eighteenth centuries in North America. Without musket, powder, and ball, Indian warriors were defenseless. They could not give up their guns and survive. Therefore, they had to hunt, trade, or plunder furs to obtain guns and munitions. Inter-Indian relationships became more brittle and dangerous in this period than they had been before contact. The fur trade, more than any other European enterprise, thrust Indians into new, unstable, and insecure relationships be-

112. For development of the arguments expressed here, see Carl Parcher Russell, *Guns on the Early Frontiers: A History of Firearms from Colonial Times through the Years of the Western Fur Trade* (Berkeley and Los Angeles: University of California Press, 1957), 10–16 and generally.

tween themselves and Europeans and with other Indian groups. Dozens of Indian groups suffered catastrophic defeats, massacres, and dispersal as pitiable refugees at the hands of Indian and, especially, European enemies. Ultimately, if we are to look for the root causes of Indian debility and dependence, they are to be found in the continuing, ruthless exercise of European military power followed by the advancing settler frontier—not the fur trade.[113]

ENVIRONMENTAL CHANGES

In the usual pattern of commercial hunters, Indians hit the most promising and closest hunting grounds first, killed off all save the most hidden or remote animals, and then moved outward to find new hunting areas. As group after group responded to market signals in the form of trade goods and trading opportunities, the pattern of intensive, devastating hunting recurred. Some furbearer species were more numerous and resilient and recovered their numbers; others, less resilient, became extinct.

Hardest hit was the beaver. Writing at midcentury, in September 1749, the Swedish naturalist Peter Kalm offered this assessment:

> Beavers are abundant all over North America and they are one of the chief articles of trade in Canada. . . . It is certain that these animals multiply very fast; but it is also true that vast numbers of them are annually killed and that the Indians are obliged to undertake distant journeys in order to catch or shoot them. Their decreasing in numbers is very easily accounted for, because the Indians, before the arrival of the Europeans, only caught as many as they found necessary to clothe themselves with, there then being no trade with the skins. At present a number of ships go annually to Europe, laden chiefly with beaver's skins; the English and French endeavor to outdo each other by paying the Indians well for them, and this encourages the latter to extirpate these animals. All the people in Canada told me that when they were young all the rivers in the neighborhood of Montreal, the St. Lawrence river not excepted, were full of beavers and their dams; but at present they are so far destroyed that one is obliged to go several miles up the country before one can meet one.[114]

Pursuit and the near extinction of the beaver in North America followed an east-to-west trajectory: in the 1660s, few beavers were to be found in coastal New England and along the lower Saint Lawrence River. As table 13.1 shows, the number of beaver pelts exported rose steeply throughout the

---

113. For a full development of this theme, see Ian Kenneth Steele, *Warpaths: Invasions of North America* (New York: Oxford University Press, 1994).

114. Pehr Kalm and Adolph B. Benson, *Peter Kalm's Travels in North America: The English Version of 1770* (New York: Dover, 1987), 534. The newly formed Swedish Academy of Sciences sent Kalm on a botanizing mission to North America at the suggestion of Carl von Linné (Linnaeus).

eighteenth century, peaking at an annual yield of 264,000 furs in the final two decades. Nineteenth-century harvests fluctuated below that level until beaver populations crashed in the 1890s.[115] The number of beavers killed to meet domestic needs of the Indians themselves and for the colonial market probably added another 50 percent to the total. Beaver harvests continued at or above this level. By 1825, beavers were extinct in southern Wisconsin, although "moderate numbers of beaver continued to be trapped in northern Wisconsin and Michigan's Upper Peninsula in the 1820's and 1930's."[116] By the 1840s, beaver populations were under pressure from Indian hunters in the Far West in Oregon and in the Canadian subarctic in the Mackenzie River drainage area. Beaver and other furbearer populations certainly plummeted as the fur frontier advanced westward.

Attached to their immediate waterways and lodges, beavers were a sedentary animal that could not readily migrate away from danger. When hunters wiped out beaver colonies, abandoned dams crumbled and created hollows of fertile soil that benefited incoming pioneer farmers. The "beaver meadow complex," formed by the temporary succession of sedges (*Carex* spp.) and bluejoint grass *(Calamagrostis canadensis)* in abandoned beaver ponds was especially important as a source of ready hay for pioneer livestock. These beaver meadows yielded up to four metric tons of hay per acre in the early period before settlers cleared land to sow English hay.[117]

The environmental effects of beaver extinction were considerable. Beavers were a keystone species whose actions determined the configuration of the entire ecosystem. They were "ecological engineers," whose tireless work created ponds that "acted as settling basins and were an important factor in the aggradation of small stream valleys."[118] The ponds retained large amounts of organic matter and eventually, by a process similar to eutrophication, became wetlands or bogs. Beaver ponds also created patches or small landscape units with distinctive vegetation (which Morgan labeled beaver meadows).[119] Beavers affected the biogeochemical cycles of temperate forest

115. Milan Novak et al., *Furbearer Harvests in North America, 1600–1984* (Ontario: Ministry of Natural Resources, 1987), 37–41. By 1898, the annual total had plunged to thirty-five hundred.

116. Jeanne Kay, "Native Americans in the Fur Trade and Wildlife Depletion," *Environmental Review* 9, no. 2 (1985): 119.

117. Gordon Graham Whitney, *From Coastal Wilderness to Fruited Plain: A History of Environmental Change in Temperate North America, 1500 to the Present* (Cambridge: Cambridge University Press, 1994), 304.

118. Ibid; C. G. Jones, J. H. Lawton, and M. Shachak, "Organisms as Ecosystems Engineers," *Oikos* 69, no. 3 (1994).

119. C. A. Johnstone and R. J. Naiman, "Boundary Dynamics at the Aquatic-Terrestrial Interface: The Influence of Beaver and Geomorphology," *Landscape Ecology* 1, no. 1 (1987).

TABLE 1   Furs Harvested in North America (Annual Averages)

	1700–1763	1780–1799	Percentage Change	1830–1849	Percentage Change
Beaver	179,268	263,976	47.3	77,654	-70.6
Raccoon	91,637	225,115	145.7	322,759	43.4
Marten	51,315	88,856	73.2	130,283	46.6
Fox	18,411	20,360	10.6	79,056	288.3
Bear	16,033	26,833	67.4	13,229	-50.7
Mink	15,730	20,680	31.5	144,719	599.8
Otter	11,525	36,326	215.2	20,169	-44.5
Muskrat	10,432	177,736	1,603.8	849,865	378.2
Lynx/bobcat	10,179	17,277	69.7	35,443	105.1
Fisher	3,373	8,480	151.4	10,412	22.8
Wolf	1,830	16,461	799.5	8,899	-45.9
Wolverine	608	1,430	135.2	1,318	-7.8
TOTAL	410,341	903,530	120.2	1,693,806	87.5

SOURCES: Data for 1700–1763 come from table 13.2, this volume. Twenty-year averages for 1780–1799 and 1830–1849 are calculated from Novak et al., *Furbearer Harvests in North America, 1600–1984*.

regimes by shifting storage of chemical elements from surrounding forest vegetation to pond sediments.[120]

A sampling of recent research suggests other possible consequences of the beaver's disappearance: Species diversity in plants, animals, and birds fostered by beaver ponds probably declined with their drying up.[121] Ducks and other waterfowl lost attractive habitat when beaver ponds drained, and they probably lost numbers as well.[122] Osprey *(Pandion haliaetus)*, who built large nests in dead tops of trees and snags near beaver ponds, lost these niches.

120. R. J. Naiman et al., "Beaver Influences on the Long-Term Biogeochemical Characteristics of Boreal Forest Drainage," *Ecology* 75, no. 4 (1994).

121. J. W. Snodgrass, "Temporal and Spatial Dynamics of Beaver-Created Patches as Influenced by Management Practices in a South-Eastern North America Landscape," *Journal of Applied Ecology* 34, no. 4 (1997); R. L. France, "The Importance of Beaver Lodges in Structuring Littoral Communities in Boreal Headwater Lakes," *Canadian Journal of Zoology* 75, no. 7 (1997); A. M. Grover and G. A. Baldassarre, "Bird Species Richness within Beaver Ponds in South-Central New York," *Wetlands* 15, no. 2 (1995).

122. D. J. Brown, W. A. Hubert, and S. H. Anderson, "Beaver Ponds Create Wetland Habitat for Birds in Mountains of Southeast Wyoming," *Wetlands* 16, no. 2 (1996); D. R. Diefenbach and R. B. Owen Jr., "A Model of Habitat Use by Breeding American Black Ducks," *Journal of Wildlife Management* 53, no. 2 (1989); P. Nummi, "The Importance of Beaver Ponds to Waterfowl Broods: An Experiment and Natural Tests," *Annales Zoologici Fennici* 29, no. 1 (1992).

River otters probably diminished in numbers as beaver ponds drained.[123] Freshwater fish declined in abundance and variety.[124]

However, reports of extinctions were exaggerated. Beavers did not disappear. In some out-of-the-way tracts, such as that discovered by Lewis Morgan in the mid-1850s, beavers flourished in great numbers (see above). Beavers were sufficiently numerous to permit continuous trapping by white settlers and substantial harvesting of beaver pelts throughout the nineteenth and on into the twentieth century. In fact, the total beaver harvest was probably as high or higher after 1800 as before. Even along the Atlantic Coast, where beavers supposedly had long been hunted out, Indian and white hunters and trappers continued to bring in beaver pelts, as well as those of other furbearers. For example, in 1763, in Newfoundland, English trappers sold about 5,700 furs, of which about 2,500 were beaver.[125]

Raccoons were even more resilient than beavers. (See table 13.2.) Although raccoon kills rose to astronomical levels by mid–nineteenth century—up to 323,000 animals per year—the species did not become extinct in its original territories. Harvests at this level certainly had a severe local impact on raccoon populations. However, the ability of raccoons to adapt to human settlement permitted the species to survive its slaughter for furs. Raccoon populations today reach densities as high as twenty animals per square kilometer.[126] Partly protected by their aquatic habitats, river otters, mink, and muskrats suffered heavy losses but survived.

Other less social and numerous furbearers were more vulnerable to sustained human predation. The original marten population, found in the colder regions of eastern North America, was probably between 2.4 and 4.7 million.[127] If this estimate is at all close to the actual total, fur trade harvests should have been sustainable. By the late eighteenth century, fur-trade hunters averaged only 89,000 marten, each year—3.7 percent of the lower bound of the estimate. By mid–nineteenth century, as white settlers began

123. D. G. Newman and C. R. Griffin, "Wetland Use by River Otters in Massachusetts," *Journal of Wildlife Management* 58, no. 1 (1994); A. P. Dyck and R. A. MacArthur, "Spacing, Movements, and Habitat Selection of the River Otter in Boreal Alberta," *Canadian Journal of Zoology* 72, no. 7 (1994).

124. I. J. Schlosser, "Dispersal, Boundary Processes, and Trophic-Level Interactions in Streams Adjacent to Beaver Ponds," *Ecology* 76, no. 3 (1995).

125. Ingeborg Marshall, *A History and Ethnography of the Beothuk* (Montreal: McGill-Queen's University Press, 1996), 75.

126. Nowak and Walker, *Walker's Mammals of the World*, 5th ed., s.v. "Raccoons."

127. My estimate is based on a total area of approximately 4.7 million square kilometers with a presumed density of .5 to 1 adult marten per square kilometer. The area includes all of Canada from the Maritimes to and including Manitoba, and all U.S. states from the East Coast as far west as and including Minnesota, Iowa, and Missouri, with the latter, Kentucky, and Virginia marking the southern boundary.

TABLE 2 Eighteenth-Century Fur Exports by Species,
1700–1763 (Annual Averages)

	English Fur Exports	French Fur Exports	Total English and French Fur Exports	Percentages
Beaver	65,427	113,841	179,268	43.8
Raccoon	18,339	73,298	91,637	22.4
Marten	19,641	31,674	51,315	12.5
Fox	13,566	4,845	18,411	4.5
Bear	3,616	12,417	16,033	3.9
Mink	7,840	7,890	15,730	3.8
Otter	4,231	7,294	11,525	2.8
Muskrat	9,783	649	10,432	2.5
Lynx/bobcat	3,872	6,307	10,179	2.5
Fisher	1,235	2,138	3,373	0.8
Wolf	1,002	828	1,830	0.4
Wolverine	470	138	608	0.1
TOTAL	149,022	261,319	410,341	100.2

SOURCES: Murray G. Lawson, *Fur, a Study in English Mercantilism, 1700–1775* (Toronto: University of Toronto Press, 1943); Innis, *The Fur Trade in Canada;* Wien, "Castor, peaux, et pelleteries dans le commerce canadien des fourrures, 1720–1790"; Phillips, *The Fur Trade.*

trapping to supplement their incomes, the annual average harvest rose to 130,000 animals—still only 5.4 percent of the total population. Nevertheless, by the end of the nineteenth century, the population crashed and marten became extinct throughout the eastern regions where they had formerly flourished.[128]

The localized intensity of commercial hunting devastated marten populations. Marten today have maximum densities of between .5 and 1.7 adult animals per square kilometer of optimal habitat. They are among the most "habitat specialized mammals in North America" and require cold-climate landscape mosaics of old-growth conifer forests to flourish.[129] The size of their home ranges and their solitary nature imply that recolonizing an area with a few survivors would have been difficult, if not impossible.

Hunting for the fur trade pushed several other species toward extinction by the early nineteenth century. Despite seemingly low annual harvests, wolves and wolverines were hit hard. The total pre-fur-trade popula-

128. Marjorie A. Strickland, "Harvest Management of Fishers and American Martens," in *Martens, Sables, and Fishers: Biology and Conservation,* edited by Steven Buskirk (Ithaca, N.Y.: Cornell University Press, 1994), 150, fig. 9.1.

129. Steven Buskirk and Roger A. Powell, "Habitat Ecology of Fishers and American Martens," in *Martens, Sables, and Fishers: Biology and Conservation,* edited by Steven Buskirk (Ithaca, N.Y.: Cornell University Press, 1994), 296.

tion of wolves was unlikely to have reached 100,000 animals in eastern North America and was probably much less.[130] Annual harvests of 16,500 wolf pelts per year in the late eighteenth century seem to have drastically depleted the population. In addition to the fur hunting by Indians, white settlers' pursuit of wolves as vermin would have pressed the animals to rapid extinction in a westward moving pattern. The wolverine suffered a similar fate. With population densities of around 1 adult animal to 200 square kilometers, losing even a few thousand animals each year was sufficient to wipe out a small original population with little or no chance of self-regeneration.

In short, the demands of the fur trade depleted beaver numbers to near extinction in much of eastern North America by the first decades of the nineteenth century and had profound consequences for the North American landscape. Fur trade hunting drastically cut the numbers of a dozen or more carnivorous furbearers. Some species recovered from remnant populations; some did not and remain extinct in much of eastern North America today. We can only speculate as to the intricate and widely diffused ecological effects caused by killing off such an array of carnivores.

The final phase of wildlife extinctions accompanied the advance of the pioneer settlement frontier. Once established, white settlers began to supplement their income by systematically trapping and hunting furbearers. To this, we may add the settlers' indiscriminate killing, often for bounty, of wolves, bears, and other large animals perceived to be a threat to livestock and humans.[131]

As with the beaver in the north, so went deer in the south. Indian commercial hunting steadily depleted the deer herds of the American Southeast.[132] If we assume that the number of deer killed each year was twice the number of exported deerskins, the scale of Indian commercial hunting becomes clearer. In the 1760s and early 1770s, Indian hunters in the Southeast probably harvested more than half a million animals per year. From its earliest years, this hunting pressure revealed itself in the contraction of deer ranges. The easily obtained coastal herds declined rapidly, followed by those of the piedmont. The Virginia and North Carolina colonial legislatures tried to formalize Indian practice by establishing open and closed seasons on deer

130. Nowak and Walker, *Walker's Mammals of the World*, 5th ed., s.v. "Dogs, Wolves, Coyotes and Jackals." Wolf population densities from contemporary studies vary from 1 per 520 square kilometers in some parts of Canada, to 1 per 73 square kilometers to 1 to 273 square kilometers in Alberta. In the Great Lakes region, researchers found stable maximum densities of 1 per 26 square kilometers. If we simply assume 1 per 100 square kilometers, the total for the cold eastern region of North America, as defined earlier, would have been 47,000.

131. Whitney, *From Coastal Wilderness to Fruited Plain*, 301–6.

132. Silver, *A New Face on the Countryside*, 96–97.

hunting east of the mountains.[133] Indian hunters were forced to range more widely each decade to pay off their accounts with the traders. Indian prosperity and well-being moved in the same secular trend over the century as that of the deer herds of the Southeast.

CONCLUSION

The rhythms of the fur trade powerfully redefined human relationships with wildlife, the forest, and the natural world in eastern North America. The interlinked ecological effects of specialized commercial hunting were most obvious in terms of the disappearance of beaver as a keystone species and deer as a highly visible ungulate and the main prey of many carnivores. Removal of the larger carnivores had an important, albeit less visible, effect as well.

The impact on human society was profound. Profits from the fur trade financed European colonization and settlement in North America. The fur trade undercut Indian resistance to European land clearing and pioneer settlement. As their entanglement in the fur trade grew, Indians became more directly dependent on Europeans and less able to resist encroachments on their lands. Disease spread by traders reduced their numbers. In effect, the fur trade emptied the landscape of humans and larger fauna in advance of the settler frontier.

As furbearers declined, so did the Indians who hunted them. Supplying furs in exchange for commodities in the marketplace, however, was not, by itself, necessarily fatal to Indian hunters, who generally displayed high levels of sophistication in this new form of exchange. Some Indian groups, such as the Hurons, flourished within the market. There is every evidence that Indians could have sustained their way of life with only modest adjustments necessary as they hunted for the world market.

In large measure, it was noneconomic forces that destroyed the Indians, not commodity production and exchange relationships. The epidemics of European-induced disease that killed many and weakened the survivors pushed Indians toward dependency. Alcohol, the European-introduced intoxicant, and the technology required to produce it also weakened and demoralized Indian societies.

It might be that producing for the fur trade made it possible for the Indians to strengthen and sustain a way of life that they otherwise would have lost much earlier and under more brutal circumstances. Unlike the Russian practice in Siberia, the North American fur and skin trade was not directly coercive. The tsars extracted furs as annual tribute from the indigenous peoples of Siberia. In contrast, the British, French, and Dutch colonial regimes

133. Ibid., 94–95.

traded goods with real value for furs and skins in a voluntary exchange with North American Indians. As workers in a global industry, laboring for low wages, North American Indians occupied a useful and profitable niche. Had they not been armed and encouraged to hunt for the fur trade, they might have suffered the fate of the Indians of Portuguese Brazil, who were either destroyed in genocidal wars or captured and impressed into servitude by the colonists and settlers of that region.

In the end, it was not participation in the fur trade that destroyed the Indians, but the European drive for colonial domination. Both British and French colonial regimes put heavy diplomatic and military pressure on successive Indian groups as they sought to create and retain allies in their struggle for territory and power. European interventions destabilized inter-Indian relations, intensified fears and insecurities, and touched off an unprecedented level of warfare in North America. The availability of ever more lethal and effective muskets from fur traders forced every Indian group to trade furs for weapons. Dissemination of muskets brought a new intensity and deadliness to Indian warfare. The final blow to most Indian groups was the advancing European settlement frontier.

During the early modern centuries, the European stocks of wild animals were much depleted in the face of expanding settlement, industrial development, and above all, agriculture. From the beginning of the sixteenth century until the end of the nineteenth, millions of lustrous beaver and other furs from North America flowed to the workshops of European furriers and hatmakers. For four centuries, Europeans protected themselves from the cold with the warmest materials available in the premodern era—and, in the case of processed beaver fur, one of the most durable. During the late seventeenth century and through the eighteenth, North American deerskins supplied lightweight, comfortable, and durable leather for trousers, gloves, and other clothing. In exchange, European traders shipped what had become cheap and abundant cloth, firearms, alcohol, and other trade goods to purchase these fabrics. The consumers and societies of western Europe were the ultimate beneficiaries of this system.[134] The forested lands of eastern North America became, in effect, a European forest preserve from which vast numbers of wildlife could be extracted and consumed.

134. For other broad comparative views, see Denys Delâge, *Bitter Feast: Amerindians and Europeans in the American Northeast, 1600–64* (Vancouver: UBC Press, 1993); and Eric R. Wolf, *Europe and the People without History* (Berkeley and Los Angeles: University of California Press, 1982).

Chapter 2

The Hunt for Furs in Siberia

By the late 1500s, after Russia's conquest of the khanate of Sibir, Siberia's vast lands lay open to exploration, conquest, and exploitation. Most of Siberia's soils, vegetation, and climate did not hold out great appeal to the Russian peasant cultivator. Instead, Siberia offered the products of the hunt to Russian frontiersmen. Russians had long hunted or purchased from indigenous hunter societies the furs of the north. Furs were one of the most valued consumption items in Russia and one of its most profitable exports.

For centuries, the temperate-zone Christian, Islamic, and Confucian worlds have demanded high-quality furs. In these colder climates, furs were valued for their luxuriously warm comfort, their visual and tactile appeal, and their scarcity and high cost. Fur wearing permitted the wearer to display high social status, power, and wealth. The primary medieval sources of supply for the finest furs were the coldest and most remote lands in northeastern Europe and northwestern Siberia. According to Janet Martin, "It was here that fur-bearing animals grew the thickest, softest pelts in the purest winter hues."[1]

Killing furbearers—as well as processing, assembling, and grading their pelts and transporting them to distant markets—was a long-standing staple of the Russian economy and a principal source of income for the nascent Russian state. In the mid–fourteenth century, the princes of Moscow, taking advantage of the weakening hold of the Mongol Golden Horde, established control over their own fur supply network. Moscow's rulers extended their military domination over the tribal peoples of Perm and Pechora to the northeast, who were required to pay tribute in fine furs. The Moscow state

---

1. Janet Martin, *Treasure of the Land of Darkness: The Fur Trade and Its Significance for Medieval Russia* (Cambridge: Cambridge University Press, 1986), 1.

negotiated arrangements with the Tatars of Kazan to permit passage of their furs through the Crimea to the Black Sea colonies of Italian merchants. Other furs found their way through Lithuania to the Hanse towns on the Baltic. Moscow became the leading fur supplier to the Ottoman realm and western Europe, as luxury furs like ermine, marten, and sable rose in popularity. Both European and Russian traders busied themselves in this vast traffic, bringing silver and gold as payment for furs.

By the beginning of the sixteenth century, despite fluctuations in routes and changing fashions in furs, the basic structural features of the northern fur trade were firmly fixed. Buoyant and growing demand by consumers fed the entire enterprise. For the consuming societies, furs continued to be a comfortable means by which to meet that most compelling human need: the visible display of high status and power combined with the appeal of warmth and comfort. Groups of foreign traders journeyed to Russian entrepôts equipped with silver and technical knowledge of northern furs. The furs were graded by species and quality by a customary schema. Russian and Tatar princes and merchants acted as middlemen in the trade. They obtained furs as tribute or in payment for iron goods, salt, or other trade goods from the indigenous peoples of the northern woods or, increasingly, Russian fur trappers. Russian traders and royal agents assembled, stored, and graded the pelts at entrepôts, which were also sites of growing state power.

Shortly after Ivan's annexation of Kazan, Russia established for the first time a direct maritime trade link with western Europe. In 1554, an English trading ship in search of an Arctic route to China landed by accident at Archangel, the White Sea port. The English captain and chief merchant, Richard Chancellor, who was brought to Moscow, opened what proved to be a successful set of negotiations with Ivan IV. The tsar gave the English traders a charter guaranteeing them free trade in his domains. The resulting Muscovy Company, a joint-stock trading company with an official monopoly on the Russian trade, established trading missions in Moscow and at Kholmogory, just south of Archangel on the Dvina River. The company sent ships each year on direct voyages between London and Archangel.

Despite a short sailing season limited by Arctic ice, Archangel proved to be an important outlet for Russian furs that generated greater profits for the Russian state monopoly. English traders also bought naval stores such as tar, timber, and hemp rope, as well as wax and hides, in return for English cloth and other goods. There remained a favorable Russian balance in the exchange that forced the English to pay the remainder with silver and gold—largely from the New World discoveries.[2]

2. Artur Attman, *The Russian and Polish Markets in International Trade, 1500–1650* (Göteborg: Institute of Economic History of Gothenburg University, 1973), 176–88.

WESTERN SIBERIA

Demand increased, but annual yields of fur in the lands around the White Sea were not keeping pace. Siberia offered the prospect of new, abundant sources of the best quality furs for both consumption and export.[3] The Russian occupation of Kazan opened up new opportunities for movement into Siberia. Driven by the prospect of fur profits, Russian frontiersmen followed the river systems north and east across the vast tracts of Siberia above the fifty-fifth parallel. Russian parties of explorers and traders trekked by boat along the rivers and by horseback, foot, and sledge on portage from one river to another. At strategic junctures, the Muscovite state, following closely after the frontiersmen, established fortified towns and administrative centers (ostrogs), to which it appointed military governors (voevody).

The first task was to annex the Tatar khanate of Sibir, already a tributary to the Russian tsar. In 1582, under the aggressive leadership of the Stroganov family, Russian forces crossed the Urals to attack Sibir, the capital, located on the Ob River. Eight hundred cossack mercenaries led by Yermak Timofeyevich defeated Kuchum, the Tatar khan, drove him into exile, and occupied Sibir. Despite continuing and bitter Tatar resistance that resulted in the death of Yermak and much of his force, the Russians persevered. In 1584, Tsar Fydor, Ivan's son and successor, sent military governors and official forces to consolidate Russian control over the Sibir khanate and its people.[4]

Moscow moved quickly to seize control of western Siberia, the lands drained by the Ob River. Private groups of Russian fur trappers and traders had already ventured along the rivers of this vast region and begun both hunting and trading for furs. With the defeat of the Tatars, Russian official and irregular expeditionary forces established fortified posts at Tobolsk in 1587, Surgut and Tara in 1594, and Obordosk the next year. Mangazeya on the Taz River, established in 1601, and Tomsk, established in 1604, became staging points for the move eastward toward the Yenisey-Tunguska River basin. Directives and funds from Moscow organized and legitimated mixed official and trader attempts to explore the Yenisey River. The tsar ordered the founding of Turkhansk at the confluence of the Yenisey and the Lower Tunguska River in 1607 and the founding of Yeniseysk to the south, just north of the confluence of the Upper Tunguska and Yenisey, in 1619.

By 1620, Russians were the dominant power in western Siberia—an area

3. Robert O. Crummey, *The Formation of Muscovy, 1304–1613* (London: Longman, 1987), 21; Henry R. Huttenbach, "Muscovy's Penetration of Siberia: The Colonization Process 1555–1689," in *Russian Colonial Expansion to 1917*, edited by Michael Rywkin (London: Mansell, 1988), 76.

4. James Forsyth, *A History of the Peoples of Siberia: Russia's North Asian Colony, 1581–1990* (Cambridge: Cambridge University Press, 1992), 32–33.

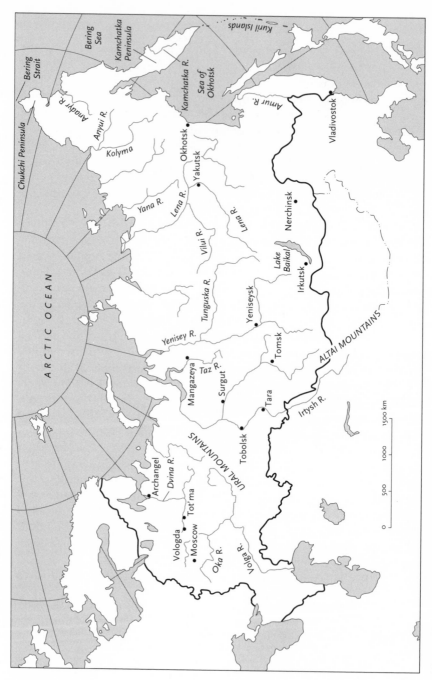

Map 3 Expansion and settlement of tsarist Russia

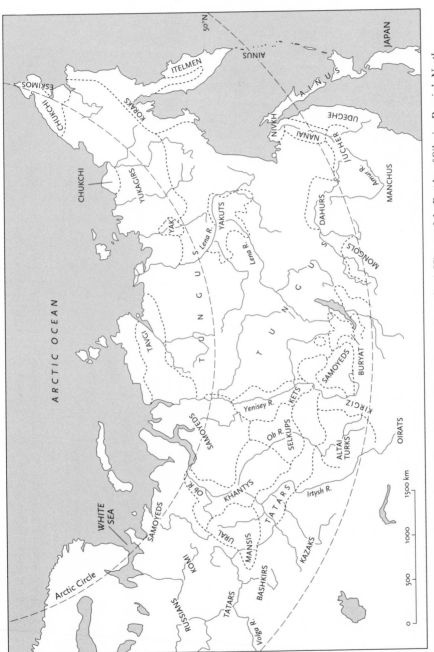

Map 4 Peoples of northern Asia, c. 1600. Adapted from James Forsyth, *A History of the Peoples of Siberia: Russia's North Asian Colony, 1581–1990* (Cambridge: Cambridge University Press, 1992), map 2, p. 17.

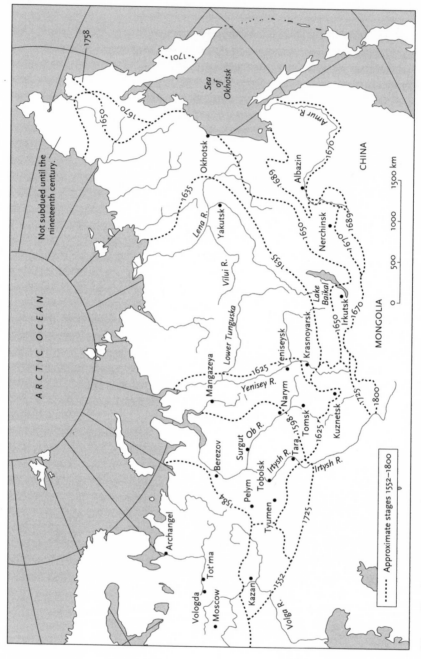

Map 5 Russian conquest of Siberia. Adapted from James Forsyth, *A History of the Peoples of Siberia: Russia's North Asian Colony, 1581–1990* (Cambridge: Cambridge University Press, 1992), map 6, p. 103.

of 2 million square kilometers. The tsar's writ ran from the Arctic Ocean to the Altai Mountains in the south and from the Urals to the valley of the Yenisey in the east. Conquest had more than doubled the territorial extent of the tsardom of Moscow.

Western Siberia's lands divided into two distinct natural regions: the frozen tundra to the north and the taiga, or marshy wet coniferous forest, below. These were Arctic and sub-Arctic lands, not all that promising for sedentary cultivation or Russian settlement. The tundra stretches forty-five hundred kilometers from one end of Siberia to the other. Above the permafrost line, the tundra lands are frozen all year round. Low temperatures and limited sunshine permit only lichens, mosses, small woody shrubs, and small herbaceous plants to grow. Having 240 days of snow each year limits animal life as well. Polar bears, foxes, rodents, owls, reindeer, and aquatic birds share space with seals and walruses on land.

South of the tundra, the western plain of Siberia is primarily taiga, a sparse forest of fir, spruce, and cedar growing over peat bogs of moss and lichen. The taiga, generally wet terrain with many lakes, streams, and marshes, is inundated in the spring by pack-ice blockages at the mouth of the Ob and other rivers. Wildlife, common to all of Siberia, includes larger mammals such as the brown bear, wolf, elk, reindeer, and lynx. The smaller furbearers—the sable, marten, beaver, ermine, and squirrel—also can be found. To the south, in the vicinity of Tomsk, the terrain dries out and aspen and birch replace conifers. These thin out into woodland-steppe formations and eventually to steppe grassland.

The small bands of Russian invaders threaded their way along western Siberia's rivers, founded fortified posts, and tried to impose new, one-sided relationships on the peoples they encountered. At first, the Siberians reacted violently to Russian demands and attacked the invaders, only to suffer bloody casualties and ignominious defeat. The killing power of Russian muskets and cannon was far superior to any weapons the Siberian natives employed. In sharp contrast to the Tatars, who terrorized and enslaved Russian settlers west of the Urals, the Siberian peoples were few, vulnerable, and divided.[5] After they submitted, the Russians forced or enticed the tsar's new subjects to help them with further expansion by serving as interpreters, guides, boatmen, and porters. Many were willing to serve as armed allies or auxiliaries and attack those neighbors with whom they had long-standing grievances.

After the Russians had demonstrated their military strength, their terms were simple. Each of the newly subdued Siberians had to offer ritual submission by means of a sworn oath to the tsar's authority. And, to confirm this, each adult male had to deliver a specified number of furs and pelts in

5. Yuri Slezkine, *Arctic Mirrors: Russia and the Small Peoples of the North* (Ithaca, N.Y.: Cornell University Press, 1994).

payment of the *iasak*, an annual tax. These were the essentials, but soldiers and colonists often forced the tsar's new subjects to help build forts, housing, and boats, to contribute other labor, or to supply foodstuffs. Russians seized and enslaved women to provide sex and domestic services for the male invaders. Although the Russians did offer gifts—metal utensils, knives, blankets, flour, tea, and especially alcohol—in return for furs, the exchange was certainly inequitable.

The total population of western Siberia in the last half of the sixteenth century probably did not exceed a hundred thousand persons, who were organized into small groups of preliterate hunter-gatherers. About half the population consisted of an estimated sixteen thousand Finno-Ugrian speakers thinly distributed across much of the western Siberian taiga. The Khantys and the Mansis—two distinct, but very similar, groups speaking mutually intelligible forms of the same language—divided the marshy spruce forestlands between the Ob and the Urals. They were organized into separate lineages, or clans, headed by a hereditary chief. Clan heads occupied forts protected by earth ramparts and stockades and amassed wealth in terms of silver objects and furs.[6] They had access to some iron and steel objects through trade. Their weapons included longbows and arrows, spears, and, for protection, mailed coats and helmets.

Ordinary Khantys and Mansis lived in log huts in the wintertime and moved to temporary hunting quarters for the summer hunting season. They used dugout or bark canoes for transport in the summer and skis for the six months or more of snow-covered winter. They hunted, but did not domesticate, reindeer for their meat and hides. They hunted and trapped sables, marten, ermines, and foxes and wore and traded their furs. Fresh, dried, and smoked fish taken from the rivers and streams supplied a considerable portion of their diet. The Khantys and Mansis, like nearly all the indigenous peoples across Siberia, apparently did not make or consume alcohol in any form.

In their spiritual beliefs, the Khantys and Mansis worshipped a Nature god, Num Torem, as well as spirits that lived in all natural phenomena. Religious rites conducted by shamans in sacred clearings involved sacrifice of reindeer and other animals. Each person had his or her own totem animal represented by designs tattooed on the person. The Khantys and Mansis were split into exogamous moieties defined by clan totems. Hunters were supposed to refrain from killing their particular totem animal. Like virtually all Siberian natives, they venerated the brown bear, who was known as the "master of the forest" and only occasionally killed and eaten. When this occurred, special rituals designed to propitiate the bear's spirit were performed before and during the village feast.

6. Forsyth, *A History of the Peoples of Siberia,* 10.

Also in western Siberia were the Samoyeds, Uralic language speakers whose numbers were similar to those of the Khantys and Mansis.[7] The Samoyeds' habitat extended across both tundra and taiga. In the extreme northern tundra, their culture was one shared by virtually all the indigenous peoples who lived in the harsh climate and terrain of northern Siberia. The Samoyeds fished and hunted seals and walruses in the long fjords of the Ob, Yenisey, and other rivers flowing into the Arctic Ocean.[8] They kept herds of domesticated reindeer to pull light wooden sledges and for clothing, meat, and milk. Their white, bushy-coated Samoyed dogs assisted in herding the reindeer. They hunted wild reindeer for meat and hides. They lived in hide-covered conical pole tents up to nine meters in diameter. These were portable and frequently were moved as groups engaged in seasonal migrations.

To the south, other groups of Samoyeds lived in the swampy taiga forests as far as the middle Ob River. In this habitat, the Samoyed lifestyle and material culture were closer to those of the Khantys and Mansi peoples. Each branch of the Samoyeds was loosely organized into confederations of lineages or clans. The latter controlled marriage patterns; access to hunting, fishing, and grazing grounds; dispute settlement, and if necessary, organization for war. For the latter purpose, temporary chiefs were accepted.

The annual flow of furs from western Siberia grew steadily and soon added substantial amounts to the tsar's revenues and generated considerable wealth for private Russian hunters and trappers. Pushed by depleted stocks of sable in western Russia, and encouraged by rising demand from Moscow, unofficial hunters and trappers, the *promyshlenniks*, and their hired armed guards moved restlessly eastward along the rivers. With extraordinary speed, the fur hunters dashed across Siberia in just a few short decades.[9]

CENTRAL AND EASTERN SIBERIA

Russian expeditions plunged eastward into the vastness of central Siberia along the three great tributaries of the Yenisey: the Lower, Central, and Upper Tunguska Rivers. In the 1620s, a band of cossacks followed the Lower Tunguska 2,400 kilometers to its source. There they found themselves on the bank of the upper Lena River. From its source near the western shore of Lake Baikal, the Lena River flows 4,400 kilometers northeastward to its great

---

7. Other, much smaller groups were the Selkups, who spoke a Samoyedic language and lived in the southeastern part of western Siberia along the tributaries of the Ob River, and the Kets, found in the Yenisey River valley.

8. Ibid., 16–17.

9. Huttenbach, "Muscovy's Penetration of Siberia."

delta on the shore of the Arctic Sea. The cossacks did not hesitate but sailed downstream (north) to explore the Lena. In 1632, they founded Yakutsk in the middle reaches of the Lena, and 720 kilometers further north on the lower Lena they built the fort of Zhigansk. The next year, the Russians reached the Lena Delta and the open sea. By the end of the decade, the cossacks had explored and built several forts on the Vilui River, the Lena tributary that flows eastward across central Siberia from its source near the Lower Tunguska. As soon as the Russians were established on the Lena, they made their by now customary demands on the indigenous peoples for ritual submission and payment of *iasak* in furs.

Midway between the Yenisey and the Lena Rivers, the sparse fir, spruce, and cedar forests of the western Siberian taiga ended. Spruce, for example, is unable to survive temperatures below minus thirty-eight degrees centigrade. From that point eastward, larger, denser forests composed of larch and pine species covered central and eastern Siberia as far as the Pacific Coast. The European larch *(Larix decidua* or *Larix europaea)* at maturity stands twenty-four to forty-two meters tall. The larch is a conifer, has reddish gray bark, and sheds its short, needlelike leaves in the fall as deciduous species do. The Scots pine *(Pinus sylvestris)* attains a height of twenty to forty meters, has a straight trunk as much as a meter in diameter, red-brown bark, and blue-green foliage at the extremities.

Two distinct peoples—the Tungus, or Evens, and the Yakuts—inhabited the 5 million square kilometers of larch and pine taiga lands comprising central Siberia. The territory and population of the Altaic-speaking Tungus, of whom there were an estimated thirty-six thousand, were by far the largest. The Tungus were originally forest dwellers in the central Siberian larch forests; they had dispersed far from their presumed homeland near Lake Baikal. They were highly mobile hunters and herders of domesticated reindeer. They used bows and arrows, protective metal armor and helmets, and iron knives and swords. They were organized into twenty or more named tribes, or clusters of clans, without hereditary chiefs.[10]

The Yakuts were a Turkic people who spoke a unitary language and are thought to have migrated from the open steppe to their compact territory in the lowlands on the upper Lena River where it intersects with the Aldan River. Here, larch forests were interspersed with meadowlands. The Yakuts, who maintained large herds of horses and cattle, practiced short-distance seasonal transhumance by moving with their animals to summer grazing lands. They were organized into a single grouping of independent clans. Each clan had a hereditary chief and shared in a common language for all Yakuts. Each clan had control over communal grazing lands and hunting and fishing grounds. At contact with the Russians, the well-organized Yakuts

10. Forsyth, *A History of the Peoples of Siberia,* 48–55.

seem to have been in the process of expanding by colonizing new lands and assimilating Tungus and other splinter ethnic groups into their domain.[11]

The fort and town of Yakutsk, built in the Yakut homeland on the Lena River, quickly became the leading Russian administrative and trade center for central Siberia. In just over a decade, by 1650, the town and its hinterland had two thousand Russians in residence. Confiscations of Yakut horses and cattle provided both mobility and meat to the colonists. Prosperous fur traders trekked to Yakutsk from European Russia to obtain the abundant furs of the region directly at the source. The traders tended to employ private Russian trappers rather than attempt to buy furs from the Yakuts or Tungus, who were overly burdened with *iasak* demands. The stream of furs sent on the yearlong river journey to Moscow increased steadily in volume.[12]

A lengthy report dated September 6, 1633, by Petr Beketov, commander of a hundred-man company *(sotnik)*, to Tsar Mikhail Federovich describes the founding of Yakutsk. The report nicely illustrates the mode and scale of Siberian conquest. According to Beketov's narration, the military governor of Yeniseysk sent him with a company of musketeers and hunter-traders *(promyshlenniks)* on "distant service" to the Lena River with supplies for one year.

The expedition actually took two and a half years, during which Beketov and his followers "suffered every deprivation," but "brought under your Sovereign Tsarist mighty hand on the Lena River many diverse Tungus and Iakut lands."[13] From their inhabitants, Beketov succeeded in collecting *iasak*, or tribute in furs, including "61 forties and 31 sables [2,471 pelts], 25 Iakut sable *shubas* [coats], 10 sable *plastinas* [pelts sewn together,] 2 beavers, 7 red fox, and one red fox pup."[14] The remainder of the report details battles with Yakut chiefs, their ultimate submission to him, the tribute exacted, and the hostages taken, as well as forts constructed and manned. At no time does Beketov appear to have had more than one hundred men under his command, and he frequently mentions sorties with far fewer participants.

In September 1633, Beketov built a fortification *(ostrog)* at Yakutsk on the Lena River "in the heart of the whole Iakut territory."[15] From here, he sent out parties to demand submission by the various Yakut princes:

11. Ibid., 55–57.

12. Ibid., 61.

13. Petr Beketov, "September 6, 1633, Report to Tsar Mikhail Federovich from the Steltsy Sotnik [Musketeer Commander] Petr Beketov Concerning His Expedition on the Lena River," in *Russia's Conquest of Siberia, 1558–1700: A Documentary Record*, edited by Basil Dmytryshyn, E. A. P. Crownhart-Vaughan, and Thomas Vaughan, vol. 1 of *To Siberia and Russian America* (Portland, Ore.: Western Imprints, the Press of the Oregon Historical Society, 1985), 136.

14. Ibid., 1:137. Sable and other furs were generally counted and packed in stacks of forty compressed between two boards. Forty to fifty sable pelts were required for a coat.

15. Ibid., 1:144.

On November 8 [1633], in accordance with the Sovereign's ukas, I, Petr[,] sent servitors on the Sovereign's service from the new ostrozhek on the Lena River to the Iakut prince Ineno-Oiun to collect iasak for the sovereign. The servitors traveled four days to reach Ineno-Oiun[,] and when they returned they reported [that] . . . this Iakut prince did not want to come under the Sovereign's mighty hand nor go to the ostrozhek, and he and his people began to attack the servitors. The servitors invoked God's mercy and fought them, and with the luck of the Sovereign they killed many Iakuts in that foray and shed their blood for the Sovereign Tsar and Grand Prince Mikhail Fedorovich [sic] of all Russia.

In the struggle they captured Prince Ineno-Oiun himself, and other . . . [missing]. In this battle the servitor Prokopii Vasilev was wounded by an arrow in his leg. They brought Prince Ineno-Oiun to the ostrozhek, and I, Petr, took him into the office and asked him why he had opposed the Sovereign Majesty. . . . The Iakut princeling said they had shot arrows at the servitors out of ignorance, that the Sovereign's men had never come to them before and that they had never even heard about the Sovereign Majesty. He said he hoped the Sovereign would have mercy now and forgive them for their transgressions. . . . I brought Prince Ineno-Oiun to take the oath, and he swore that he and all his people would serve loyally under the Sovereign's mighty hand for all time, and that they would pay iasak.[16]

The encounter closed when the Yakut prince handed over twenty sable pelts as his first payment of tribute to the tsar.

The lure of more furs sent Russian frontiersmen pressing on to the east with scarcely a pause. As the nineteenth-century tsarist historian Slotsov puts it, "The Iakutsk authorities, drawn to yasak [iasak] as surely as a magnet to the pole, went on sending out their scouts to track down any human retreat which had not yet been subjected to yasak."[17] Yakutsk, two-thirds of the way from the Urals across Siberia, became the jumping-off point for further Russian exploration and conquest. From Yakutsk, there were two onward routes. The first marched southeast 720 kilometers through mountainous country inhabited by Tungus peoples to the Pacific Ocean. In 1648, Russian contingents founded two coastal settlements, Okhotsk and Tauisk, on the shores of the Sea of Okhotsk.

The second, far more arduous, route to the northeast extended 2,400 kilometers across forest, tundra, and mountains as far as the Chukchi Peninsula thrusting out into the Bering Strait. The route followed an intricate pattern that made optimal use of the great rivers of the northeast. From Yakutsk, the Russians trekked overland to the source of the Yama River, took boats north along the Yama as it flowed to the Arctic, left the middle Yama for an over-

16. Ibid., 1:145.
17. Quoted in Forsyth, A History of the Peoples of Siberia, 75.

land trek to the source of the Aiazeya River, built boats and moved with the current as it flowed eastward, left the Aiazeya at its northward bend, trekked to the lower Kolmya River, floated with the northerly current of the Kolmya to its intersection with the Anyui, pushed against the current upriver eastward to the Anyui's source, and then trekked overland to float along the upper Anadyr River as it flowed eastward to the Bering Sea. As early as 1649, a Russian expedition traversed this route and founded the town of Anadyrsk on the upper Anadyr River, 300 kilometers from the coast.[18] By the mid-1600s only the Chukotsk and Kamchatka Peninsulas were left undisturbed.

Along this northeastern route, the Russians encountered a new set of indigenous peoples, whose population probably did not exceed forty thousand persons. First, they discovered a neolithic people they called collectively Yukagirs. From west to east, these were the Khoromos, Yandins, Uyandins, Shormobas, Omoks, Lawrens, Chuwans, and Anauls, who all spoke the same language, one unrelated to any other known human language. Each named group consisted of clans or patrilineages named after a single male founder. Under the guidance of a powerful shaman, the Yukagirs worshipped the clan ancestor.

These groups divided into the "reindeer Yukagirs" and the "settled Yukagirs." The reindeer Yukagirs, who had no domesticated reindeer, moved with the wild reindeer herds of the region from the taiga forests in May as they grazed the tundra vegetation, and they followed the herds back toward the forests in August each year. When the herds congregated for mating in the fall, the Yukagirs organized killing drives and slaughtered great numbers for meat and hides. The "settled Yukagirs" lived in log cabins or lodges along the rivers and subsisted by fishing and hunting elk. The Yukagirs, like nearly all peoples in Siberia at the time, believed strongly in the notion of spirit guardians or "master" spirits of natural phenomena. The spirit guardians of the reindeer and the elk in particular had to be propitiated by various rites and rituals.

Further to the northeast, where the Russians reached the mouth of the Kolmya River, they first encountered settlements of Asiatic Eskimos along the frozen shore. The Siberian Eskimos, like their counterparts across the Bering Strait, were a coastal, winter people whose life was consumed with hunting seals, walruses, and whales. Interspersed among the Eskimos were the Chukchi and Korak peoples. Some had adopted a life of sea hunting virtually identical to that of the Eskimos and lived in permanent coastal settlements. Others, who herded reindeer, spent the year in a transhumance pattern similar to that of the Yukagirs. The Chukchi and Korak peoples were the dominant inhabitants of the eponymous Chukchi Peninsula, the easternmost extremity of Siberia, which thrust into the Bering Strait.

18. See ibid., 134, map 7.

FURS, TRIBUTE, AND THE RUSSIAN STATE

Moscow's modest investment in ongoing Siberian conquest was more than amply repaid. The quantity of sable and other furs that flowed to Moscow from the new lands became one of the most valuable liquid assets of a cash-starved state. Devoid of domestic gold- or silver-producing mines, and lacking in much exportable agricultural and industrial production, the early modern Russian monarchy relied on the sale of furs to obtain coined and uncoined precious metals for its treasury. The tsar also used furs from his stores to reward exceptional service by his officials, nobles, and clergy; to make diplomatic gifts; and to make special purchases abroad of strategic or luxury goods.[19] Furs were not used to pay salaries or for other ordinary disbursements within Russia, because the tsar wanted to realize profits from the export price in Moscow.

Some thirty elite merchants in Moscow, appointed by the tsar, purchased furs, usually of the best quality, from royal stores and were permitted to export these furs to foreign markets. Foreign merchants arriving in Moscow had to give first refusal to the tsar's agents for their goods. Any purchases made from their stocks were paid in furs.

Moscow set up a network of customs posts at the border of Siberia, in every *ostrog*, and at portage points and other strategic locations along the main Siberian river routes.[20] The regime recruited heads of customs posts from older Russian fur-trading towns west of the Urals, such as Ustuig, Vologda, Sviazhsk, Tot'ma, Sol Vyehgodsk, and Moscow itself. These were "sworn men," or responsible notables with fur-trading experience, elected by the assemblies of these towns and sent for one- to two-year terms to Siberia. They were independent of the military governors. They were responsible for appropriating the best one of every ten pelts carried by traders or hunters, for storing these furs, and for shipping them to Moscow along with the tribute furs demanded from Siberian native hunters. Traders entering Siberia with goods for sale were charged a similar 10 percent tax, paid either in money or in kind.

Total yearly state revenue from Siberian furs grew steadily, from twelve thousand rubles in 1589 to a plateau of one hundred thousand rubles per year or more for the middle decades of the century, 1640 to 1680; the figure declined to an average annual return of seventy-eight thousand rubles in the 1690s.[21] These very large sums, calculated on the original Siberian price of

19. Raymond Henry Fisher, *The Russian Fur Trade, 1550–1700* (Berkeley and Los Angeles: University of California Press, 1943), 130.

20. George Vjatcheslau Lantzeff, *Siberia in the Seventeenth Century: A Study of the Colonial Administration* (Berkeley and Los Angeles: University of California Press, 1943), 135.

21. R. H. Fisher, *The Russian Fur Trade*, 114.

furs, not the export price, constituted between 7 and 10 percent of the state's rising income until the 1680s, when fur revenues began to drop off.[22] Fur revenues defrayed total state expenditures in Siberia, with a comfortable margin to spare.[23] By far, the greater portion of pelts taken by native hunters was appropriated by the tsarist state—not purchased by private traders.

The primary duty of Siberian military governors was to collect the *iasak*, levied in furs on every fit native Siberian adult male between eighteen and fifty years of age. Russian settlers were exempt from this tax, derived from an older Tatar practice that connoted subordination and defeat. Each group of Siberian natives that had submitted to the tsar was forced every year to pay the stipulated number of good-quality unfinished furs, preferably sable, which was the standard. In theory at least, each *iasak* payer should have hunted and trapped the furs himself. If sable pelts could not be obtained, the state would accept marten, beaver, otter, fox, ermine, lynx, wolf, or even squirrel at fixed ratios to sable.

The number of sables to be paid varied by district and over time. Originally set high, at ten to twelve sables per man per year, by the early 1600s the average was closer to five pelts. By midcentury the rate had dropped to three pelts per man in western Siberia. The state pragmatically adjusted its demand to the realities of declining sable populations.

Tsarist officials identified and fixed the territory occupied by each distinct ethnic and linguistic group as a tax district, or *volost*. Contiguous *volosts* were grouped into larger units with a Russian *ostrog* at the center that served as seat for the military governor. At the time of initial submission, as illustrated in the Beketov document quoted above, the Russians took two measures to ensure payment of the *iasak:* first, they exacted a solemn oath of allegiance to the tsar that included a commitment to pay the *iasak;* and second, they took one or two of the leading men from each *volost* hostage and kept them captive at the *ostrog.* Periodically the Russians exchanged their hostages for new ones. The Russians provided food for hostages, who were confined, often chained, and guarded to prevent escape or rescue. Nonpayment of the *iasak* by their group meant indefinite captivity or abuse and even death.

After the hunting season, by late fall and early winter, delegations of Siberians came from nearby *volosts* to the *ostrog* with the required number of furs to pay the *iasak.* They also presented additional furs to the military governor and his staff as a gift *(pominki)* in honor of the tsar. *Pominki* payments seem to have been retained as a personal perquisite by the *voevody* and his

22. Ibid., 120.
23. Ibid. For 1699, fur receipts in Siberia were 74,982 rubles against total expenditures of 54,086 rubles. The state collected an additional 56,538 rubles in money, so that the Siberian surplus that year was actually 77,434 rubles. Therefore, the fur revenues were almost entirely profit to the state.

staff. Before the natives handed over their *iasak* furs, the military governor
was obliged to display the hostages from that *volost* as evidence of their good
health and condition. Finally, the Russians feasted the natives with food and
strong alcoholic drinks and gave them gifts. The latter consisted of beads,
grain, iron knives and axes, and cloth—but not guns, ammunition, or alcohol. These gifts, although much anticipated by the *iasak* payers, were scarcely
equivalent to what the Russians would have had to pay in barter if the Siberians were free to trade rather than forced to pay a tax. If any furs remained
after the official payments, the governor or his staff usually offered to buy the
surplus either for the treasury or for their private accounts.

To make collections from remote *volosts* or from some of the more mobile
nomadic groups, especially in eastern Siberia, the Russians resorted to erect-
ing networks of small blockhouses *(zimov'e)* in regions distant from the primary towns. Official parties traveled to collect the *iasak* at these points.[24]
Around 1629, for instance, the *iasak* collectors sent to certain nomadic tribes
from Mangazeya (on the Taz River) would enter a *zimov'e* (usually a simple
cabin with a stove adapted for wintering) and there await the natives with the
furs. The natives, two or three at a time, would approach the place and throw
the furs through the window. On their side of the window, the *iasak* collectors would show the hostages, whom they had brought along for this purpose
from the *ostrog*, and throw back some beads, tin, and bread. Both sides regarded each other with extreme suspicion, because, as is stated in one of the
voevody's reports, "the natives are afraid of being seized as hostages, while the
serving men are afraid of being murdered." As this description suggests,
iasak collection by tsarist officers was an adversarial, often brutal, expropri-
ation of the products of the hunt from the weak indigenous peoples of
Siberia. They hunted sable and other furbearers to avoid punishment, not
for the incentives of trade goods and profit.

Submission to the Russians immediately forced Siberian natives into a
new mode of hunting, carried out under duress, with a new set of priorities
that designated sable as the most desirable prey animal. The *iasak* could be
paid most efficiently by trapping or killing sable, followed by other furbearers according to the decreasing value assigned by the Russians. The *iasak* dis-
torted the long-standing hunting patterns and the prey selections of the
Siberians. The Khantys, Mansis, Samoyeds, Yakuts, Tungus, and Yukagirs had
previously taken furbearers and either used or traded their furs, but not with
the same desperate intensity. The energy they had expended in killing animals for meat was diverted to killing furbearers—especially sables.

The Siberian sable *(Martes zibellina)* shares many characteristics with the
European pine marten *(Martes martes)* and the American marten *(Martes*

24. Lantzeff, *Siberia in the Seventeenth Century,* 128–29.

americana).[25] Sables occur across 7 million square kilometers of Siberia's cold taiga forests, from the Dvina River eastward to the Pacific Coast.[26] Sables are superbly equipped to withstand cold temperatures, with adaptations such as furred feet and use of protected microhabitats. However, they cannot thrive in areas with high summer temperatures or in broadleaf forests. It is likely that their range increased somewhat to the south with the fall in temperature during the early modern centuries.[27]

These animals are small, forest-dwelling carnivores; males weigh between .8 and 1.8 kilograms and females reach .7 to 1.5 kilograms. They have slender, long, supple bodies and elongated tails. Their winter fur consists of long, silky, lustrous guard hair with dense underfur. Their coat colors vary from light brown to dark brown. Their most important prey are voles *(Clethrionomys rutilis* or *Clethrionomys gapperi)*, but they routinely kill and eat weasels *(Mustela sibirica* and *Mustela nivalis); mice* (Arvicolidae); pikas; small, tailless hares *(Ochotona* spp.); chipmunks *(Eutamias sibericus); squirrels;* the Siberian jay and other birds; and spawning salmon.[28] In winter, sables will even kill and eat grouse (Tetraonidae) sheltering in snow holes and, in deep snow, musk deer *(Moschus moschiferus)* ten times their weight. They also gather and consume pine nuts from the Siberian pine species *(Pinus siberica* and *Pinus pumila),* honey, and many types of bush berries and fruits. Adult sables are energetic hunters and foragers who cover long distances as they hunt by day and night.

Sables are solitary nesting and burrowing animals. Females select brood or maternal nests to occupy through much of the spring and into the summer. Both adult males and females in the summer and autumn move around to a number of nests and resting sites. Both sexes occupy permanent nests from December to April. These consist of sometimes lengthy burrows through the snow leading to round chambers usually placed under the trunk or roots of a tree.

The animals have few natural predators and may live up to fifteen years. Reproduction is on an annual cycle. Mating takes place from June to August, and birth of one to five kits per litter occurs in April or May. The total gestation period is actually 250 to 300 days because of delayed implantation; the actual development of the embryo requires only twenty-five to forty days.

25. Steven Buskirk, ed., *Martens, Sables, and Fishers: Biology and Conservation* (Ithaca, N.Y.: Cornell University Press, 1994), 2.

26. Nikolai N. Bakeyev and Andrei N. Sinitysn, "Sables in the Commonwealth of Independent States," in *Martens, Sables, and Fishers: Biology and Conservation,* edited by Steven Buskirk (Ithaca, N.Y.: Cornell University Press, 1994), 246.

27. Ibid., 248.

28. Steven Buskirk, "Diets of, and Prey Selection by, Sables *(Martes zibellina)* in Northern China," *Journal of Mammalogy* 77 (1996).

The young kits wean at seven weeks and attain adult body weight by five months.

Sables are fiercely territorial and sedentary animals. Barring fires or other disasters, they spend their entire lives in a well-defined range, within which they annually vary their nests and hunting territories. As the Russian biologists Solokov and Belousev comment, "The area inhabited by an individual sable is relatively small, 2–3 intermingled wood mounts, the heads of 2–3 neighboring rivulets, often a mountain taiga stream whose inflows drain an area of about 22–28 square versts [23.5 to 29.9 square kilometers]—this is the area where it [the sable] is born, lives and dies."[29] This may be an extreme statement of the sable's range, since other reports suggest that density may be as high as 1.5 sables per square kilometer in some pine forests and reduced to 1 animal per 25 square kilometers in larch forests.[30]

Sables were especially vulnerable to human predation during the winter when their burrows and nests were visible and their inhabitants could be readily caught and killed. However, collecting enough pelts to meet the *iasak* quota meant that Siberian hunters had to trek long intervals between one sable home range and another. Filling the annual quota for a single hunter killed off the sable population in areas measuring tens to hundreds of square kilometers. Because sables were solitary, territorial, sedentary, and slow-reproducing animals, once gone they were unlikely to be replaced by others. Each year, meeting the *iasak* required travel over wider tracts of territory with steadily growing stress and greater certainty that the quotas could not be met.

RUSSIAN HUNTERS AND TRADERS

Important as the state's tax demand on the native Siberian hunters was, however, Moscow's collection of sable and other furs did not come close to the furs taken by private traders who employed Russian trappers in Siberia. For example, in 1631 the tsar's fur treasury sent out furs worth 42,000 rubles: 18,000 rubles from tolls and 24,000 from the *iasak* on Siberian natives.[31] These data suggest that, in that year, the private Russian traders and hunters produced furs worth 180,000 rubles, or seven and a half times the value of the 24,000 rubles' worth of furs paid in *iasak* by Siberian native hunters. Of the total 204,000 rubles' worth of furs exported from Siberia in that year,

29. Quoted in S. U. Stroganov, *Carnivorous Mammals of Siberia* (Jerusalem: Israel Program for Scientific Translations, 1969, available from the U.S. Department of Commerce Clearinghouse for Federal Scientific and Technical Information, Springfield, Va.), 221.

30. Ronald M. Nowak and Ernest P. Walker, *Walker's Mammals of the World*, 5th ed. (Baltimore: Johns Hopkins University Press, 1991), s.v. *Martes zibellina*.

31. Paul Bushkovitch, *The Merchants of Moscow, 1580–1650* (Cambridge: Cambridge University Press, 1980), 117.

state-owned furs were valued at 42,000 rubles (20.6 percent) and private traders' furs totaled 162,000 rubles (79.4 percent).

Native hunters faced direct competition from the Russian trappers who poured into Siberia. Russian merchants traveled themselves or sent their agents to Siberia to engage in a brisk private trade, but the indigenous peoples seem to have had little part in it. Many private Russian hunter-traders (*promyshlenniks*), whose hunting grounds had been depleted, crossed the Urals to take furs from the rich Siberian hunting grounds. Some came as members of expeditions financed and organized by traders; some came in self-financed groups of hunters. Most were experienced hunters whose families and villages had long been involved in commercial hunting in the Russian north. Areas such as Pomorye, the region surrounding the White Sea, prospered from profits made by its hunters in Siberia. Customs records suggest that 2,000 or more Russian hunters moved into Siberia each season. Large numbers moved beyond the Lena River into eastern Siberia. For example, in 1642, 839 Russian hunters heading east passed through Yakutsk.[32]

In Siberia, fur hunting and trapping took place in winter, when pelts were generally in their best condition. Young sables born in March and April each year had grown sufficient hair on their coats by the following winter to be worth taking. Hunting parties traveled in boats on the rivers to the hunting grounds before the winter freeze. In contrast to most Siberian natives, who hunted furbearers with bow and arrow, the Russians adopted trapping methods on a large scale.

At the onset of winter, Russian hunting bands divided into two- or three-man teams with agreed-on territories. They built numerous trap pits that consisted of deep holes dug in the ground surrounded by a palisade of six-foot stakes. At a single narrow entrance, they suspended a board baited with fish or meat. As soon as the animal alighted on the entrance board, the board turned and threw the animal into the pit. Each group made dozens of traps that they checked regularly. The hunters bludgeoned any animals found, reset the traps, skinned their prey, and smoked the pelts. An alternative method involved nets and dogs. The hunter tracked individual sables in the snow to their nest in the ground or in a tree, put a net around the site, and waited—sometimes for a full day—for the sable to emerge and become entangled in the net. Then the dog would kill the trapped animal. At times, when confronted with groups of sable holes, hunters used smoke to drive the sables into the open.[33]

Such methods as these produced massive harvests when applied by large numbers of Russian hunters. In newly opened tracts, such as the Lena River area in the 1640s, each man in a hunting party might take as many as 120

32. R. H. Fisher, *The Russian Fur Trade*, 94.
33. Ibid., 156–57, supplies a description of methods from the early 1700s.

sables in a season.[34] Before the town burnt in 1643, Mangazeya on the Taz River was the dominant internal fur market for Siberia. In 1641, those private Russian traders returning to European Russia passed through customs at Mangazeya with 62,882 sable furs. Returns for the same year from Yeniseysk, to the south, amounted to 36,030 sable pelts carried by traders or hunters.[35] In 1702, the tsarist regime did a financial survey that produced total figures for pelts exported from Siberia at the end of the century. According to this record, in 1698 the total number of pelts sent to European Russian towns was 256,837, and for 1699 the number was 489,900.[36] Throughout the seventeenth century, a plausible Siberian harvest—including iasak and private hunting—would have ranged between 200,000 and 300,000 sable pelts every year.

Slaughtering fur-bearing animals in such numbers assuredly depleted animal populations. Since market demand and prices for Siberian furs increased steadily throughout the seventeenth century, it was cost-effective for many Russian hunters to search out hunting grounds bypassed in the initial rush eastward.[37] They were able to obtain profitable harvests in areas on the tributaries of the great rivers that still had sizeable animal populations. It was this steady process of hunting out all available areas behind the moving frontier that bolstered the total annual catch and helped exhaust the fur-bearing stocks in Siberia.

State pressure on indigenous hunters did not relent in spite of protests and declining iasak returns. Between the 1620s and 1690s, iasak collections from western Siberia declined by about 45 percent.[38] In 1638, Tsar Mikhail Federovich noted, "The voevodas [military governors] write to the Sovereign from Siberian towns that they cannot obtain any more furs. They report that these Siberian towns and ostrogs are experiencing a depletion of sables and other furbearing animals because the iasak-paying forest dwelling natives have trapped all the available animals."[39] The tsar's solution for that problem was to send his officers eastward to the Lena River area. By the 1690s, sables had vanished as far east as the vicinity of Yakutsk on the Lena River.[40]

During the 1690s, the Chinese market for furs, with its nearly insatiable

34. Ibid., 98.
35. Bushkovitch, The Merchants of Moscow, 121–22.
36. R. H. Fisher, The Russian Fur Trade, 180. In 1698, the tithe equaled 16,800 and the iasak 105,837; in 1699, the tithe was 42,200 and the iasak was 109,900.
37. Richard Hellie, "Furs in Seventeenth-Century Muscovy," Russian History 16 (1989). See p. 187, fig. 12, for the north and fig. 13 for Siberia. Prices at Moscow rose slowly but steadily throughout the century. See p. 186, fig. 11.
38. R. H. Fisher, The Russian Fur Trade, 102.
39. Basil Dmytryshyn, E. A. P. Crownhart-Vaughan, and Thomas Vaughan, Russia's Conquest of Siberia, 1558–1700: A Documentary Record, vol. 1 of To Siberia and Russian America (Portland, Ore.: Western Imprints, the Press of the Oregon Historical Society, 1985), 171.
40. R. H. Fisher, The Russian Fur Trade, 107.

demand, opened to Russian fur traders. The territorial interests of tsarist Russia and Qing China collided in the Amur River valley. China prevailed and forced Russia out of the Amur Valley in a dispute settled by the Treaty of Nerchinsk in 1689. One article of the treaty provided that private traders from each country could trade in each other's territory. The Chinese market paid high prices for all varieties of Siberian furs. Ermine and wolverine commanded better prices than sable or fox—although the latter sold well. In return, traders could bring back porcelain, silk, gold, silver, tea, precious and semiprecious stones, and ivory.[41] Given the distances involved, Siberian furs were the only commodity available to Russia to exchange for these highly prized goods.

In the late 1690s, Peter the Great, anxious to engross the potential profits of the China fur trade and concerned by the state's inability to obtain the finest-quality sables as the supply decreased, imposed a state monopoly on all export sales of furs from Russia and on all sable and fox furs in the domestic market. This new arrangement simply shifted the source of pressure and did not inhibit private Russians from hunting for furs. The new monopoly ended only in 1762, by which time dwindling harvests had reduced the monopoly's importance for state revenues.

Overall, Russian and foreign demand for sable drove Siberian expansion. Of the furs, sable was most heavily valued and traded. Over a 125-year period for which information survives, sable accounted for just under 95 percent of the total monies paid for furs in sales at Moscow.[42] The Moscow price of sable pelts, that benchmark of the Russian fur trade, rose steadily at a rate of 1.68 percent per year between 1600 and 1719. As Richard Hellie comments, "Certainly, this constant rise in the price of sable reflects relentless, ruthless trapping, without the slightest notion of conservation, of the Russians' most valuable fur crop."[43]

CONQUEST AND SETTLEMENT

Why did the Russians prevail so quickly and easily over such a vast territory? First, and perhaps most important, the indigenous peoples were few and poorly organized. A generally accepted official Russian count for tribute purposes puts the indigenous population of all Siberia at only 227,000 in the

41. Ibid., 225.

42. Hellie, "Furs in Seventeenth-Century Muscovy," 69–70, and table 4.8. All sable transactions totaled 2,469 (58.9 percent), from 4,191 total fur transactions. Total monies paid for sable in those transactions amounted to 1,631,047 rubles (94.7 percent) of a total expenditure of 1,723,205 rubles for furs.

43. Richard Hellie, *The Economy and Material Culture of Russia, 1600–1725* (Chicago: University of Chicago Press, 1999), 62, fig. 4.4.

1600s.[44] Even allowing for substantial underestimation by the widely scattered Russian officials, it is doubtful that the total early modern Siberian population exceeded 300,000 persons.

For the Siberians, who were organized into hundreds of discrete groups that lacked centralizing state structures, unified, large-scale effective resistance to the Russians was impossible. With technological capacities that at best encompassed some use of iron and steel, their weaponry could not match Russian firearms. To varying degrees, each group fought. Some groups fought desperately and some occasionally won victories, but overall they could not defeat the Russians. Both resistance and flight remained futile.

New diseases also weakened and demoralized the indigenous peoples of Siberia. The worst of these was smallpox "because of its swift spread, the high death rates, and the permanent disfigurement of survivors."[45] Smallpox first reached western Siberia in 1630. In the 1650s, it moved east of the Yenisey, where it carried away up to 80 percent of the Tungus and Yakut populations.[46] In the 1690s, smallpox epidemics reduced Yukagir numbers by an estimated 44 percent. The disease moved rapidly from group to group across Siberia. Death rates in epidemics reached 50 percent of the population. The scourge returned at twenty- to thirty-year intervals, with dreadful results among the young. Venereal disease, called "the Russian disease" by the natives, spread widely as Russian intruders engaged in sexual relationships with native women. Venereal disease sharply reduced fertility and sent indigenous populations into decline. Other, airborne infections such as measles hit hard at the Siberians. Finally, alcoholism seems to have taken hold in populations that had not previously known its use, and it contributed to an increasing cultural and social malaise.[47]

Because the indigenous populations were so weak, the manpower required to defeat them was relatively low. Russian exploration and conquest was the work of small parties of audacious private trappers and state servicemen. Groups of only 20, 30, or 50 tsarist musketeers or cossacks routinely defeated larger forces of Siberians. Moscow sent relatively few men to Siberia. When, in 1636, the tsar was strapped for manpower by the race into central Siberia, he doubled the Siberian cadre of troops and officials, and the total number rose to a paltry 5,004 men (from 2,735 serving a decade earlier).[48]

44. Forsyth, *A History of the Peoples of Siberia,* 71, table 5.1.

45. Alfred W. Crosby, *Ecological Imperialism: The Biological Expansion of Europe, 900–1900* (Cambridge: Cambridge University Press, 1986).

46. James Forsyth, "The Siberian Native Peoples before and after the Russian Conquest," in *The History of Siberia: From Russian Conquest to Revolution,* edited by Alan Wood (London: Routledge, 1991), 82–83.

47. Ibid., 82.

48. Lantzeff, *Siberia in the Seventeenth Century,* 67.

After the initial phase of conquest and fur trading, Russian settlers did find their way to even the most distant and remote parts of Siberia. Apart from state officials and soldiers, hunters, and trappers, Siberia began to draw peasant migrants. Parts of the southern taiga forest in western Siberia lent themselves to sedentary plow cultivation. These attracted Russian pioneer settlers, who clustered near the Ural Mountains in Tobolsk district. By 1670, there were 7,586 peasant farmsteads with some 34,000 settlers occupying land after cutting and burning the taiga forest in that region.[49] Another area of peasant settlement and grain cultivation was located on the upper Ob River around Tobolsk.

In central and eastern Siberia beyond the Yenisey River, large areas under permafrost discouraged widespread Russian peasant migration. Some agricultural settlement occurred around Yeniseysk in the 1620s, in areas of black earth around Krasnoyarsk in the 1630s, and in pockets of good soil along the Angara and Ilim Rivers in the 1650s.[50] Officials imported many of these peasants to grow grains to feed their settlements. Native Siberians' resentment over peasants grabbing and clearing their hunting grounds found expression in numerous complaints and even violent incidents.

The Russian population of Siberia grew steadily. The number of male peasants rose from 49,000 in 1678, to 173,912 in 1719, to 365,050 in 1762, and to 600,368 in 1811.[51] From these data, we can do a crude estimate of the growth of total agricultural area in Siberia. If each peasant pioneer occupied 20 hectares with his household area, arable land, hayfields, and woodlots (somewhat more than the 10–17-hectare average claimed by peasants in the Russian heartland), the totals for those years are as follows: 9,800 square kilometers in 1678, 34,782 square kilometers in 1719, 73,010 square kilometers in 1762, and 120,074 square kilometers in 1811. Although even the 1811 total is less than 1 percent of the total land area of Siberia (which covered 13.5 million square kilometers), in absolute terms the area of agricultural settlement was significant. Especially in western Siberia, Russian pioneers burnt and cleared forests, plowed for grain cultivation, and grazed their livestock—and thereby altered the existing habitat.

IMPACTS ON INDIGENOUS PEOPLES

As animal populations dropped in eastern Siberia, the living standards of the Tungus, Yakuts, and other eastern groups also worsened. Disease, the tsar's continuing demand for *iasak* payment in sable furs, and Russian brutality and

49. Forsyth, *A History of the Peoples of Siberia*, 45; David Moon, "Peasant Migration and the Settlement of Russia's Frontiers, 1550–1897," *The Historical Journal* 40, no. 4 (1997): 877.
50. Ibid., 64.
51. Moon, "Peasant Migration and the Settlement of Russia's Frontiers," 863, table 1.

corruption all exacted a heavy toll on native populations across Siberia. A 1744 memorial written by Heinrich von Fuch, a political exile with extended experience among the Yakut and Tungus peoples of northeastern Siberia, eloquently protested their hardships suffered as furs became harder to harvest. When von Fuch departed Siberia, he "promised the Iakuts and Tungus, who had petitioned me, that I would report these conditions to Imperial authorities."[52] He points out, "At first there were plenty of furbearing animals there, but now there are no sables and not many foxes in those Iakut lands, from the shores of the [Arctic] ocean all the way south to the great Lena River."[53]

Moreover, contagious disease had devastated the Siberians—"when they are stricken with smallpox they die like flies." Even more devastating was the inflexibility of Russian officials who forced survivors to pay the *iasak* owed by their dead relatives. According to von Fuch:

> I personally knew several wealthy Iakuts who had to pay for four or five of their dead relatives. They were so impoverished that before I left they had to forfeit all their livestock and horses, and sometimes pawn their wives and children [to Russian officials]. Some of them hang or drown themselves. This is a natural consequence because a local native works very hard in the forest all winter and suffers hunger and cold until he traps enough to pay his iasak and make gift[s of furs] to the iasak collector and his assistants. If in addition to this he is forced to pay the iasak for those who have died or who have run off, first he loses all his livestock, then his wives and children. He cannot hunt without horses, so he commits suicide or runs off. Then the collectors find his relatives and force them to pay. The collectors take everything until the natives are destitute.[54]

Von Fuch recommended that the *iasak* payers be permitted to submit fixed numbers of squirrel and wolverine pelts instead of the diminished sable and fox.

Greedy Russian officials exacted large illegal bribes and gifts from the natives that were often equal to the amount of the *iasak* paid. If officials were not paid what they demanded, they "then take the native's wives and grown children to work for them. They also take the nets, axes, tools, boats, bows and arrows. Sometimes they take the clothes right off the backs of the natives, and beat and torture them secretly in their iurts [encampments]."[55] Perhaps most deplorably, according to von Fuch, the native peoples had no recourse, no representation, no means by which their ill treatment could be protested

52. Ibid., 187.
53. Dmytryshyn, Crownhart-Vaughan, and Vaughan, *Russia's Conquest of Siberia*, 1:170.
54. Ibid.
55. Ibid., 1:173.

effectively. The military governors were invariably influenced by their local native interpreters, who benefited from the existing corrupt system.

The native Siberian population did not disappear, in spite of Russian brutality and the ravages of smallpox and other diseases. For western and eastern Siberia combined, the total native population recorded in 1790 was 303,395 persons.[56] The 1790 total is slightly more than the estimated preconquest population of 227,000. Part of the increase may be accounted for by the inclusion of a growing number of mixed-race, Russian-indigenous persons counted as Siberians by officials.

KAMCHATKA AND THE PACIFIC

The search for new sources of fur led the Russians to further eastward advances in the first half of the eighteenth century. In 1696, a cossack commander, Vladimir Atlasov, led an overland expedition out of Anadyrsk fort on the Anadyr River in northeast Siberia on an eighteen-hundred-kilometer trek south into the Kamchatka Peninsula. Two years later, Atlasov returned with 3,640 sable pelts taken as *iasak* from the Itelmen—the natives of Kamchatka—or trapped by members of the expedition. The numerous Kamchatka sables were larger than ordinary Siberian varieties, and their furs brought higher prices at market. The Russians soon returned to obtain more furs. Over the next quarter century, a steady stream of Russian cossacks followed the long, arduous route to Kamchatka, forced the Itelmen to submit to the tsar in time-honored fashion, and exacted *iasak*.

The Kamchatka Peninsula is one of the most unstable regions on earth, with its twelve active volcanoes and the earthquakes and tidal waves associated with frequent volcanic eruptions. In the 1690s, the birch and larch forests of the Kamchatka River plain supported a sizeable human population, perhaps thirteen thousand Itelmen people (called Kamchadals by the Russians). These Paleo-Siberian language speakers used bone and stone implements, hunted reindeer, fished salmon, hunted seals, and carried out modest horticulture. The Itelmen were a warrior people accustomed to tough internecine warfare among themselves, who lived in villages fortified by palisades to protect themselves against interlineage raiding.[57]

The lengthy circuitous land route to Kamchatka was made hazardous by attacks from the northern Korak peoples, who had obtained firearms by this time. Lack of a defined sea route impeded exploitation of the peninsula's resources. Finally, in 1716–1717, after several failed attempts, the cossack Kozma Sokolov successfully navigated from Okhotsk to the peninsula, and

56. Forsyth, *A History of the Peoples of Siberia*, 115, n. 14.
57. Ibid., 132–33.

the land route was virtually abandoned. Okhotsk became Russia's chief Pacific port until the mid–nineteenth century.[58]

Apparently unchecked by the imperial authorities, the cossacks treated the Itelmen with contempt and cruelty that went well beyond the usual Russian practice in Siberia. They extorted furs far in excess of the numbers specified for payment of the *iasak* and brutally punished those Itelmen who did not meet their demands. If the Itelmen could not hand over the demanded furs, the cossacks seized and enslaved Itelmen women and children. In 1724, the Russians at the Upper Kamchatka and Big River forts possessed among them 209 Itelmen slaves.[59] The cossacks also forced Itelmen to use their sled dogs and canoes to transport seaborne supplies to Russian forts.

Itelmen resentment against cossack brutality caused numerous small-scale violent attacks that the cossacks punished ferociously. This ongoing hostility triggered three large-scale rebellions, in the periods 1706 to 1713, 1731 to 1732, and 1741 to 1742. Even though the Itelmen acquired firearms and developed effective war chiefs, they did not prevail. Punitive campaigns and massacres of the Itelmen followed each of these uprisings. Despite the unrest, the flow of sable furs from Kamchatka continued and the sable population declined steadily. Itelmen numbers dropped too: from 13,000 when the Russians arrived in the 1690s to about 6,000 by 1767. The smallpox epidemic of 1768–1769 reduced that number to about 3,000 at its end. Many of the Itelmen were in fact of mixed Russian-Itelmen descent by that time.[60]

SEA OTTERS IN THE PACIFIC

Russian interest in the Pacific Coast intensified when Peter the Great sent Captain Vitus Bering on the first Kamchatka exploration in 1725, just before the tsar's death. Bering sailed along the Kamchatka coast as far north as what came to be called the Bering Strait, before turning back.[61] The second Kamchatka expedition (1733–1734), led by Bering and A. I. Chirikov, brought a wave of new settlers to Okhotsk and the Pacific Coast. In 1738, Bering sent ships from Okhotsk to Kamchatka and then to the Kuril Islands. In 1739, a second expedition to the south reached Hokkaido in Japan. On June 4, 1741, Bering sailed from Kamchatka for America across the Bering Sea. He commanded one twenty-four-meter sailing vessel built in Okhotsk, the *Svyatoy Petr*, and Chirikov commanded its sister ship, the *Svyatoy Pavel*. Although the

58. James R. Gibson, *Feeding the Russian Fur Trade: Provisionment of the Okhotsk Seaboard and the Kamchatka Peninsula, 1639–1856* (Madison: University of Wisconsin Press, 1969), 9–11.

59. Forsyth, *A History of the Peoples of Siberia*, 135.

60. Ibid., 140–43.

61. T. Armstrong, "Bering's Expeditions," in *Studies in Russian Historical Geography*, edited by James H. Bater and R. A. French (London: Academic Press, 1983), 175–95.

ships became separated, each commander landed on North American soil safely by mid-July—Bering in the Gulf of Alaska and Chirikov near Prince of Wales Island. Chirikov returned safely to Kamchatka by mid-October. Bering landed erroneously on an uninhabited island (Bering Island) two hundred kilometers east of Kamchatka. After his ship wrecked offshore, Bering died from an illness, and the crew spent nearly a year there until they built a new vessel and sailed home. The rebuilt ship sailed to Kamchatka in August 1742, wintered over, and finally arrived in Okhotsk in June 1743.

The reconstructed *Svyatoy Petr* returned with several hundred sea otter pelts taken on Bering Island during the crew's long sojourn. They reported that great numbers of sea otters were to be found along the coasts of the islands in the Bering Sea. So luxurious were these furs that they brought the astounding price of eighty to one hundred rubles each when sold in Siberia. The best sea otter pelts were nearly 2 meters long and .7 meters in width when stretched before drying. Their fur was rich jet black and glossy, with a slight intermixture of white hairs that conveyed a muted silver color in the background. The normal price steadied at about double that of sable pelts, or four rubles per skin. So much in demand were sea otter furs in China that formerly land-bound Siberian traders and hunters took to the sea in pursuit of the sea otter.

The sea otter *(Enhydra lutris)* lives in shallow waters with kelp and shellfish beds along the coasts of the northern Pacific from Hokkaido in northern Japan to southern California. Grouped in schools of seventy-five to a hundred, sea otters eat crabs and fish in summer and sea urchins and mollusks in winter. They are slow to reproduce, since females bear only one pup each year. Although mammals, they spend most of their lives in the water and come ashore to rest primarily at night and in times of hard winds and foul weather. During fair weather they go far to sea and sleep afloat. Generally, they were best hunted at sea during the fair weather season of the North Pacific, from May to June of each year. So soundly did they sleep that they could be approached within very close range by experienced hunters.

Russian entrepreneurs paid to have sailboats hastily built and designed at Okhotsk and other ports. Each boat carried forty to seventy crew members operating on shares. A single trip lasted two years or more because the hunters spent the winter on the Commander Islands. Here, they hunted sea cows for meat and sea lions and fur seals for their hides. The following summer, the boats sailed to the Aleutians, where they operated from one of the small beaches. They forced the Aleuts to join the hunting parties formed by the Russians and to net or harpoon sea otters. The crews put to sea in the Aleut *baidaras* or umiaks, which were made from the hides of sea cows and held six to eight men. In the course of a summer, they could take 100 or more pelts per crew member for the return to Okhotsk. A full load of furs

returned ten thousand to thirty thousand rubles, or twice the cost of outfitting an expedition.[62]

Between 1743 and 1800, Russian hunters made 101 officially counted voyages to the Aleutian Islands, the Commander Islands, and Alaska. The half-
century harvest (1743–1798), from which tsarist officials took their 10 percent tax, amounted to 186,754 pelts. As early as 1750, sea otters had
disappeared from the coast of the Kamchatka Peninsula; by 1780, they had
disappeared from the Kuril Islands; and by the 1790s, their numbers on the
Aleutians had perceptibly dropped. The North Pacific shores of Alaska
marked the terminus for the Siberian hunt for furs.

ENVIRONMENTAL EFFECT OF THE RUSSIAN CONQUEST

The Russian advance into Siberia noticeably changed the faunal composition of the entire region from the Ob River to the Kamchatka Peninsula.
With every passing decade, Russian and native hunters further depleted the
sable population all the way across Siberia. Was this a significant loss that
caused major changes in Siberian ecosystems? Probably not. The sable was
not a keystone species equivalent to the American beaver or even a dominant
carnivore in Siberia.[63] That role can be assigned to larger animals such as the
bear or wolf. The sable's disappearance might have reduced pressure on its
many prey species. However, so many species prey on smaller rodents that
the effect would be virtually impossible to measure. The Siberian weasel may
have increased its numbers and pines might have had better seed distribution when sables stopped eating, and thereby killing, pine nuts.[64] The ecological consequences of the sable's departure were diffuse and hard to de-
tect in the historical record.

Perhaps more significant is the fact that, with the Russian advance into
Siberia, other furbearers, especially carnivores, came under new hunting
pressures. Over twenty species of furbearers were sold, many for substantial
prices, on the Moscow market.[65] Moscow transactions data, however, under-
state the intensity with which Russian and native hunters pursued bears,
wolves, wolverines, foxes, bobcats, cats, otters, minks, ermines, and weasels.
Some furs, like ermine, were preferred and were sold to the Chinese market.
Most of the remainder were immediately fabricated into clothing or sold on

62. J. R. Gibson, *Feeding the Russian Fur Trade*, 24–33.

63. For a discussion of keystone species, see M. E. Power et al., "Challenges in the Quest for
Keystones," *BioScience* 46 (1996).

64. I am grateful to Steven Buskirk for making these points in a personal communication.

65. Hellie, *The Economy and Material Culture of Russia*, 53–54. Foxes, at 11.2 percent of
recorded transactions, and marten (5.8 percent) were prominent in sales at Moscow. Noncar-
nivores included beavers, at 5.6 percent of the total transactions, and squirrels, at 7.7 percent.
Transactions involving other animals combined were no more than 2 to 3 percent, if that.

local and regional markets for domestic consumption. As sable catches declined, it is likely that Russian and native Siberian hunters put more effort into taking these other species. Human predation can easily have a deleterious effect on relatively small populations of carnivores, whose average population densities are only 3 percent of those of their prey.[66] The end result of this stepped-up effort would have been the depletion of the wolf, usually considered a keystone carnivore because of its size and effect on herbivores, and similar reductions in virtually all smaller carnivores. Whether surges in herbivore prey populations occurred in early modern Siberia as a result—and if so, to what extent—is an unanswered question.

Finally, as the hunt thrust out into the Pacific Ocean, the war on the sea otters had a significant ecological effect on the coastal fauna around its rim. The sea otter is a "conspicuous predator in nearshore communities of the northeastern Pacific Ocean" and can be considered a keystone species for those communities.[67] When sea otters were plentiful, they preyed heavily on the invertebrate herbivore the sea urchin *(Strongylocentrotus polyacanthus)*, whose populations live in shallow waters. When sea otters reduced sea urchin populations, these herbivores no longer heavily grazed kelp or macroalgae *(Alaria fistulosa, Laminaria* spp., and *Agarum* spp.), and kelp forests grew luxuriantly. The kelp canopy in turn provided important food and cover for a wide range of fish and other species. Intensified human hunting in the Aleutians reversed this sequence. Sea urchin populations shot up and grazed kelp and other macroalgae to a remnant layer and reduced fish and other coastal marine populations.[68]

CONCLUSION

A century and a half after the 1552 conquest of Kazan, the Russian tsar ruled over all Siberia. The early modern Russian state rarely wavered in its expansionist resolve as, decade after decade, Moscow mobilized resources and deployed military force in service of expansion into Siberia. Russian frontiersmen, some of them directly employed by the state and some of them private

66. Steven Buskirk and Gilbert Proulx, "Furbearers, Trapping, and Biodiversity" (manuscript, 2000).

67. James A. Estes, Norman S. Smith, and John F. Palmisano, "Sea Otter Predation and Community Organization in the Western Aleutian Islands, Alaska," *Ecology* 59 (1978): 822. This is the classic statement of the sea-otter-as-keystone-species argument.

68. James A. Estes and David O. Duggins. "Sea Otters and Kelp Forests in Alaska: Generality and Variation in a Community Ecological Paradigm," *Ecological Monographs* 65, no. 1 (1995). Despite criticisms, the theory remains robust and its applications have been extended beyond the original rocky shore habitats investigated by Estes. R. G. Kvitek et al., "Changes in Alaskan Soft-Bottom Prey Communities along a Gradient in Sea Otter Predation," *Ecology* 73 (1992).

entrepreneurs, carried out an audacious feat of exploration and ruthless conquest.

The tsars, heads of a centralizing and aggrandizing regime, maintained continuity of purpose from reign to reign. In large measure, Moscow's determination can be explained by the fact that the world fur market continued to send out strong demand signals. The regime reaped high returns from the furs demanded of Siberian natives as a tax. A large, perhaps even dominant, share of fur profits went to the private sector. Violent, hardy, private fur trappers and traders had much to gain by pushing deeper and deeper into Siberia to gain access to untapped stocks of sables and other furbearers. The profits obtained in the form of furs amply repaid the costs of this great national venture.

Whatever their numbers, the indigenous peoples of Siberia did not flourish or prosper under early modern Russian rule. The pressures they endured and the cultural and social devastation that ensued was nearly identical to those faced by the Indians of North America, described in the previous chapter. Aside from the strains they suffered in paying the *iasak,* the natives of Siberia became increasingly dependent on Russian-produced and -traded consumer goods. They developed a taste for and need for bread, became addicted to alcohol and tobacco, and relied on firearms and purchased ammunition. They lost possession of their choicest hunting grounds and fishing rights after taking fraudulent loans from settlers. They found the settlers competing with them in gathering such edible forest produce as the nuts from the cones of Siberian pine as well as honey from wild bees. Many natives were reduced to dependency and beggary on the outskirts of Russian settlements.[69] Others retreated to more distant, less productive areas, in the hope that they could avoid these pressures.

Active, commercial hunting by both Russian settlers and indigenous peoples stripped the larger carnivores from the Siberian landscape. What for Russians began in the sixteenth century as commercialized hunting of sables in western Siberia had, by the late eighteenth century, intersected with the world hunt for sea mammals in the northern oceans.

69. Forsyth, *A History of the Peoples of Siberia,* 157–58.

Chapter 3

Cod and the New World Fisheries

From the Baltic to the Barents Sea, the fishing grounds of the northeastern Atlantic and Arctic had long produced valuable catches of cod for European markets. Fishermen had identified and were exploiting each of the major populations of cod in the northwestern Atlantic. Since the thirteenth century, there had been a long-distance trade in stockfish—dried and salted cod—dominated by merchants of the Hanseatic League. From Icelandic waters, European fishermen pushed onward to discover gratifyingly copious stocks of cod, a familiar resource, off Labrador and Newfoundland.

In the 1490s, Basque fishermen apparently sailed regularly across the icy waters of the North Atlantic to take codfish from coastal waters ("the banks") of Newfoundland, Nova Scotia, and southern Labrador. Between 1497 and 1502, the exploratory voyages of the English John Cabot and Portuguese Gaspar Corte-Real made visible, and excited interest in, the transatlantic route to the northeast coast of North America.[1] Greater numbers of fishing vessels from a greater number of European ports sailed each year to the fishing grounds off Newfoundland. The New World fishery became a new industry that consumed considerable European capital and entrepreneurial energy. The fisheries tapped into a vast natural resource virtually unused by the sparse Indian and Eskimo populations of the region.

Cod, with its rich protein, was one of the great prizes of the New World. The New World fisheries were a self-renewing resource of the greatest abundance.[2] Every year over the next half millennium, the fishing fleets of the

---

1. Felipe Fernández-Armesto, K. N. Chaudhuri, and Times Books, *The Times Atlas of World Exploration: Three Thousand Years of Exploring, Explorers, and Mapmaking* (New York: Harper-Collins, 1991), 74–75.
2. A recent book on the cod fisheries is Mark Kurlansky, *Cod: A Biography of the Fish That*

Old World caught coldwater New World codfish, preserved them, and carried them home to put cheap, nutritious protein on the food markets of western Europe. Cod became a staple food for African slaves laboring in the sugar fields of the West Indies. Cod enriched the diet of the colonial settlers of New York, New England, and Canada. Even after three centuries of intense fishing, the great stocks of codfish seemed inexhaustible to the humans who preyed on them.

THE PREY

The adult Atlantic codfish *(Gadus morhua)* is a species of coldwater fish belonging to the order Gadiformes, akin to haddock, pollock, hake, and whiting. The adult fish has a heavy body and large head, blunt snout, and a distinctive barbel under the lower jaw tip. It has a square tail with three dorsal and two distinct anal fins. Colors vary from grayish to reddish tones speckled with small, round, indistinctly edged spots. A distinctive, pale lateral line runs down the body. Atlantic cod studied today mature sexually at a median age of 1.7 to 2.3 years and have body lengths measuring 32 to 41 centimeters. They may live twenty or more years and attain lengths up to 1.3 meters and bodyweights as high as 25 to 35 kilograms. The largest recorded codfish caught in modern times was taken in 1895 and weighed 95.9 kilograms.[3]

The cod is an ideal fish for human consumption. Its flesh is white, firm, and gelatinous without being fatty, and the relatively few bones are easily removed. Raw cod flesh is 17.8 percent protein. Most important, codfish can be preserved almost indefinitely by sun drying and salting. When the water is removed, the salted, dried cod is 62.8 percent protein.[4] Cod can also be preserved wet for a limited period after being caught, by heavy salting (pickling) of the eviscerated, headless carcass. Cod eggs, or roe, are nutritious and palatable either fresh or smoked. Cod livers produce an edible oil rich in vitamins.

Cod follow annual migration patterns tied to the reproductive cycle and seasonal temperature changes in the water. Mature and juvenile cod spend

---

Changed the World (New York: Walker and Company, 1997); A. R. Michell puts New World fishing in the general context of the early modern European fisheries of Western Europe. "The European Fisheries in Early Modern History," in *The Economic Organization of Early Modern Europe,* edited by E. E. Rich and Charles Wilson (Cambridge: Cambridge University Press, 1977).

3. Michael P. Fahay and Northeast Fisheries Science Center, *Essential Fish Habitat Source Document* (Woods Hole, Mass.: U.S. Department of Commerce National Oceanic and Atmospheric Administration, National Marine Fisheries Service, Northeast Region, Northeast Fisheries Science Center, 1999), 2.

4. Agricultural Research Service, U.S. Department of Agriculture, Nutrient Data Laboratory Home Page, USDA Nutrient Database for Standard Reference (Release 13), 1999. In 100 grams of salted, dried Atlantic cod, there are 62.82 grams of protein.

their winters offshore along the submerged continental shelf clustered on rough-textured banks or shallow grounds with water 40 to 130 meters in depth (rarely, as deep as 200 meters) and at temperatures usually between −1.5° and 10° C. The blood plasma of cod freezes at −0.7°C; however, the juvenile and adult fish produce antifreeze proteins that permit survival in waters nearly down to the freezing point of seawater (1.8°C).

In late winter or early spring, cod follow one of a number of distinct migration routes separated by deepwater trenches. Upon arrival inshore, the cod stocks concentrate in dense numbers along the coast in predictable locations, or grounds, of fifty meters depth or less. Currently off Newfoundland, huge, dense schools of cod leave the deeper wintering areas in early spring "and follow tongues of deep, relatively warm, oceanic waters ('highways') across the shelf to summer feeding areas inshore."[5]

In early June to July, depending on location, the codfish temporarily abandon their zooplankton diet when they make contact with massive schools of capelin (*Mallotus villosus*), small, silvery, smeltlike fish heading toward the shore to spawn. Voracious after their own spawning, codfish pursue the capelin inshore, where they are vulnerable to the hand lines and jiggers of inshore fishermen. The inshore season lasts from one hundred days in southern waters to less than sixty days off Labrador. Concentrations of cod move inshore along the coast during the summer and return to deeper, offshore waters along the banks in the winter. Some larger cod prefer colder and deeper water and return to the offshore banks by early autumn to spend the winter.

The peak spawning season occurs as migration begins, but spawning may take place anytime between November and July. Fertilized females release several million eggs in water temperatures between 5° and 7°C. The buoyant pelagic eggs drift on the water surface for an average of two to three weeks before hatching larvae. Optimal temperatures for incubation are between 2° and 8.5°C; the upper bound is 12°C. The emergent larvae, 3.3 to 5.7 millimeters in length, also pelagic, drift from a near-surface depth to depths of 75 meters. The larvae feed on zooplankton until they reach 20 millimeters in length and their fin rays are formed. Optimal temperatures range from 4° to 12°C. The larvae are vulnerable to a wide range of predators, including spiny dogfish, sea raven, hake, halibut, flounder, and adult cod.

As they age, larvae move deeper, until they reach the ocean bottoms as first-year juvenile codfish. Juveniles, especially in the first and second years, cluster in areas of spawning activity at depths of 25–75 meters. Often, they cluster to try to avoid cannibalism by adult cod. Larger juveniles overwinter on the banks with adult cod. Both juveniles and adults consume a varied diet, including zooplankton, especially copepods, as well as shrimp, crabs,

5. Fahay and Northeast Fisheries Science Center, *Essential Fish Habitat Source Document*, 1.

and small fish such as capelin, herring, and juvenile redfish. Cod predators, apart from humans, primarily are large sharks.

Self-sustainable stocks of *Gadus morhua* are found across the North Atlantic and Arctic Oceans. In the northeast, there are six distinct cod habitats: At the northern limits of its range, between 80° and 62° north latitude, the northeast Arctic cod stock inhabits the Barents Sea as far north as Svalbard and migrates south to spawn along the west coast of Norway.[6] The western Greenland stock extends south from Disko Bay (69° north) to the tip of Greenland (60° north) at Cape Farewell.[7] The Icelandic–eastern Greenland stock centered on 65° north latitude has spawning grounds located between Iceland's west coast and Greenland.[8] Two self-sustainable Faroe Island stocks have been identified along the 62° parallel.[9] The North Sea stock stretches between the 61° and the 51° parallels.[10] Just to the east, two distinct bodies of cod live in the Baltic Sea.[11] All these stocks had long been known and exploited by European fishermen before the opening of the New World cod fisheries in the late 1400s.

6. Odd Nakken, "Causes of Trends and Fluctuations in the Arcto-Norwegian Cod Stock," in *Cod and Climate Change: Proceedings of a Symposium Held in Reykjavík, 23–27 August 1993*, edited by Jakob Jakobsson and the International Council for the Exploration of the Sea, ICES Marine Science Symposia, v. 198 (Copenhagen: International Council for the Exploration of the Sea, 1994), 213, fig. 1.

7. Erik Buch, Svend Aage Horsted, and Holger Hovgard, "Fluctuations in the Occurrence of Cod in Greenland Waters and Their Possible Causes," in *Cod and Climate Change: Proceedings of a Symposium Held in Reykjavík, 23–27 August, 1993*, edited by Jakob Jakobsson and International Council for the Exploration of the Sea, ICES Marine Science Symposia, v. 198 (Copenhagen: Denmark International Council for the Exploration of the Sea, 1994).

8. Sigfus A. Schopka, "Fluctuations in the Cod Stock off Iceland during the Twentieth Century in Relation to Changes in the Fisheries and Environment," in *Cod and Climate Change: Proceedings of a Symposium Held in Reykjavík, 23–27 August 1993*, edited by Jakob Jakobsson and the International Council for the Exploration of the Sea, ICES Marine Science Symposia, v. 198 (Copenhagen: International Council for the Exploration of the Sea, 1994).

9. S. H. I. Jakupsstovu and Jakup Reinert, "Fluctuations in the Faroe Plateau Cod Stock," in *Cod and Climate Change: Proceedings of a Symposium Held in Reykjavík, 23–27 August 1993*, edited by Jakob Jakobsson and the International Council for the Exploration of the Sea, ICES Marine Science Symposia, v. 198 (Copenhagen: International Council for the Exploration of the Sea, 1994).

10. Henk Heesen and Niels Daan, "Cod Distribution and Temperature in the North Sea," in *Cod and Climate Change: Proceedings of a Symposium Held in Reykjavík, 23–27 August 1993*, edited by Jakob Jakobsson and the International Council for the Exploration of the Sea, ICES Marine Science Symposia, v. 198 (Copenhagen: International Council for the Exploration of the Sea, 1994).

11. Ole Bagge and Fritz Thurow, "The Baltic Cod Stock: Fluctuation and Possible Causes," in *Cod and Climate Change: Proceedings of a Symposium Held in Reykjavík, 23–27 August 1993*, edited by Jakob Jakobsson and the International Council for the Exploration of the Sea, ICES Marine Science Symposia, v. 198 (Copenhagen: International Council for the Exploration of the Sea, 1994).

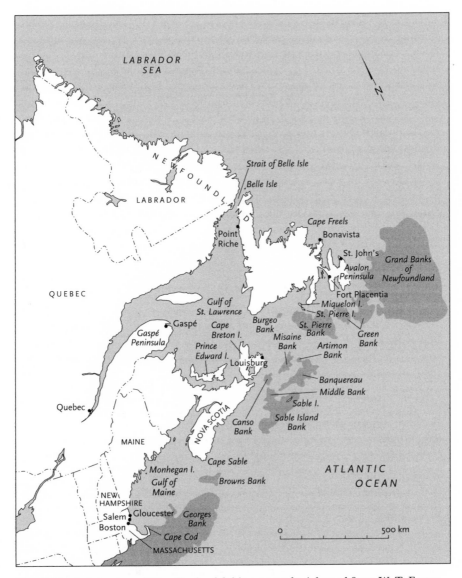

Map 6 North Atlantic and New England fishing grounds. Adapted from W. T. Easterbrook and Hugh G. J. Aitken, *Canadian Economic History* (Toronto: Macmillan Co. of
Canada, 1967), p. 28.

In the northwest, the New World cod habitats do not extend as far north into the Arctic Ocean as do those in the northeast. New World cod habitats, however, are found much further to the south. Self-sustaining cod stocks are found in several areas. The Labrador and Newfoundland stocks inhabit the area from 61° to 43° north along the east coast of Labrador to the banks off the east and southern coasts of Newfoundland.[12] Between 52° and 45°, the Gulf of Saint Lawrence shelters two cod stocks, a northern and a southern, each of which spends the spring and summer months in the gulf for spawning but migrates to areas just outside it for the winter.[13] An eastern and a western stock inhabit offshore waters along the Scotian shelf, off the southeastern coast of Nova Scotia between 46° and 42° latitude.[14] The Gulf of Maine stock (44° to 42°) is found in the offshore waters marked by Cape Sable (in Nova Scotia) to the north and Cape Cod to the south.[15] The Georges Bank stock (42° to 40°) is linked to the southern New England–mid-Atlantic stocks that terminate at 35°, at Cape Hatteras.

THE EARLY NEW WORLD COD FISHERY

Breton, Norman, and Spanish and French Basque fishermen dominated New World cod fisheries throughout the sixteenth century. A smaller number of Portuguese and English vessels crossed the North Atlantic each season.[16] The fishery divided into two approaches: the offshore, or banks, fish-

12. C. T. Taggert et al., "Overview of Cod Stocks, Biology, and Environment in the Northwest Atlantic Region of Newfoundland, with Emphasis on Northern Cod," in *Cod and Climate Change: Proceedings of a Symposium Held in Reykjavík, 23–27 August 1993,* edited by Jakob Jakobsson and the International Council for the Exploration of the Sea, ICES Marine Science Symposia, v. 198 (Copenhagen: International Council for the Exploration of the Sea, 1994).

13. Ghislain A. Chouinard and Alain Frechet, "Fluctuations in the Cod Stocks of the Gulf of St. Lawrence," in *Cod and Climate Change: Proceedings of a Symposium Held in Reykjavík, 23–27 August, 1993,* edited by Jakob Jakobsson and International Council for the Exploration of the Sea, ICES Marine Science Symposia, v. 198 (Copenhagen, Denmark International Council for the Exploration of the Sea, 1994).

14. Kenneth T. Frank, Kenneth F. Drinkwater, and Fredrick H. Page, "Possible Causes of Recent Trends and Fluctuations in Scotian Shelf/Gulf of Maine Cod Stocks," in *Cod and Climate Change: Proceedings of a Symposium Held in Reykjavík, 23–27 August 1993,* edited by Jakob Jakobsson and the International Council for the Exploration of the Sea, ICES Marine Science Symposia, v. 198 (Copenhagen: International Council for the Exploration of the Sea, 1994).

15. Fredric M. Serchuk et al., "Fishery and Environmental Factors Affecting Trends and Fluctuations in the Georges Bank and Gulf of Main Atlantic Cod Stocks: An Overview," in *Cod and Climate Change: Proceedings of a Symposium Held in Reykjavík, 23–27 August 1993,* edited by Jakob Jakobsson and the International Council for the Exploration of the Sea, ICES Marine Science Symposia, v. 198 (Copenhagen: International Council for the Exploration of the Sea, 1994).

16. Portuguese participation in the early New World cod fisheries seems to have been limited. Darlene Abreu-Ferreira, "Terra Nova through the Iberian Looking Glass: The Portuguese-

ery and the inshore, or sedentary, fishery. The first produced wet, salted, actually pickled fish; and the second, sun-dried, salted fish.

As its name implies, the offshore fishery exploited the banks located well offshore from Labrador, Newfoundland, Nova Scotia, and New England.[17] European fishermen preyed on stocks of fish found lying near the ocean bottom in a dozen or more shallow offshore banks. Well-provisioned ships loaded with salt set off from Atlantic ports as early as January each year. Consumers in France, Italy, Spain, and Portugal had long been accustomed to, and enjoyed, pickled fish. In addition, sea salt could be had cheaply in the Bay of Biscay and along the coasts.

Ships and crews were not large for the period. Ships known as bankers ranged from forty to one hundred tons capacity and carried fifteen to twenty men, who were both seamen and fishermen. Captains steered by latitude, guided by readily available charts. They identified the banks by soundings as well as by sightings of seabirds hovering over concentrations of fish.

During the voyage, the crew erected an outboard staging along one side of the ship. When they reached the banks, the leather-apron-clad crew members, each sheltered by an upright half-hogshead stood on the outboard staging to fish. Each man cast two lines simultaneously to within a few feet of the bottom. Baiting his hooks with cod entrails or pieces of herring, each might take twenty-five to as many as four hundred codfish a day. Most of the cod caught in the sixteenth and seventeenth centuries probably ranged between four and fifteen kilograms—substantially larger than those taken today. The very largest specimens were close to two meters in length and more than a hundred kilograms in weight.

When caught, the fish were dressed, thrown in a salting tub for several days, and then packed in the hold between layers of salt.[18] As soon as the boat was full, carrying from twenty thousand to twenty-five thousand heavily salted "wet," or "green," codfish, the captain returned to his home port to sell them. If he arrived in time for the Lenten season in France and the Mediterranean countries, his profits soared. Banker vessels could make two or even three trips to the offshore fishery before the season closed.

Sun drying and lightly salting offered an alternative means of preserving the catch. By the 1540s, the sedentary, or inshore, fisheries had begun on the eastern coast of Newfoundland. Sun-dried cod kept better and found an excellent market in the Mediterranean countries. The inshore fishers timed

---

Newfoundland Cod Fishery in the Sixteenth Century," *Canadian Historical Review* 79, no. 1 (1998).

17. Charles de La Morandière, *Histoire de la pêche française de la morue dans l'Amérique septentrionale (des origines à 1789)* (Paris: Maisonneuve et Larose, 1962), 1:27–32.

18. Harold Adams Innis, *The Cod Fisheries: The History of an International Economy*, rev. ed. (Toronto: University of Toronto Press, 1954), 47–48.

their spring departure from European Atlantic ports to precede the massing of capelin and cod inshore in early summer. Inshore vessels were large, up to 250 or even 300 tons capacity, and had crews of up to 150 men. At the end of a five- to six-week, two-thousand-mile voyage, the fishing vessels pushed through offshore ice to land in one of dozens of sheltering harbors and coves on Newfoundland or along the mainland.

After securely mooring their ship, the crew built a covered timber wharf with tables for cleaning fish, huts for the crew, and several chest-high, thirty-meter or more, open wooden drying racks along the shore. As soon as the shore facilities were complete, the crew unloaded fifteen or more open fishing boats, ten to twelve meters in length, equipped with sails and oars. They dug mussels from the beach for bait, then caught herring and, when they arrived, spawning capelin.

Early every morning, each small boat, crewed by three to four men, set out to fish the shallows just off the coast. They used hand lines up to sixty meters in length, to which were attached weights and baited hooks. The cod were readily hooked; they were hauled into the boat and the lines recast. When the crew had a full boatload, they returned to the fishing wharf. On the wharf, a "header" dexterously gutted and decapitated each fish and carefully saved the liver for its oil in a separate container. Next, a "splitter" cut the fish lengthwise and removed the backbone. Young helpers stacked and brushed the fish sections with salt on a wooden board. After salting, the stacked fish were taken to the drying table and exposed to the sun.

As the season progressed, freight vessels turned up in each harbor to buy dried fish and carry them back to European markets. By September, this annual cycle was largely complete as each fishing vessel packed up the last of its catch in its own hold and sailed for home.

By the late 1500s, New World cod fishing had become an important industry for early modern Europe. Basque maritime entrepreneurs flourished in the fisheries. For example, Adam de Chibau, a prominent French Basque merchant, mobilized funds from a consortia of fellow merchants to send eight fishing vessels on repeated voyages to Newfoundland between 1601 and 1611. These were evidently profitable. De Chibau maintained a high and influential position as a burgess in local society and left an estate worth 30,000 ducats when he died.[19]

Interest in the industry's potential ran high in official and mercantile circles, and reports about the cod fishery proliferated. For example, in 1578, the English traveler Anthony Parckhurst described in a letter to M. Richard Hakluyt "the sundry navies that come to Newfoundland or Terra nova [sic],

19. Michael M. Barkham, "French Basque 'NewFound Land' Entrepreneurs and the Import of Codfish and Whale Oil to Northern Spain, c. 1580 to c. 1620: The Case of Adam de Chibau, Burgess of Saint-Jean-de-Luz and 'Sieur de St. Julien,' " *Newfoundland Studies* 10, no. 1 (1994).

for fish."[20] Parckhurst lists, in what was probably an underestimate, 150 French and Breton vessels totaling 7,000 tons capacity, 50 Portuguese vessels at 3,000 tons, more than 100 Spanish vessels at 5,000 to 6,000 tons, and 50 English vessels with unspecified tonnage, for a total of 350 or more boats with 17,000 or more tons capacity fishing for cod in that year. Research published in 1997 suggests that the totals were probably much larger. In 1580, an English intelligence operative estimated in a report that 500 French vessels engaged in the New World fisheries.[21]

After 1580, when the Danish monarch imposed hefty license fees on boats in Icelandic waters, numerous English West Country fishermen shifted from Icelandic to North American waters. During this period, however, Spanish and Portuguese New World fishing for cod dwindled to insignificance. To some extent, this decline was due to the wars between Spain and England. In the last two decades of the sixteenth century, English raiders and pirates harassed and captured Spanish and Portuguese fishing vessels off Newfoundland.[22] When the war ended in 1604, the Anglo-Spanish treaty of that year granted English traders permission to bring New World codfish into Iberian markets.[23] Thereafter, Spanish fishermen could not compete successfully with the French and English.

The annual flow of wet and dry codfish was a welcome addition to the European diet. Vigorous distribution networks and far-flung markets for New World cod quickly emerged. For example, Bordeaux, along with Rouen and La Rochelle, was a major center for outfitting and supplying New World fishing vessels (largely Basque) and a leading entrepôt for returning ships laden with cod. By midcentury, Bordeaux traders were buying tons of cod and shipping it along the rivers of Aquitaine to Cahors, and to Toulouse and Mont-de-Marsan. By then, cod had "become the market leader among commercially-available salt fish in the country around Bordeaux, overtaking sardines, herring and salmon, not to mention its medieval competitor, hake from Brittany."[24]

Cod's appeal lay partly in its palatability. Consumers preferred it to the other salt fish. Partly it was price. Cod, for example, sold for less than half the price of hake in this period. River toll records and notarial sales contracts for salt fish show that cod had become a consumer staple by the end of the century.[25]

20. Innis, *The Cod Fisheries*, 9–10.
21. Laurier Turgeon, "Bordeaux and the Newfoundland Trade during the Sixteenth Century," *International Journal of Maritime History* 9, no. 2 (1997): 8.
22. Ralph Greenlee Lounsbury and the Kingsley Trust Association, *The British Fishery at Newfoundland, 1634–1763* (New Haven: Yale University Press, 1934), 28–31.
23. Innis, *The Cod Fisheries*, 92.
24. Turgeon, "Bordeaux and the Newfoundland Trade during the Sixteenth Century," 21.
25. Ibid., 22; 28, table 4.

SEVENTEENTH CENTURY

During the seventeenth century, English fishing fleets, directly supported by the English state and mercantile communities, moved aggressively to gain a foothold in the inshore dried fish industry in the southeastern corner of Newfoundland. The English fleet challenged the French industry in size and scale. Dried cod from Newfoundland became the basis of a three-cornered trade between Newfoundland, Spain, and England. In Harold Innis's trenchant comment, "Cod from Newfoundland was the lever by which [England] wrested her share of the riches of the New World from Spain."[26]

Slowly, small populations of more or less permanent inhabitants grew up around the fishing harbors in Newfoundland and Nova Scotia. These "winterers" stayed behind when the fishing boats left and lived off the land. The French established colonies with small contingents of troops in Nova Scotia and on the Avalon Peninsula at Fort Placentia in Newfoundland. The British set up a colony at Saint John's. However, settlement was not critical to the annual operation of the inshore fisheries. Year after year, the fleets came, caught and processed their catches, and departed.

Exploitation of the New World fisheries grew substantially when English and French mariners discovered the prolific fishing grounds of New England. During the sixteenth century, European fishermen had hardly touched the New England stocks. It was only after a series of exploratory voyages made by English and French mariners that the value of this resource became better known. The first English expedition, that of Bartholomew Gosnold in 1602, arrived in Maine waters and sailed south along the coast until it reached the great peninsula of present-day Massachusetts. As a member of the party commented, "Neere this Cape we came to anchor in fifteene fadome, where wee tooke great store of Cod-fish, for which we altered the name, and called it Cape Cod."[27] Gosnold returned with high praise for the richness of the New England coastal waters, which he deemed superior to those of Newfoundland.[28] Stimulated by these reports, merchant syndicates and individual entrepreneurs organized several more English voyages and attempts to found colonies of settlement. In the same years, Virginian colonists from Jamestown sent fishing expeditions north to the New England banks to obtain badly needed food for their settlement.

The French, too, were actively involved in reconnaissance. From New

26. Innis, *The Cod Fisheries*, 52.

27. Faith Harrington, " 'Wee Tooke Great Store of Cod-Fish': Fishing Ships and First Settlements on the Coast of New England, 1600–1630," in *American Beginnings: Exploration, Culture, and Cartography in the Land of Norumbega*, edited by Emerson W. Baker (Lincoln: University of Nebraska Press, 1994), 194.

28. Raymond McFarland, *A History of the New England Fisheries, with Maps* (Philadelphia: University of Pennsylvania; New York: D. Appleton and Company, 1911), 31–32.

France, Samuel de Champlain commanded a carefully planned and exe-
cuted exploration of the New England coast in 1605. Champlain's surveys
resulted in the publication of accurate maps of the New England coast that
included descriptions of harbors, water depths, and location of fishing
banks. All these accounts praised the virtues of New England. The southern
fisheries boasted relatively shallow fishing grounds close to shore, numerous
large codfish for the taking, and good shore sites for drying and processing.

In the 1620s, cod fishing off New England's shores—although it engaged
only a fraction of the number of boats that sailed for Newfoundland—had
become an alternative destination for West Country English fishermen. By
the end of the decade, there were at least ten seasonal fishing stations in use
from Maine's Monhegan Island in the north as far south as Cape Ann off
Massachusetts. Each year between January and March, forty to fifty fishing
vessels left Plymouth, Falmouth, or other English West Country ports for the
New England banks; they returned by September fully laden with codfish.

In the 1640s, partly as a result of the English Civil War, colonists who had
begun to settle coastal villages started a commercial fishery that soon supplanted that of the English fishermen.[29] Operating in smaller boats,
seventeenth-century colonial cod fishers tapped the mid-Atlantic and Gulf
of Maine cod stocks. They set up shore stations to produce dried cod from
inshore fisheries. By 1675, there were reportedly 440 boats and one thousand
colonial fishermen operating in the New England inshore fishery.[30] This
fleet was producing some 60,000 quintals (6,250 metric tons) of dried fish
per year.

Enterprising New England traders profited by sending their own vessels
bearing dried fish, timber, and other commodities directly to Mediterranean
Europe and the West Indies. In the latter part of the century, New England
merchants also carried flour, meat, and other provisions, as well as West Indies sugar and rum, north to Newfoundland settlements.

The New World cod fisheries grew in size, capital investment, and production in the seventeenth century. In 1677, for example, 109 English vessels
sailed to Newfoundland for the inshore fishery. When they arrived, they deployed 892 four-man boats. Settlers wintering on Newfoundland put another
337 fishing boats in the water. The total number of cod landed by English
fishermen in that year produced 238,000 quintals (12,138 metric tons) of
dried codfish for British or wider European markets. The average return

29. Douglas R. McManis, *Colonial New England: A Historical Geography* (New York: Oxford
University Press, 1975), 102–7; Daniel Vickers and the Institute of Early American History and
Culture, *Farmers and Fishermen: Two Centuries of Work in Essex County, Massachusetts, 1630–1850*
(Chapel Hill: University of North Carolina Press, for the Institute of Early American History
and Culture, Williamsburg, Va., 1994), 98–99.

30. Vickers and the Institute of Early American History and Culture, *Farmers and Fishermen*,
100.

load per vessel was 2,183 quintals (111.4 metric tons) of dried fish, and the average production per five-man rowed fishing boat was 194 quintals that year.[31] In general, each five-man boat (three in the boat and two ashore) employed in the British inshore dry cod fishery was expected to produce about 200 quintals (10.2 metric tons) of dried fish each season.[32]

Newfoundland settlers ("planters") put one-third (340) of the boats in the water, and seasonal vessels from England represented two-thirds (708), for an average of 1,048 each season—a presumed workforce of 5,240 fishermen. The average catch was 214 quintals (10.9 metric tons) per boat, or 11,232 tons in a good year. These averages disguise considerable fluctuation between good seasons and poor seasons. Annual catches sank as low as 125,000 quintals (6,375 metric tons) in 1684 and went as high as 347,000 quintals (17,697 metric tons) in the bumper year of 1692.[33] Since the numbers of boats were relatively constant, these variations probably reflect natural fluctuations in cod numbers rather than the intensity of the fishing effort—at least in this period.

French production and capacity was similar to that of the English. In 1664, an official inventory prepared for Colbert listed seventeen ports that had sent 352 fishing vessels to the New World. Of these vessels, the report specifically identified 120 as bankers (*pêche errante*), which had brought back wet, salted fish from the offshore fishery, and 232 as *pêche sédentaire* of the inshore fishery, which had caught and processed dried fish.[34] If we presume a per-vessel average return of 2,000 quintals of either dried or wet fish carried back to France, then in a good year, a fleet of that size should have produced 264,000 quintals (13,464 metric tons) of heavily salted wet cod and 464,000 quintals (23,673 metric tons) of dried codfish. The total combined would have been 37,137 tons of cod in a good year.

In 1704, the fishing convoy returning from inshore fishing at the French settlement of Plaisance consisted of 43 vessels of 5,741 metric tons crewed

31. C. Grant Head, *Eighteenth Century Newfoundland: A Geographer's Perspective* (Toronto: McClelland and Stewart, 1976), 63. Head writes, "In 1677, the total cod landings in English Newfoundland produced more than 220,000 quintals of dried fish, and this was probably typical of that decade." The number of vessels and boats comes from table 3 in D. H. Cushing, *The Provident Sea* (Cambridge: Cambridge University Press, 1988), 70. I have used Pope's adjusted figures for the 1677 catch (see below).

32. Peter Pope, "Early Estimates: Assessment of Catches in the Newfoundland Cod Fishery, 1660–1690," in *Papers Presented at the Conference Entitled "Marine Resources and Human Societies in the North Atlantic since 1500," October 20–22, 1995* (St. John's, Newfoundland: The Institute of Social and Economic Research, Memorial University of Newfoundland, 1997), 11.

33. Ibid., 30, table 2. I have recalculated Pope's figures using the total catch figures he provides to arrive at a nine-year average. For 1682, I used 203,500 quintals, splitting the difference between his higher and lower estimates for that year.

34. De la Morandière, *Histoire de la pêche française de la morue dans l'Amérique septentrionale*, 1:315. The figure for inshore vessels is 132, which I take to be an error for 232.

by 1,508 men. This fleet brought 123,000 quintals (6,273 metric tons) of dried fish to French ports. This works out to 2,860 quintals (146 metric tons) per vessel, or 81.6 quintals (4.2 metric tons) per man fishing, considered to be "fort abondante."[35]

These data suggest that in the seventeenth century the English and French fishing fleets carried an average of 35,000 metric tons of dried codfish and 12,000 tons of wet codfish for sale to European consumers each year. A smaller quantity of less desirable codfish was beginning to be taken up by Barbados and other West Indies sugar islands to feed a growing slave population. The Canary and Madeira Islands also imported fish, as well as other commodities, from New England. In addition, a growing settler population along the North American coast, over 100,000 persons by 1700, certainly consumed a share of the catch.[36]

THE EIGHTEENTH CENTURY

French and British exploitation of the New World cod fisheries intensified in the eighteenth century. The flow of fish to Europe and the Caribbean quadrupled. The French New World fisheries continued despite two significant imperial defeats inflicted by the British in 1713 and 1763. Although the terms of the 1713 Treaty of Utrecht forced the French out of Newfoundland and Nova Scotia, they retained Cape Breton Island and the right to catch and dry fish along the western shore of Newfoundland. That the French negotiated tenaciously for New World fishing rights as part of the postwar settlement attests to the economic value of the cod fishery.

After 1713, the French consolidated their maritime holdings by establishing the city of Louisburg on Cape Breton Island as a headquarters for the inshore fishery, and by occupying Ile Saint Jean (Prince Edward Island) and the Gaspé Peninsula.[37] French fishing vessels also traveled north to Labrador. In 1719, five hundred fishing vessels sailed from a dozen French ports for the North American cod fishery. Approximately half engaged in inshore fishing for cod to dry and half in offshore banks fishing for wet cod.[38] A few additional vessels sailed out from Quebec. For a half century, the French

35. Ibid., 1:498.
36. The population of New England was about 93,000 in 1700. McManis, *Colonial New England*, 68–69, table 1. For English Newfoundland, there was a total of 3,450 permanent inhabitants in 1715; see Head, *Eighteenth Century Newfoundland*, 256. Total population in New France in 1700 was less than 6,000 persons. Quebec, by far the largest town, had only 2,000 settlers in 1700. Raymond Douville and Jacques Donat Casanova, *Daily Life in Early Canada*, 1st Amer. ed. (New York: Macmillan, 1968), 82.

37. De la Morandière, *Histoire de la pêche française de la morue dans l'Amérique septentrionale*, 2:643–82.
38. Innis, *The Cod Fisheries*, 169.

cod fishery flourished as a vigorous competitor to the English fishery. In 1745, clearly a good year, the French fishery produced 1.1 million quintals (56,100 metric tons) of dried fish for sale in Mediterranean markets, 15,600 tons of wet cod (3.9 million fish weighing 4 kilograms each, counted individually for the Parisian market), and 689,400 gallons of cod liver oil.[39]

The Treaty of Paris in 1763 forced the French to give up their colonial settlements on the mainland as well as Cape Breton and Prince Edward Islands. The French did retain possession of the two small islands of Saint Pierre and Miquelon, just south of Newfoundland, as a fishing base.[40] The British permitted French fishing vessels seasonal landing privileges along the shore of Newfoundland between Point Riche in the west to Bonavista in the north. Despite these setbacks, by the 1770s the French fleet had nearly returned to its former numbers and productivity. French inshore fishermen marketed an average of 361,258 quintals (18,425 metric tons) of dried salt cod per year and the banks fishermen brought back another 100,000 to 130,000 quintals (5,100 to 6,630 metric tons) of wet fish for the Parisian market.[41]

After 1713, the English fishery grew rapidly. Newfoundland remained a busy island fishing platform off the coast of North America that produced an ever increasing tonnage of fish for Europe and the West Indies. The diplomatic accord turned over the inshore fishery on Newfoundland's southern coast, previously worked by the French, to English fishermen. Political stability encouraged English expansion into previously untapped inshore fisheries along the inland coast from Cape Freels to Cape Saint John. The number of three-man fishing boats put in the water each season rose to around twenty-two hundred by the early 1770s. The annual catch from the enlarged inshore cod fishery of Newfoundland produced double the seventeenth-century levels, or 500,000 quintals (25,500 metric tons) of sun-dried fish, in the 1740s. Thereafter, average production rose only slightly, to 550,000 quintals (28,050 metric tons) in the 1770s.[42]

English fishermen and their backers, stimulated by rising market demand, sent vessels for the first time to the offshore banks to fish directly from shipboard. Unlike the French, they had no home market for heavily salted wet cod and required dried fish for the southern European market. The English bankers necessarily had to salt their catch heavily at sea to keep it from spoiling in the weeks required to fill their holds. But in a new departure, the bankers then pulled in to Newfoundland beaches, washed off their fish and

39. Ibid., 168.
40. Ibid., 183–85; de la Morandière, *Histoire de la pêche française de la morue dans l'Amérique septentrionale*, 2:731.
41. Innis, *The Cod Fisheries*, 182.
42. Head, *Eighteenth Century Newfoundland*, 65, 70, 140.

had them sun-dried before export. An official report of 1726 describes the process:

> The Country Ships that come here to fish upon the Banks, generally leave England [in February] & are in the some time [sic] in March, the first thing they doe is Land their Stores, & make choice of a Stage & flakes belonging to it, what they call a Ships Room. . . .
>
> Their first trip to the Bankes [sic] is generally the beste, the coldness of the Season allowing them to stay the longer out: as they catch the fish they Split them & Salt 'em then lay 'em down in the Ships hold, where they lay till they goe into the Harbour, they [sic] they take them out & Spread them upon the Fleakes, where they lay for a day or two if the Weather will allow. . . . Some time after this they lay them together in small heaps about a dozen or 14 of them . . . & Spread them again in the mornings; after that they put them up into larger heaps, what they call piles, & from thence leave them as they require & the Weather will allow, until they are fit to goe aboard ship.[43]

By the early 1770s, the English offshore fishery deployed 150 to 200 bankers, which together generated around 100,000 quintals (5,100 metric tons) of dried fish each year.

SETTLEMENT ON NEWFOUNDLAND

Newfoundland moved slowly toward a colony of settlement. Had fishing not been available to settlers, the island's harsh climate and skimpy soil would have discouraged European settlement. Cod fishing provided an adequate living—especially for migrants from Ireland, who became a substantial portion of the settled population. The island's summer fishing-season population jumped from six thousand persons in the early eighteenth century to twenty-five thousand by the 1740s and remained at that level for the remainder of the century.[44] Gradually the proportion of wintering to migratory summer residents grew to half in the 1770s. Women and children constituted only one-fourth of the resident population—single male laborers continued to dominate through the century.

After 1713, other resources were exploited commercially for the first time. Settlers constructed weirs and used seines to catch Atlantic salmon when they came up streams to spawn in July. They strung large nets along the coastal headlands in December, waited for shoals of seals to approach, and then pulled up the nets at the right moment. Seal oil, like cod oil, was very much in demand. Both salmon fishing and sealing provided substantial

---

43. Ibid., 73–74.
44. Head, *Eighteenth Century Newfoundland*, 56, 232.

additional income, especially in the northern areas of the island. Relatively small numbers of furs also augmented Newfoundlanders' income.[45]

Settlers were slow to move inland from the coast, even though colonists were given clear title to lands they occupied and cultivated. Clause VII of the Parliamentary Act to Encourage the Trade to Newfoundland in 1699 provided permanent title for lands used by settlers and offered protected seasonal use of beach sites to migratory fishermen. Total cultivated land on the island was just over a thousand hectares in the early 1770s. Given low yields and poor soil, the cultivated area did not produce enough food for the year-round inhabitants, let alone the summer migratory influx. Massive amounts of food imports were essential. Bread, biscuits, flour, pork, beef, peas, butter, molasses, and rum were the staples.[46] In 1763, American traders and shippers sent to Newfoundland ports over 1 million pounds of breadstuffs, 653 barrels of pork, 19,580 gallons of molasses, and 57,420 gallons of rum—the latter from the West Indies. English West Country merchants shipped breadstuffs, peas, sugar, beer, cider, and cheese. Irish traders sent hundreds of barrels of butter, pork, and beef. Just how dependent Newfoundland was on imports became apparent when American imports ceased and English shipping dwindled during the American Revolutionary years.

The slow pace of settlement and cultivation, however, did not prevent steady, cumulative deforestation. In 1500, the forests, while not all that impressive in size, did cover most of the island's land surface. In the coastal areas frequented by fishermen, mature conifers, eighty to one hundred years old, reached twenty to thirty feet high and had diameters measuring four to five inches at breast height. Trees in the interior forests were considerably larger. By the 1770s, the coastal forests had been stripped away for fuel and building needs and the interior forests were under active assault.[47]

THE NEW ENGLAND FISHERY

Like that of Newfoundland, the colonial New England cod fishery burgeoned during the 1700s. Unlike in Newfoundland, however, the fisheries were not the only, or even the principal, form of commercial production. Under the stimulus of continued immigration—which caused New England's population to rise from 93,000 persons in 1700 to 539,000 in 1770—land clearing on the settler frontier proceeded at an impressive pace during the century.[48] Domestic and foreign demand for fish and timber, two of the region's principal exports, continued to run high.

45. Ibid., 74–76.
46. Ibid., 130, 146.
47. Ibid., 45–46.
48. McManis, *Colonial New England*, 68–69.

Between 1675 and 1725, the New England fishery transformed itself from a purely regional inshore fishery into a much larger long-distance maritime industry. New England retained its local fisheries but also sent large deepwater fleets to compete with British and French fishing vessels in the waters of first Nova Scotia and then Newfoundland and Labrador. New England shipowners and entrepreneurs invested in more expensive, larger ketches and schooners. They adopted the fast, seaworthy, fore-and-aft-rigged, two-masted, 20- to 100-ton fishing schooner developed on the New England coast.[49] Depending on the season and the captain's strategy, vessels might sail to the Newfoundland offshore grounds or they might work Georges Bank off Cape Cod or any of the other smaller grounds off the New England coast.[50] Another several hundred boats were engaged in the mackerel and herring fisheries.

Boston and Salem, whose merchants financed the trade and owned many vessels, exported the bulk of dried codfish. Marblehead and Gloucester emerged as the busiest of the twenty or so fishing towns along the coast in Massachusetts, New Hampshire, and Maine. During the pre–Revolutionary War years, the New England cod fisheries employed nearly five thousand men in more than 665 vessels.[51] The average annual catch from 1768 to 1772 grew to more than 300,000 quintals (15,300 metric tons) of dried cod per year.[52] In the early 1770s, New England ships sent an average of 123,308 quintals (6,289 metric tons) of dried salt cod per year to southern European markets.[53] Together, southern European and West Indies markets paid an annual average of 152,155 pounds sterling for New England fish in the period 1768–1772.[54]

During the American Revolution, pressure on the fishing grounds eased as seafaring energies were diverted to war, and the total catch fell off consid-

49. Vickers and the Institute of Early American History and Culture, *Farmers and Fishermen,* 143–52.

50. Robert Greenhalgh Albion, William A. Baker, and Benjamin Woods Labaree, *New England and the Sea* (Middletown: Wesleyan University Press, for the Marine Historical Association Mystic Seaport, 1972), 28–29.

51. McFarland, *A History of the New England Fisheries,* 112.

52. Laurier Turgeon, "Fluctuations in Cod and Whale Stocks in the North Atlantic during the Eighteenth Century," in *Papers Presented at the Conference Entitled "Marine Resources and Human Societies in the North Atlantic since 1500," October 20–22, 1995* (St. John's, Newfoundland: Institute of Social and Economic Research, Memorial University of Newfoundland, 1997), 90.

53. James G. Lydon, "Fish for Gold: The Massachusetts Fish Trade with Iberia, 1700–1773," *New England Quarterly* 54 (1981): 544–45, table 2. The figure is based on compilation of customs figures from New England and Newfoundland.

54. John J. McCusker, Russell R. Menard, and the Institute of Early American History and Culture, *The Economy of British America, 1607–1789, with Supplementary Bibliography* (Chapel Hill: University of North Carolina Press, for the Institute of Early American History and Culture, Williamsburg, Va., 1991), 108.

erably. After 1783, French, British, and American fishing fleets returned in their former numbers.

THE MARKET FOR CODFISH

Europeans came to rely on cheap, ample supplies of North American dried and salted fish as a staple of their diet in the early modern centuries. This was especially timely, since, throughout Europe after 1500, meat consumption declined dramatically from its late medieval levels.[55] During the sixteenth century and most of the seventeenth, the price of codfish in North American and European markets moved upward. Daniel Vickers has constructed a combined index for codfish prices in North America and Spain for the period 1505–1892. The base period is 1784–1800 = 100. The index is worked out in prices converted to silver equivalents. From a low of 19 in 1505, the cod price index climbed to 72 in 1598. The index spiked at 101 in 1629. For the next forty years, until 1669, it remained at a plateau, with an annual average of 85.[56] After 1670, the cod price index began a slow decline, until prices reached a mid-eighteenth-century trough in the 40 to 60 index range. Presumably, this decline resulted from greatly increased output from the fisheries. Interruptions in fishing caused by the American and French Revolutions and the Napoleonic Wars forced cod prices to over 100 during the period 1790 to 1815.

Contemporaries fully recognized the importance of cod. In a report to the English Admiralty published in 1615, Richard Whitburne writes:

> And . . . I should here set downe a valuation of that fish (cod) which the French, Biscaines, and Portugals fetch yeerely from this coast of Newfoundland and the Banke . . . usually making two voyages every yeere thither . . . (to which places and to the coast of Canady [Canada] which lieth neere unto it and yeerely sent from those countries more than 400 saile of ships).
>
> It would seeme incredible, yea some men are of opinion, that the people of France, Spain, Portugall and Italy could not so well live if the benefit of the fishing upon that coast and your Majesties other dominions were taken from them.[57]

New World dried and salt cod became an important element in what is today recognized as the healthful Mediterranean diet.

In an average year during the seventeenth century, 47,000 metric tons of

55. Massimo Livi Bacci, *Population and Nutrition: An Essay on European Demographic History* (Cambridge: Cambridge University Press, 1990), 93–95.
56. Daniel Vickers, "The Price of Fish: A Price Index for Cod, 1505–1892," *Acadiensis* 25, no. 2 (1996): 101. I have calculated the average index for 1629–1669 from appendix 1.
57. Harold Adams Innis, *Select Documents in Canadian Economic History* (Toronto: University of Toronto Press, 1929), 16. Whitburne was present in Newfoundland in 1615.

codfish arrived in European markets. When sold, the codfish could, in theory, have supplied 136.3 billion kilocalories per year, or 373.4 million kilocalories per day, to European consumers.[58] Most of the loads went to France, Spain, and Italy, which together had a combined population of approximately 40 million persons in 1650. If we assume that 80 percent went to markets in these three countries, the equivalent of 376 million 100-gram portions would have been sold. This works out to 9.4 portions consumed per person per year, each with an energy value of 290 calories and 62 grams of protein for dried cod, or 18 grams of protein for wet cod.

In theory, then, codfish should have been readily available and affordable for ordinary consumers. This does seem to have been the situation. Data compiled in the 1930s by Earl Hamilton on commodity prices and wages for the early modern period confirm this. For example, for the period 1601 to 1650 in Andalusia in Spain, calculations made from Hamilton's annual data show that the average price of dried codfish was 4 *maravedi* (a Spanish copper coin) per 100 grams, tuna fish was 4.5 *maravedi*, and mutton was 5.7 *maravedi*.[59] That is, of the most common types of meat and fish, codfish was the cheapest. It was routinely sold in Andalusian markets in this period.

Even an ordinary urban laborer could afford it. Over the fifty-year period, a day laborer in Andalusia averaged 150.2 *maravedi* wages per day. A 100-gram portion of dried codfish would have consumed only 2.7 percent of his day's wages; a 250-gram portion, only 6.7 percent. Codfish prices in other regions in Spain were similar to those in Andalusia. Rising imports of codfish and declining prices during the eighteenth century imply that codfish retained its role as a cheap and accessible food for most Europeans.

New World cod imports rose steadily in the course of the eighteenth century. The combined average annual French and English output of dried codfish for the period 1701 to 1789 was 41,354 metric tons.[60] To this we may

58. John Komlos, "The New World's Contribution to Food Consumption during the Industrial Revolution," *Journal of European Economic History* 27 (1998). According to table 3 on p. 74, the Newfoundland fishery sent 40 percent of its total exports, or 21,228 metric tons of fish, to England every year, and these fish contributed 50 million kilocalories per day to the British diet. This works out to 859,713.6 kilocalories per year per metric ton, or only 859.7 kilocalories per kilogram. This seems low, since USDA Nutrition Laboratory figures given earlier show 290 kilocalories per 100 gram portion of dried salt codfish. I have used the figure 2,900 kilocalories per kilograms, or 2.9 million kilocalories per ton.

59. Earl J. Hamilton, *American Treasure and the Price Revolution in Spain, 1501–1650* (Cambridge: Harvard University Press, 1934). Average prices for dried codfish are calculated from annual data in appendix 5, table A. According to the customary measurement (Libra carnicera) of codfish, 32 ounces = 920.32 grams. Wages are calculated from appendix 7, table C. Coins are *maravedis* of pure copper, issued from 1603 through 1650.

60. Turgeon, "Fluctuations in Cod and Whale Stocks in the North Atlantic during the Eighteenth Century," 166, table 1. Turgeon found combined data for English and French catches for a total of thirty-one years between 1677 and 1789.

add an average 9,072 metric tons for the New England fishery. The dried fish total, 50,246 tons, was 143 percent higher than the 35,000-metric-ton average for the seventeenth century.[61] If we assume that wet fish shipments continued at one-third the volume of dried fish shipments, this would have added 13,800 tons, for a combined total of 55,000 tons (rounded). Using the calculation applied earlier for the seventeenth century, for a population grown to 49 million, this would have made available 11.2 100-gram portions of dried codfish per capita per year—a distinct increase from 9.4, the seventeenth-century figure.

The catches were moving upward. Between 1785 and 1790, combined English and French fleets shipped 54,437 metric tons per year and New England vessels carried 20,027 tons, for a total of 74,464 tons.[62] If we assume that wet fish shipments continued to average about one-third the volume of dry fish shipments, this puts the combined dry and wet fish total in the latter half of the century at about 100,000 metric tons per year—roughly double that of the seventeenth century. With 80 percent, or 80,000 tons, delivered in these countries, the number of portions rose to 16.3 per capita in the 1780s. As codfish deliveries increased, prices dropped, to the benefit of the consumer.

IMPACT OF THE COD FISHERY

Was the early modern catch sufficiently large to have an impact on cod stocks and the maritime ecosystem? Most historians and biologists have assumed that catch levels prior to twentieth-century industrial fishing were well within a sustainable yield for the entire stock of codfish in the waters off the North American coast. Only after five centuries, when the annual catch quadrupled to over 800,000 metric tons during the 1960s, did the population crash due to overfishing.[63]

Early modern cod landings were well below the late-twentieth-century figure. D. H. Cushing, basing his calculation on intermittent data on numbers of fishing vessels, concludes that, each year, "up to 250,000 tonnes of fish fresh from the sea were taken from about 1580 to 1750."[64] Peter Pope, who

61. Vickers and the Institute of Early American History and Culture, *Farmers and Fishermen*, 154, table 4.

62. The highest combined English and French totals occurred in the five years between 1785 and 1789, when the annual live catch averaged 245,502 metric tons live weight for these two fleets alone (Turgeon, "Fluctuations in Cod and Whale Stocks in the North Atlantic during the Eighteenth Century," 106).

63. Pope, "Early Estimates," 26.

64. Cushing, *The Provident Sea*, 74–75. Cushing assumed that each quintal equaled 112.2 pounds. However, a quintal of dried fish "from the sea (after heading, splitting and drying)" equaled 227 kilograms (500 pounds) of fresh fish (ix). Under this formula, divide the number of quintals of dried fish by .224, or multiply by 4.46, to arrive at the live catch weight. To convert live catch weight into dried fish output, multiply by .224. De la Morandière, however, asserts

used both catch and total fleet tonnage data, concludes that "the total live catch at Newfoundland in this period appears to have been in the order of 200,000 metric tonnes."[65] This figure is four times the 50,000 metric tons adopted by biologists who had earlier reconstructed historical trends for cod catches.

Pope suggests that fishing at the 200,000-metric-ton level had been going on since the last half of the sixteenth century. He states that human predation at this scale probably did not have much of an impact on total cod stocks in the region, but that "European fishers may have already been putting pressure on local stocks by 1600."[66] These pressures probably made cod scarce on Newfoundland's English shore, "and fishers made, on average, only about 60 percent of the catch per boat that they had come to expect."[67]

Landings did not remain at the 200,000-metric-ton level but continued to rise. By the late 1780s, European deliveries alone amounted to 75,000 metric tons of dried fish and another 25,000 tons of wet cod (see above). Additional landings fed domestic markets in Canada and the North American colonies. The European numbers alone imply a 180 percent increase, to a 360,000-ton live catch, and the total catch might well have doubled to 400,000 tons.[68]

At the same time, fishing pressure diffused over a wider area and bore upon new cod stocks. A new commercial fishery grew up in New England in the late 1600s that exploited previously ignored codfish stocks in the mid-Atlantic, Gulf of Maine, and Georges Bank regions. Doubling the catch probably did not double landings of the Newfoundland stock—although it is likely that landings from that stock had increased by the late eighteenth century.

More recently, however, scholars have "begun to challenge commonly held assumptions concerning the time frame over which Newfoundland cod have been overexploited."[69] It has long been observed that the overall size of codfish catches had begun to shrink by mid–eighteenth century.[70] Even in

---

that dressing and drying would remove 80 percent of the water from each carcass. In his view, a 2-kilogram codfish after drying would weigh only 350 grams. According to his calculations, the ratio drops to .175 for conversion. De la Morandière, *Histoire de la pêche française de la morue dans l'Amérique septentrionale*, 1:183.

65. Pope, "Early Estimates," 24.

66. Ibid., 27.

67. Ibid.

68. Dried weight is multiplied by 4.46, and the weight of wet cod is unadjusted.

69. Jeffrey A. Hutchings, "The Nature of Cod *(Gadus morhua)*: Perceptions of Stock Structure and Cod Behavior by Fishermen, 'Experts,' and Scientists from the Nineteenth Century to the Present," in *Papers Presented at the Conference Entitled "Marine Resources and Human Societies in the North Atlantic since 1500," October 20–22, 1995*, edited by Daniel Vickers (St. John's, Newfoundland: Institute of Social and Economic Research, Memorial University of Newfoundland, 1997), 170.

70. Cushing, *The Provident Sea*, 75.

this early period, catches at inshore fisheries declined if fished too severely. Some of the Newfoundland bays seemed to have had limits to the sustainable local catch. According to C. Grant Head:

> [There is] a tendency for the total inshore catch to not exceed a certain maximum for any long period of years. Note especially the case of Trepassy and St. Mary's, where at cycles of ten to fifteen years catches rose above 18,000 quintals, but never remained above that magnitude for more than about five years. . . . In Placentia Bay, this magnitude can be placed at about 60,000 quintals, on the Southern Shore at about 80,000 quintals, at St. John's at about 50,000, in Bonavista Bay at 30,000 and in Fogo and Twillingate district at 25,000. It is here suggested that these figures represent a maximum sustainable yield of the inshore fishing resources of each area, using the traditional fishing technology.[71]

In response to local scarcities, cod fishers moved to new, unexploited coastal regions. In the mid– to late eighteenth century, they moved across the Strait of Belle Isle to the inshore waters of eastern Labrador. In the late eighteenth century, resident Newfoundlanders intensified fishing along the island's Petit Nord, or North Shore. Perhaps the most dramatic spatial expansion came with intensified, industrialized offshore fishing.

Fish biologists have articulated a more sophisticated understanding about codfish stocks and their population configurations and dynamics. They have been negotiating between two extreme views: One long-standing popular and scientific view holds that all codfish in the entire North Atlantic region belong to a single stock that, until very recently, was thought to be nearly inexhaustible. Since codfish are "cosmopolitan wandering vagrants" within this vast region, each codfish is interchangeable with another. Only the total number of fish taken by human predation matters. In the other view, long held by fishermen with a local ecological understanding honed over generations of close observation, cod are territorial animals "unwilling to wander and[,] when they do, instinctively driven to return to their place of birth to reproduce."[72] This model implies that there are discrete cod substocks, or breeding populations, identified with particular inshore spawning grounds and annual migration patterns that can be depleted by excessive fishing.

The emerging view is of a complex system in which there are self-sustaining stocks—Newfoundland, Gulf of Maine, Saint Lawrence, Georges Bank, mid-Atlantic—that constitute separate breeding populations (listed above). However, codfish within each stock are not an undifferentiated mass. The larger stocks contain breeding populations that must be managed as separate entities. The substocks exhibit complex migratory patterns in the course of each year. According to Jeffrey A. Hutchings, "Cod tend to dif-

71. Head, *Eighteenth Century Newfoundland,* 66.
72. Hutchings, "The Nature of Cod," 172.

fer in the timing and nature of their spawning and feeding behaviour. They also tend to differ by age; some age groups engage in feeding migrations and return to spawning areas while others remain more stationary."[73] Younger cod are more likely to remain inshore while larger cod migrate to feed.

The timing, distance, and direction of migrations may be determined by the size, age structure, local food supplies, and competition for food by other species. If food supplies change, migrations may also change. Some individuals may move from one stock to another. Heavy fishing at particular spawning sites may well have sharply depleted specific substocks and even encouraged migration. As human fishing removed larger, more mature fish from each substock, the chances of abrupt swings in the reproductive rate increased. In short, even at the seemingly "moderate" levels of the 1600s and 1700s, fishing altered the age (and perhaps gender) structures, size, weight, and spawning and feeding habits, and the overall size of codfish stocks in the North Atlantic.

Apart from annual fishing, the codfish stocks were subject to other forces that helped determine their size, distribution, and rate of reproduction in the early modern period. It is possible that early modern whaling in this region had a positive effect on codfish numbers. Basque whalers largely fished out bowhead and right whales *(Balaena mysticetus)* and *(Balaena glacialis)* from the waters around Newfoundland and Labrador by the early 1600s.[74] Thereafter, northern French Basques continued the whale fishery in the area around the Gulf of Saint Lawrence, but at a much reduced catch level. Both whales and cod occupy a similar position on the trophic food web. They both feed heavily on crustacean zooplankton—primarily copepods, euphausiids, and mysids. Eliminating large herds of whales could well have freed zooplankton for cod consumption and fostered an increase in codfish stocks by the end of the sixteenth century.[75]

COLDER WATERS

A larger issue is that of climate change. What effect did Little Ice Age cooling have on the northern oceans generally and on the cod fisheries of the New World specifically? Evidence adduced by Hubert Lamb, and more recently by A. E. J. Ogilvie and J. Jonsson, from historical annals, cod fisheries catch data, and coastal sea ice accumulation around Iceland, Greenland, and the Faroe Islands strongly suggests that a substantial cooling of the

73. Ibid., 173.
74. See chapter 16.
75. John J. Burns et al., *The Bowhead Whale* (Lawrence, Kans.: Society for Marine Mammalogy, 1993), 229–32.

northeastern Atlantic took place in the early modern centuries.[76] This change had a demonstrable, unfavorable effect on the Icelandic–eastern Greenland codfish stocks.

Generally speaking, even though cod is a boreal fish, warmer water temperatures (below an upper limit) favor higher rates of reproduction in codfish. Cod also will shift their grounds from colder, less favorable waters to warmer waters when necessary. It is likely that Icelandic cod populations were reduced from what they had been in the warmer medieval period. Codfish in the Icelandic stock seem to have responded unfavorably to colder water temperature in this period—probably because of the vulnerability of the cod eggs and larvae to colder conditions. Female cod spawn in temperatures from 5° to 7°C. Larvae require temperatures above 5°C and do better at even higher temperatures. The larval food supply could have been hard hit as well. If normal Atlantic Ocean waters were invaded by extremely cold polar waters that transported and preserved ice, the primary production of phytoplankton would have been sharply reduced and zooplankton populations would have collapsed, as they did in the 1960s.[77]

For Iceland, Jonsson assembled smoothed annual trends in cod catches, estimated by a qualitative index derived from the Icelandic annals, and compared these with reconstructed ocean temperatures from monthly sea ice data. His data show distinct correlations between reduced fishing output and colder temperatures. For the post-1600 period, Icelandic cod catches are "in fairly good agreement with estimated temperature variations, showing long-term fluctuations of 50–60 years."[78] During the first half of the seventeenth century, water temperatures rose in some years to above 5°C, and cod catches rose accordingly. In the second half of the century, temperatures plummeted to a low of 2.5°C in the mid-1690s, and catches fell in response.[79]

---

76. H. H. Lamb, "Climatic Variation and Changes in the Wind and Ocean Circulation: The Little Ice Age in the Northeast Atlantic," *Quaternary Research* 11 (1979): 12, fig. 9; A. E. J. Ogilvie, "Documentary Evidence for Changes in the Climate of Iceland, A.D. 1500 to 1800," in *Climate since A.D. 1500*, edited by Raymond S. Bradley and Philip D. Jones, rev. ed. (London: Routledge, 1995), 105, fig. 5.4. See also D'Arrigo and Jacoby, "Dendroclimatic Evidence from Northern North America," 302, fig. 15.4.

77. J. Jonsson, "Fisheries off Iceland, 1600–1900," in *Cod and Climate Change: Proceedings of a Symposium Held in Reykjavík, 23–27 August 1993*, edited by Jakob Jakobsson and the International Council for the Exploration of the Sea, ICES Marine Science Symposia, v. 198 (Copenhagen: International Council for the Exploration of the Sea, 1994), 14.

78. Ibid., 15.

79. Lamb, "Climatic Variation and Changes in the Wind and Ocean Circulation," 15. The coldest episode appears to have been "between 1675 and 1700[, when] the water temperatures prevailing about the Faroe Islands presumably were on overall average 4° to 5°C below the average of the last 100 years, an anomaly 4 or 5 times as great as that shown by the thermometer observations of the time in central England, where the coldest decade (1690s) averaged about 1.5°C below the warmest decades in the earlier part of this century."

Warmer temperatures in the first half of the eighteenth century improved catches—with the usual year-to-year fluctuations. Another period of severe cold in the 1750s reduced catches so much that many Icelanders died of hunger. Better conditions followed for the period 1766–1779, only to be succeeded by colder temperatures and reduced catches for the remainder of the century. During the first half of the nineteenth century, there was a "gradual, but irregular, increase in temperatures" that resulted in better catches.[80]

Presumably the same colder conditions and broad pattern of temperature fluctuations with southward movement of polar waters occurred in the northwestern Atlantic during the early modern centuries. However, New-foundland, unlike Iceland, does not lie at the northern limits of the cod's range. The waters undoubtedly became colder, but their impact on cod eggs, larvae, and food supplies may not have been as pronounced. Maybe cod reproduction was affected and populations were reduced overall in New World stocks because of the colder climate after 1500—but it is simply not possible to demonstrate this.

To date, no long-term correlation between temperature and catches sim-ilar to that done for the Iceland fisheries has been constructed for New-foundland or any of the New World fisheries. Before 1700, annual catch data are intermittent at best and vary from one national fishery to another. Short-term attempts to link catch data with temperature are suggestive but show anomalies. For example, Pope has calculated the catch rate per boat from both planters and seasonal fishermen at Newfoundland for the espe-cially cold last quarter of the seventeenth century. He has catch and boat data for nine years between 1675 and 1698. Seven years show an average rate of 185 quintals (9.4 metric tons) dried fish produced per boat—well below the 200-quintal (10.2-ton) norm.

However, in 1692, English fishermen pulled in catches that averaged 350 quintals (17.8 metric tons) per boat, and in 1698 their catches averaged 285 quintals (14.5 metric tons).[81] The 1692 catch may be attributed to a warmer period for the spawning season after a cold December and January. But the winter of 1697–1698 "became famous for its severity," with its painfully low temperatures and twenty to thirty heavy snowfalls seen in New England. Massachusetts Bay froze from January to March. A half century later, Peter Kalm, the Swedish naturalist, found Americans agreeing that the winter of 1697–1698 "was the coldest and severest which they had ever felt."[82] More-

80. Jonsson, "Fisheries off Iceland," 8, fig. 2.
81. Pope, "Early Estimates," 30, table 2.
82. Karen Ordahl Kupperman, "Climate and Mastery of the Wilderness in Seventeenth-Century New England," in *Seventeenth-Century New England: A Conference,* edited by the Colonial Society of Massachusetts (Boston: The Society, distributed by the University Press of Virginia, 1984), 31–32.

over, none of these correlations attempts to account for the possibility that fog, storms, and ice dangers could have reduced fishing activity and catches in an age of oar and sail.

Temperature changes certainly must have had an influence on the distribution and population dynamics of the cod stocks of the northwestern Atlantic. Tracking these changes, however, with incomplete information is another matter. Even today, using much more precise and full climate data, fish catch numbers, and a variety of fish-tracking data, it is difficult for biologists to identify short-term and long-term effects of temperature changes on cod populations. Niels Daan observes:

> We have to be aware that climate influences not just cod, but also all other species of the Subarctic ecosystem. Therefore any relation between climate and cod stocks will be mediated through a complex structure of abiotic and biotic processes operating in the ecosystem. As a consequence, we cannot expect simple mechanics; in fact, the effects of climate change are likely to be so complex and unpredictable that we cannot just accept without question any simple relationship which might appear to explain much of the variation observed in cod stocks.[83]

CONCLUSION

The New World fishing industry is an example of the steady evolution of human maritime capacity since the medieval centuries, and, more generally, of the growing capacity of early modern economic institutions and the ever greater reach of the world market. After 1500, several western European societies developed new large-scale, offshore, commercial fisheries for New World cod. Never before in human history had fishing fleets regularly, every year, made such voyages—traversing thousands of kilometers of open, dangerous water across the North Atlantic—to return with great loads of codfish. To operate at this distance demanded extraordinary entrepreneurial, organizational, seafaring, and shipbuilding skills. The industry's demand for capital was large; so also was its need for labor. The tonnage of North American cod taken, processed, and consumed in Europe and its colonies climbed steadily.

In the face of prolonged colder temperatures throughout the early modern centuries, overall codfish stocks, despite local scarcities, remained abundant and easily caught. Fishing intensity and total catches fluctuated, but the

---

83. Niels Daan, "Trends in North Atlantic Cod Stocks: A Critical Summary," in *Cod and Climate Change: Proceedings of a Symposium Held in Reykjavík, 23–27 August 1993*, edited by Jakob Jakobsson and the International Council for the Exploration of the Sea, ICES Marine Science Symposia, v. 198 (Copenhagen: International Council for the Exploration of the Sea, 1994), 269.

resource continued. Overall output moved steadily upward decade after decade. Every year thousands of tons of highly palatable, nutritious protein fed people of all classes in North America and Europe. The average sizes of codfish caught, however, did decline from century to century. Continued, steadily intensifying, and basically unregulated fishing changed the age composition, the average size, and probably the behavior of codfish in the various New World stocks. So numerous were codfish and so resilient, however, that it took five hundred years for human fishing to cause the stocks to crash—as they did in the 1980s.

Chapter 4

Whales and Walruses
in the Northern Oceans

Before 1500, favorably situated coastal communities around the world killed and consumed whales in a largely passive, opportunistic enterprise. Shore-based fishing communities in Arctic waters off the east and west coasts of North and South America, Siberia, South Africa, New Zealand, Japan, and northern Europe intercepted whales as they made their migratory rounds each year.[1] The whales taken were those vulnerable species that appeared regularly in coastal waters and were slow-moving enough to be taken by men in small boats wielding harpoons and lances or even nets. The greater part of the catch went for subsistence needs, although all whaling groups were engaged in limited trading and exchange networks. For these communities, whales were a substantial source of meat, as well as oil for illumination and heat and whalebone for artifacts. The total catch was relatively modest and does not seem to have posed a serious threat to whale stocks. If climatic changes or other developments changed the numbers or direction of whale migrations, these communities were forced to adapt. They did not really have the means to pursue whales throughout their migratory journeys.[2]

Commercialized early modern whale hunting was a departure. For the first time in human history, hunters actively pursued whales on the open sea in regions far distant from their homes. Each summer season, European and North American whalers made the dangerous voyage into western Arctic and

1. Richard Ellis, *Men and Whales*, 1st ed. (New York: Knopf, 1991).
2. For right whale hunting by Indians along the southeastern Atlantic coasts of North America, see Lewis H. Larson, *Aboriginal Subsistence Technology on the Southeastern Coastal Plain during the Late Prehistoric Period* (Gainesville: University of Florida Press, 1980), 145–62. I am indebted to my colleague Peter Wood for this reference. For Northwest Pacific coast whale hunting among the Tlingit-speaking peoples of North America, see Alvin M. Josephy, *America in 1492: The World of the Indian Peoples before the Arrival of Columbus* (New York: Knopf, 1992), 55–60.

sub-Arctic waters to the limits of pack ice in search of whales, walruses, and seals. Simultaneously, the intensified, systematic shore-based whaling along the eastern coast of North America, on both Japanese coasts, and along northern Europe added to the catch. Industrial whaling in the northern oceans heavily exploited a resource that, like the codfish, had been only lightly hunted by humans. Whales and, to a lesser extent, walruses and seals became new commodities in the early modern world economy. Europe, in particular, obtained access to abundant marine resources that were free for the taking. In its new form, whaling was a spectacular and profitable aspect of the world hunt—a market-driven enterprise. Demand for whale oil and whalebone was sufficient to send increasing numbers of men and ships into northern waters. By mid–eighteenth century, the hunt for whales enlarged to include new stocks of different species in the southern oceans.

THE PREY

The prey that first drew commercial European hunters into northern Arctic waters was the walrus *(Odobenus rosmarus),* hunted for its extended ivory tusks, tough, thick hide, and copious fat. Immense numbers of walruses, a gregarious species, lived in the pack ice in herds of several thousand closely packed individuals. Walruses are large animals. Adult males reach 270 to 356 centimeters in length, 150 centimeters in height, and weigh between eight hundred and seventeen hundred kilograms; females are somewhat smaller. This species is generally cinnamon brown with coarse hair covering a tough, wrinkled skin that is about 2–4 centimeters thick over most of the body; beneath this lies a layer of blubber that on the chest measures about 10 centimeters thick. The walrus has a ponderous, rounded body with thick fore flippers and hind flippers, each having five digits. It has a rounded head with small eyes and a muzzle with a large, thick mustache. Both sexes have distinctive tusks, which reach 100 centimeters in length in males and 80 centimeters in females. Nearly the entire tusk is ivory (dentin), and a single tusk in an older male can weigh five kilograms or more.

Shallow waters across the Arctic Ocean and its adjoining seas constitute the usual habitat of the walrus. Walruses haul themselves out of the water to rest on the ice and, in summer, sometimes on beaches and rocky islets. The animals live in huge herds ordered by dominance hierarchies established by males. They migrate south as the pack ice expands in the winter and return north in the spring as the ice recedes. They feed by diving to depths of ten to fifty meters to forage on the ocean bottom for clams and mussels and a wide array of other invertebrates and, occasionally, take fish and seals. They mate in winter and have a total gestation period of fifteen to sixteen months. In early summer, from mid-April to mid-June, mothers give birth to a single calf. Lactation lasts up to two years, and extremely strong mother-calf bonds are maintained. Full maturity comes at 9–11 years for females and 15 years for males. Maximum longevity is about 40 years.[3]

Early modern whalers hunted two closely related species of large whales: the bowhead, or Greenland, whale *(Balaena mysticetus)* found in Arctic and sub-Arctic waters, and the right whale *(Balaena glacialis)*, distributed world-wide along the coasts of Europe, Asia, Africa, and the Americas. Occasion-ally, the gray whale *(Eschrichtius robustus)* was captured. Later, by mid–eighteenth century, American whalers pursued sperm whales *(Physeter macro-cephalus)* worldwide in a new phase of the industry. However, bowhead and right whales, not distinguished as separate species until the 1860s, remained primary targets before 1800. Over several centuries, open-water whalers, sail-ing in previously uncharted northern seas, developed a narrowly focused un-derstanding of the behavior and habitat of these animals.

Why were these two species of whales the primary quarry? First, they were immense creatures. Mature animals could reach eighty to one hundred met-ric tons in weight but were, for all their size, inoffensive and timid. Second, they were valuable. Each bowhead or right whale contained thick layers of blubber that could be converted to oil, and had hundreds of extended 3–5 meter baleen, or whalebone, plates of a tough, pliable, strong plasticlike ma-terial for industrial use. (European whalers reserved all possible space on their ships for blubber, oil, and whalebone. They consumed only a little of the meat, if any, and simply discarded the remainder.) A single carcass was a rich prize that could be had merely for the cost of hunting it down. Third, they were vulnerable. Both species were slow swimmers who followed regu-lar migratory routes in pursuit of food in the summer and winter seasons. Of-ten these routes brought them close to shore. Air breathers, they spent time on the surface, often sleeping, where they could be sighted and attacked. Fourth, they could be retrieved when killed. Most bowheads and right whales did not sink when they were killed, but stayed buoyant; their carcasses could be processed in the water or towed back to shore. Finally, they were abun-dant. Various reconstructions put the Arctic bowhead population prior to in-dustrial whaling at approximately 50,000 to 60,000 and the right whale pop-ulation at about 80,000 animals worldwide.[4] With these numbers, the bowhead whales formed the largest standing stock of biomass of any mam-

3. Ronald M. Nowak and Ernest P. Walker, *Walker's Mammals of the World*, 5th ed. (Baltimore: Johns Hopkins University Press, 1991), s.v. "walrus."

4. For bowhead whales, see Douglas A. Woodby and Daniel B. Botkin, "Stock Sizes Prior to Commercial Whaling," in *The Bowhead Whale*, edited by John J. Burns, J. Jerome Montague, Cleveland J. Cowles, and the Society for Marine Mammalogy (Lawrence, Kans.: Society for Ma-rine Mammalogy, 1993), 387. For right whales, see Roger Payne, *Among Whales* (New York: Scrib-ner, 1995), 269, citing M. Klinowska, "Dolphins, Porpoises, and Whales of the World," in *The IUCN Red Data Book* (Gland, Switzerland: IUCN, 1991). See also Kim E. W. Shelden and David J. Rugh, *The Bowhead Whale, Balaena mysticetus: Its Historic and Current Status* (Seattle: National

mal in the Arctic, estimated at 2 million metric tons—far more than that of the other two numerous mammals north of the fifty-seven-degree parallel: ringed seals and caribou.[5] Surprisingly, for such a large animal, bowheads, along with other baleen whales, are only at the third trophic level. On average, each bowhead whale consumes about a hundred metric tons of zooplankton each year. Bowhead whales engulf huge quantities of tiny crustaceans (copepods, euphausiids, and mysids) that in turn feed on phytoplankton, algae, and other primary biomass in the ocean.[6]

Bowhead populations are conventionally divided into five stocks, or distinct regions of commercial exploitation. (These may have been distinct breeding populations, but marine biologists are not certain on this point.)[7] From west to east, these are the Okhotsk Sea and Bering Sea stocks in the western Arctic and northern Pacific, and the Davis Strait, Spitsbergen, and Hudson Bay stocks in the eastern Arctic and northern Atlantic. Early modern European whalers first hunted the Spitsbergen and later the Davis Strait whales, but commercial hunting of the small Hudson Bay stock and the western Arctic bowheads did not begin until mid– to late nineteenth century. Two methods of extrapolation suggest a minimum size of 25,000 bowheads for the Spitsbergen population in the early sixteenth century, and 11,000 for the Davis Strait stock, for a total of 36,000 bowhead whales.[8] It is these relatively few animals and their descendants who became the quarry for a three-hundred-and-fifty-year hunt that ended in their extinction in eastern Arctic waters.

The bowhead derives its name from the bowlike shape of its enormous mouth that constitutes two-sevenths to one-third of its total body length. Lacking a dorsal fin, the bowhead has two short, broad flippers and extended tail flukes that average one-third of body length. The whale's paired blowholes are protected by a high crown that affords a defense against ice. The arch, or bow, of the mouth rises to accommodate the baleen plates used to trap zooplankton in the whale's mouth. These plates form in two rows, one on each side of the mouth. Each main plate, or lamina, has adjacent minor

Marine Mammal Laboratory, National Marine Fisheries Service, National Oceanic and Atmospheric Administration, 1997).

5. John J. Burns et al., *The Bowhead Whale* (Lawrence, Kans.: Society for Marine Mammalogy, 1993), 1. The editors calculate that sixty thousand bowhead whales, if similar to modern bowheads, would total 2,020,000 metric tons, and that the stock would have consumed 5,720,000 tons of planktonic food annually. This is a greater amount of food than required for an estimated 7 million seals, which would consume 560,000 metric tons, or required for 4.3 million caribou, which would consume 800,000 tons.

6. Lloyd F. Lowry, "Foods and Feeding Ecology," in *The Bowhead Whale*, edited by John J. Burns, J. Jerome Montague, Cleveland J. Cowles, and the Society for Marine Mammalogy (Lawrence, Kans.: Society for Marine Mammalogy, 1993), 229–30.

7. Woodby and Botkin, "Stock Sizes Prior to Commercial Whaling," 387.

8. Ibid., 401, table 10.4. The Hudson Bay stock is put at 575 animals.

plates and baleen hairs to aid in closure. The total number of plates in each animal may reach 330 or more on each side.

The bowhead is predominantly black in color with a consistent white chin patch and scattered, nonpigmented white streaks or mottling across its body. Beneath the epidermis and dermis lies a dense, thick layer (up to 28 centimeters) of adipose and fibrous tissue referred to as blubber. The innermost layer of the skin, or hypodermis, is a soft tissue that connects the skin with the muscles and other organs. (The hypodermis permits whalers to readily strip the layer of blubber intact from the carcass.) The eyes, covered with movable lids, are located low on either side of the head. The ear channels lie just below the eyes. This warm-blooded, air-breathing mammal has enormous lung capacity and the strength to sustain itself in extended dives as it searches for subsurface plankton clouds.[9]

Bowheads inhabit largely icy Arctic waters in the region of the Atlantic between 60 and 85 degrees north and in the Pacific between 50 to 75 degrees. They tend to live on the edge of the ice pack. They swim under the ice surface in leads of open water and are powerful enough to breach ice cover up to sixty centimeters thick in order to breathe. Each spring season, segregated by sex and age class, bowheads move in loosely assembled herds north to reach largely ice-free continental shelf waters; they retreat slowly southward in the autumn as the ice cover advances. Migration speeds are slow, with travel averaging four kilometers per hour.

Bowhead whales are gregarious animals who communicate among themselves with a remarkable repertoire of low-frequency calls and songs as well as by blows and slaps on the water.[10] These whales live long—forty years or even far more—and have few natural enemies. Only the fast-swimming killer whales *(Orcinus orca)* are known to attack bowheads. Ice entrapment is the other occasional threat to bowheads, who can reach a point where they simply cannot break thickened ice cover.[11] As befits their size, bowheads have a slow reproductive cycle and a low annual reproductive rate.[12] Females sexually mature late, when they are about fifteen years of age (and measure 12.5

9. Jerrold T. Haldiman and Raymond J. Tarpley, "Anatomy and Physiology," in *The Bowhead Whale,* edited by John J. Burns, J. Jerome Montague, Cleveland J. Cowles, and the Society for Marine Mammalogy (Lawrence, Kans.: Society for Marine Mammalogy, 1993).

10. Bernd Wursig and Christopher Clark, "Behavior," in *The Bowhead Whale,* edited by John J. Burns, J. Jerome Montague, Cleveland J. Cowles, and the Society for Marine Mammalogy (Lawrence, Kans.: Society for Marine Mammalogy, 1993).

11. L. Michael Philo, Emmett B. Shotts Jr., and John C. George, "Morbidity and Mortality," in *The Bowhead Whale,* edited by John J. Burns, J. Jerome Montague, Cleveland J. Cowles, and the Society for Marine Mammalogy (Lawrence, Kans.: Society for Marine Mammalogy, 1993).

12. William R. Koski et al., "Reproduction," in *The Bowhead Whale,* edited by John J. Burns, J. Jerome Montague, Cleveland J. Cowles, and the Society for Marine Mammalogy (Lawrence, Kans.: Society for Marine Mammalogy, 1993).

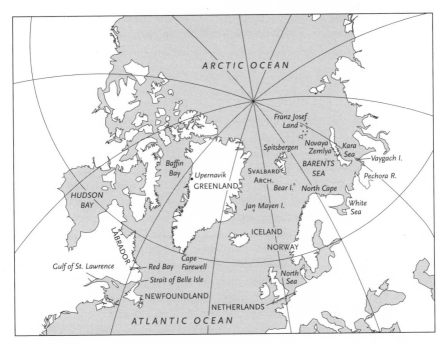

Map 7 Whaling areas of the Northern Hemisphere

to 14 meters in length). Adult females calve every three to four years. Mating and conception occur in late winter and early spring. Gestation, while not known with certainty, is estimated to last thirteen to fourteen months. The nursing calves, which are born in April and May, accompany their mothers during the spring migration to the summer feeding grounds. Weaning occurs by twelve months or so. Bowhead calves grow slowly by comparison with other whale species.

Right whales, slightly smaller, share many of the physical and behavioral characteristics of bowheads. This species' mouth is nearly as large, but not as arched, as that of the bowhead. Right whales have similar baleen plates, are black in color with an irregular white belly patch, and lack a dorsal fin. Most strikingly, they are born with callosities, or "keratinous lumps and bumps," distributed across the face and head.[13] Since these callosities do not change over time, they permit confident identification of individuals. Unlike bowheads, the right whale is widely dispersed. Right whales have been found

13. Richard Ellis, *Men and Whales*, 1st ed. (New York: Knopf, 1991), 7. This work has excellent illustrations of various types of whales.

in every ocean and along the coasts of every continent, including Antarctica. Today, they exist in remnant populations totaling no more than one or two thousand animals.[14]

INDIGENOUS ARCTIC WHALING

Between 1200 and 1600 C.E., throughout the circumpolar Arctic and sub-Arctic, the Inuit (Eskimo) peoples were the most skilled and aggressive hunters of whales and other marine mammals. In contrast to the reindeer-hunting peoples of northern Eurasia or the caribou-hunting Indians of North America, the Inuits relied on the sea as their main source of subsistence. Highly specialized Inuit technology and intimate knowledge of the harsh, ice-locked environment permitted them to survive and even to live in relative comfort—much to the amazement of those Europeans who first ventured into the northern oceans. The latter were intrigued by how the Eskimos used oil from marine mammals for heat and light, stayed warm and mobile in fur and skin clothing, and took shelter in rapidly constructed snow houses that provided warmth in a frozen environment. They admired the fast and buoyant sealskin kayaks propelled by double-bladed paddles and the speed and endurance of sled dogs that pulled enormous loads on efficient, runnered sledges with seeming ease. They were impressed by the Eskimos' navigational and hunting skills displayed in the trackless land of ice and snow as they pursued the walrus, seal, and polar bear.

The indomitable Eskimos, with their cheerful resilience and skill in coping with the Arctic's hazards, became a symbol of a relatively benign, admirable, savage state for the early modern world. As European explorers and whalers recorded more ethnographic detail about Eskimo life, Inuits became stock figures in an emerging taxonomy of savage peoples. The Eskimo hunter who braved the Arctic ice and ocean waters in search of marine mammals became a trope for a superb, but limited, form of human adaptation to the most severe environment in the world.

The fully developed Arctic medieval and early modern hunting culture that depended on marine mammals and engaged in intensive whaling is known by archaeologists as the Thule culture. First appearing in the northern Bering Strait region and the Chukchi Sea coast of Alaska about 900 C.E., the Thule supplanted the Punuk and the Birnirk cultures. Over the next few hundred years, it spread rapidly westward into Siberia, as well as eastward

14. Robert L. Brownell et al., *Right Whales: Past and Present Status: Proceedings of the Workshop on the Status of Right Whales, New England Aquarium, Boston, Massachusetts, 15–23 June 1983* (Cambridge, Eng.: International Whaling Commission, 1986).

across all of Arctic North America as far as Labrador and Greenland.[15] Evidence for a warming trend around 1000 to 1200 C.E. has led to speculation that reduced sea ice may have opened up summer routes for migratory whales all the way across from the Bering Sea to Greenland. The ensuing abundance of whales may have encouraged dispersal of Inuits and the Thule culture. Other archaeologists have posited population growth and internecine warfare as possible push factors.[16]

The Russian anthropologist I. I. Krupnik has suggested a cyclical series of adaptations to Arctic climatic change in which warming trends attracted whales and walruses into northern waters and thereby permitted Eskimos to hunt these large mammals. During cooling trends, the large mammals retreated to southward waters, and the importance of fishing and of hunting caribou, reindeer, and seals rose.[17] The Eskimos hunted and used all accessible Arctic land and sea animals, from birds and foxes to whales. The emphasis put on each species depended on both the relative effort needed under specific circumstances and the energy return expected. The latter phase of Thule culture, between 1400 to 1600 C.E., was a cooling period during which Arctic hunters found whales less abundant and adapted accordingly.[18]

Despite contraction of the whales' ranges, however, whaling retained its central significance for Thule-era peoples. Favorably situated coastal settlements continued to hunt whales and walruses until the seventeenth century. Simply put, the economic return for whale hunting was very large indeed. According to Krupnik:

> Eskimo subsistence, like most human economies, did not escape a general evolutionary tendency toward using ever more productive, stable, and at the same time, more labor-intensive, resources in the environment. Hunting the largest sea mammal[s] such as whales and walrus required more complex hunting technology and organization, but compared to other subsistence activities yield[ed] a maximum harvest in the shortest period of time. Yet, without sufficient labor resources to store large amounts of meat quickly, the hard-won

15. Sam W. Stoker and Igor I. Krupnik, "Subsistence Whaling," in *The Bowhead Whale*, edited by John J. Burns, J. Jerome Montague, Cleveland J. Cowles, and the Society for Marine Mammalogy (Lawrence, Kans.: Society for Marine Mammalogy, 1993), 584. Thule cultural dominance of the Arctic reached its height in the thirteenth through sixteenth centuries, known as the "Baleen Period" in American archaeology. See also Robert McGhee, "Thule Prehistory of Canada," in *Handbook of North American Indians*, edited by William C. Sturtevant (Washington: Smithsonian Institution, 1978).

16. Ibid.

17. I. I. Krupnik, *Arctic Adaptations: Native Whalers and Reindeer Herders of Northern Eurasia* (Hanover, N.H.: University Press of New England, for Dartmouth College, 1993), 189–90.

18. Ibid. Krupnik speaks of the "decline of aboriginal whaling, the resumption of sealing and caribou hunting, and the desertion of large coastal villages during this period throughout the entire Eskimo ecumene from Chukotka to Greenland" (188).

catch would rot. So, utilizing such "feast-or-famine" meat supplies also required considerable additional energy to create large food reserves.[19]

Only settled, relatively densely populated communities could mobilize the human energy to hunt whales successfully. Whaling was very much a community endeavor, with communal sharing of the proceeds among all its members. Successful whale-hunting communities probably obtained well over half their food and fuel requirements from butchered whales. Calculations made on faunal remains from two Somerset Island sites in the Canadian Arctic suggest that food from whales "equaled the food from all other animals combined."[20] Feeding sled dogs—each of whom, when working, required as much food as an adult human—was made considerably easier by success in the whaling season.

The huge size of the bowhead whale, the primary target for Arctic hunters, meant that success could be measured by annual kills of only a few animals for each community. Along the Chukchi Peninsula, for example, archaeologists working with identifiable remains at coastal settlements estimate the annual kill at about 10 to 15 bowheads per year before European contact. Along the Alaskan coast, the total may have reached 45 to 60 animals. In the eastern Canadian Arctic, the annual kill was about 25 to 30 whales per year. Along the Labrador coast, hunters took 4 to 5 animals per year. For the entire west coast of Greenland, indigenous hunters took perhaps 10 animals per year; no estimate has been made for the east coast. In short, the total estimate for Arctic hunters in the late Thule period is no more than 120 to 130 animals captured per year.[21] This includes both the Spitsbergen and Bering Sea stocks of bowhead whales.

Archaeological remains show that hunters deliberately pursued immature animals whose carcasses were more manageable when landed. Yearling bowhead whales—seven to ten meters in length and 5,000 to 13,000 kilograms in weight—were the preferred targets. One reason may well have been that, despite the admitted sophistication of Eskimo whaling technology, capturing fully adult bowheads stretched its limits. For bowheads, body weight did not increase in linear fashion as body length extended. A mature adult might gain another seven to ten meters in length, reaching a total of 17 meters, but gain proportionately far more weight, reaching 80,000 to 85,000 kilograms.[22] Contrary to popular belief, selection of immature animals was probably not as damaging to the whale herds as taking mature animals in

19. Ibid., 190.

20. Allen P. McCartney and James M. Sevelle, "Thule Eskimo Whaling in the Central Canadian Arctic," *Arctic Anthropology* 22 (1985): 42.

21. Stoker and Krupnik, "Subsistence Whaling," 591–97.

22. Allen P. McCartney, "Whale Size Selection by Precontact Hunters of the North American Western Arctic and Subarctic," in *Hunting the Largest Animals: Native Whaling in the Western*

their reproductive years—especially for large mammals with such slow rates of reproduction. Selective capture of yearlings was probably less disruptive than attacking the adult population.[23]

The total array of organizational skills and technical innovations that made whale hunting successful was impressive: Inuit whalers used *umiaks*, walrus- or sealskin-covered boats (with flotation devices under the seats) that carried six to eight paddlers, a steersman, and one or two harpooners in the bow. Several of these boats, working in unison, approached a sighted whale in silence in order to make the first harpoon strike at close range. The harpoon, attached to a thirty-meter seal-hide line, had a roughly two-meter wood or bone primary shaft with an attached short foreshaft of the same materials and a detachable swivel head of bone or ivory. Inserted in the head was a slate or iron blade. The harpoon head detached from the harpoon proper when it struck the whale and swiveled within the wound to hold firmly within the animal's flesh. The harpoon shaft floated free and was recovered later. The harpoon line was attached to two or three floats made of whole, inflated sealskins that created a drag equivalent of 90 to 135 kilograms. At the strike, the harpooner threw the floats and line overboard. These floats marked the whale's whereabouts when it dived and helped the whalers to anticipate its next surfacing, when it could be attacked again. Whalers also used more powerful sea anchors or chutes made out of whalebone or baleen to exhaust the whale and slow its escape. As often as necessary, the whalers put more harpoons into the whale as the pursuit continued.

At the kill, the whalers, who sometimes climbed on the beast's back, drove four-meter-long lances with sharpened stone heads into the brain, the heart, or the lungs of the animal. Lancers in faster and more maneuverable kayaks sometimes aided boat crews in the kill.[24] Once the whale had been killed, the whalers lashed its fins close to its body and towed it to the shore. If possible, they hauled the whale out of the water using dogs, men, and lines; if not, they butchered the carcass in shallow water using large flensing knives with blades of polished slate. Butchering and hauling the proceeds required the services of nearly the entire community for a day or more. The meat and *muktuk* (blubber with skin attached) was stored in pits dug in the permafrost.

In a good year, whaling produced surpluses that could be traded with other, nonwhaling Eskimo communities more reliant on caribou or reindeer. Whale oil provided badly needed fat for caribou hunters, whose diet consisted of lean meat most of the year, and helped to balance out years when caribou stocks fell or were nonexistent. Surplus caribou skins, with

---

Arctic and Subarctic, edited by Allen P. McCartney and the Canadian Circumpolar Institute (Alberta: Canadian Circumpolar Institute, University of Alberta, 1995), 99.

23. Krupnik, *Arctic Adaptations*, 238.

24. Ibid., 586–88.

their hollow hairs, offered whale hunters desirable fur and skins for high-insulating, cold-weather clothing. These were the principal items exchanged in vigorous trading networks across the Arctic.[25]

It is doubtful that human predation in the Thule period had more than a slight impact on the stocks of whales in the Arctic. Climatic change and food availability would have been the major determinants of the numbers of whales—not human hunting.[26] As stated earlier, the total catch by Arctic whalers was probably no more than a hundred or so animals per year. Limited catches partly reflected the limitations of the whaling technology employed and the modest numbers of people involved.

Existing archaeological remains do not support the notion that precontact Eskimo populations were much larger than those counted in the nineteenth and twentieth centuries. There is no evidence of large-scale mortality from new diseases of the sort seen in societies to the south and, therefore, no reason to suspect large precontact populations.[27] It is unlikely that more than a few thousand people across Arctic and sub-Arctic Eurasia were directly involved in whale hunting in any single year, and probably there were fewer. And, even with some offtake of whale oil by larger populations in a trading network, the overall human pressure on whale stocks was modest—a situation that would change rapidly in the next centuries.

THE BASQUES

The Basques, who inhabit the coastline of the Bay of Biscay, in a region bisected by the national boundary between France and Spain, have enthusiastically hunted whales since the early medieval centuries. Overall, forty-seven coastal villages and towns in French and Spanish Basque country relied on offshore whaling to supplement fishing until the supply of right whales ended in the early nineteenth century. Many towns have municipal seals and coats of arms that proclaim a proud history of whaling.[28]

The Basques hunted migrating right whales that came close to shore between October–November and February–March. (Basque whale hunting

25. Gene W. Sheehan, "Whaling Surplus, Trade, War, and the Integration of Prehistoric Northern and Northwestern Alaskan Economies, A.D. 1200–1826," in *Hunting the Largest Animals: Native Whaling in the Western Arctic and Subarctic*, edited by Allen P. McCartney and the Canadian Circumpolar Institute (Alberta: Canadian Circumpolar Institute University of Alberta, 1995).

26. Sue E. Moore and Randall R. Reeves, "Distribution and Movement," in *The Bowhead Whale*, edited by John J. Burns, J. Jerome Montague, Cleveland J. Cowles, and the Society for Marine Mammalogy (Lawrence, Kans.: Society for Marine Mammalogy, 1993), 313.

27. Krupnik, *Arctic Adaptations*, 221.

28. Ellis, *Men and Whales*, 47.

was virtually identical to that practiced by the Eskimos of the Arctic against bowhead whales, described above.) Fishing cooperatives erected lookout towers and placed full-time lookouts on duty throughout the season. When whales were sighted, the whalers launched small rowing boats in pursuit. If fortunate and skillful, they got close enough to harpoon and kill their prey and then towed the carcass back to shore. Harpooners aimed first at calves, which were easily hit, so that the mothers would come to their aid and then be taken. Each whale taken was a bonanza for a small village, since the whalebone, oil, and meat were all valuable and could be either consumed or sold.[29] The catch taken by these methods was modest in number. A fishing village that took a whale each year would consider itself fortunate. Catch statistics from the village of Zauraz in the Spanish Basque country for the period 1500 to 1550 show a total of thirty-three whales for the fifty years. However, this rate was halved in the second half of the century.[30]

The high point of offshore Biscay whaling seems to have been the sixteenth century, which was followed by a gradual decline in the catch thereafter. Offshore whaling certainly continued but became subordinate. Probably around 1500, if not before, Basque whalers set out from the Bay of Biscay in larger ships searching for new whaling grounds in the North Sea as far as Iceland.[31] Confident of their hunting skills and well aware of possible profits to be made, the Basques were the first to begin industrial, early modern whaling. Local investors and financiers from as far away as Bordeaux and New Rochelle put up the funds necessary to build and outfit specially equipped whaling vessels and pay their crews for extended periods of time. In part, this initiative accompanied the pursuit of codfish into northern waters by Basque and other fishermen as stocks declined in the Bay of Biscay. To some degree, lowered catches by offshore whaling methods also may have pushed the expansion.

Basque whalers did not stop at Iceland. By the early sixteenth century, they had begun sailing directly across the Atlantic to exploit new cod fishing and whaling grounds off Labrador and Newfoundland. The first recorded voyage made by northern French Basques to Terranova, or "New Land," was in 1517. By the 1530s, as many as twenty Basque vessels made the transat-

29. Alex Aguilar, "A Review of Old Basque Whaling and Its Effect on the Right Whales (*Eubalaena glacialis*) of the North Atlantic," in *Right Whales: Past and Present Status: Proceedings of the Workshop on the Status of Right Whales, New England Aquarium, Boston, Massachusetts, 15–23 June 1983*, edited by Robert L. Brownell, P. B. Best, John H. Prescott, the New England Aquarium Corporation, and the International Whaling Commission (Cambridge, Eng.: International Whaling Commission, 1986).

30. Ibid., 194, table 3.

31. Jean Pierre Proulx and the Canadian Parks Service, *Basque Whaling in Labrador in the Sixteenth Century* (Ottawa: National Historic Sites Parks Service, 1993), 12.

lantic journey each year.[32] The primary whaling site was the narrow Strait of Belle Isle between the west coast of Newfoundland and the Labrador coast. Material remains from the first whaling station in North America at the present-day harbor of Red Bay on the Labrador coast confirm the presence of Basque whalers. On Saddle Island, located in the mouth of Red Bay, archaeologists discovered foundations from several blubber-rendering tryworks sites, a site where coopers built casks for whale oil, hundreds of pieces of red Spanish roofing tile, Spanish majolica ceramics, glassware, iron tools, and a cemetery holding remains of 140 whalers.[33]

The most remarkable finds, however, have been those of several Basque whaling ships and boats sunk in Red Bay Harbor. Firmly identified is the *San Juan*, a three-masted, ninety-foot galleon sunk while loading barrels of whale oil during a gale in 1565 and whose insurance policy is still extant in Spanish archives. Contemporary references permit identification of another seven ports along the same stretch of coast, for a total of eight Labrador whaling settlements occupied. After a two-month journey across the Atlantic, large whaling galleons arrived in June or July of each year at Belle Isle for the four- to five-month summer and autumn season. A typical Basque whaler of 250 tons capacity might have a crew of fifty or more sailors, craftsmen, and skilled harpooners and flensers. The galleons were not used to hunt whales, but were moored in the harbor to serve as living quarters and storehouses. The whalers built, or used already built, tiled roof tryworks on land, where copper cauldrons were positioned over great ovens. Each whaling captain sent out fully equipped whaleboats (called shallops) with six- or seven-man crews to patrol the straits in regular shifts.

When a whale was sighted, the boat crew tried to get between the whale and the open sea and to come upon the animals from behind. At a distance of seven to eight meters or even closer, if possible, the harpooner thrust the detachable harpoon head into the whale's body. When the wounded whale began to dive, the crew paid out a three-hundred-meter line of rope attached to the harpoon head. Usually the whale surfaced before the entire rope was used up, but wooden floats were attached to the end of this line so that the whale could be kept in sight if this did happen.[34] Sometimes boats with additional lines were able to add their length to the original line.

This began a bloody, prolonged embrace between whale and boat crew in which the final outcome was not at all certain. Many whales escaped. They

32. Ibid., 15–16. Notarial documents in Bayonne, Bordeaux, and La Rochelle confirm these voyages.

33. James A. Tuck and Robert Grenier, *Red Bay, Labrador: World Whaling Capital, A.D. 1550–1600* (St. John's, Newfoundland: Atlantic Archaeology, 1989).

34. Proulx and the Canadian Parks Service, *Basque Whaling in Labrador in the Sixteenth Century*, 53–57.

dove under the ice and loosened the harpoon in their frantic maneuvers. If the harpoon held during several dives and surfacings, the boat crew was able to get close enough to the tiring whale for the harpooner to thrust lances aiming for the animal's heart or lungs. When he succeeded, the whale thrashed in its death paroxysm—the most dangerous point for the hunters in their small boat—and, when dead, usually floated on the surface of the water.

The whalers then towed the carcass to the harbor, where they lashed it to the side of the whaling galleon. Flensers with huge knives cut the blubber off the whale in strips and carried it into shore to be heated in the cauldrons of the tryworks. The resulting oil, cooled, skimmed, and strained, was poured into newly built wooden barrels. The Spanish barrel in use had a capacity of around 180 to 200 liters of oil and a loaded weight of 250 kilograms. The whalers also removed the baleen plates and stored them carefully on board ship.

Analysis of hundreds of whale skeletal remains found on land and underwater at Red Bay suggest that the Basque whalers killed roughly equal numbers of bowheads and right whales, whose ranges overlapped in this region. During the summer, the whalers probably took right whales at the northern extent of their range; in the later autumn months, referred to as the "second season," they captured bowheads as they migrated into southern waters.[35] By far the greatest number of whales identified were fully mature adult whales, not calves.[36] Sources contemporary to the time state that each whale carcass yielded between 70 and 140 barrels of oil.

Toward the end of the season in November and December, most whaling captains had succeeded in filling their vessels with whale oil and were preparing to return to their home ports in the Bay of Biscay. Whaling galleons, between two hundred and seven hundred tons displacement, could carry 600 to 1,500 Spanish barrels of whale oil on the return voyage. Perhaps twenty to thirty whaling galleons made the Terranova journey each season.[37] At an average of 85 barrels of oil per whale and 1,000 barrels per vessel, the median catch could have been 12 whales per voyage. Commercially valuable baleen plates probably averaged three hundred or so per whale and could be

35. Stephen L. Cumbaa, "Archaeological Evidence of the Sixteenth Century Basque Right Whale Fishery in Labrador," in *Right Whales: Past and Present Status: Proceedings of the Workshop on the Status of Right Whales, New England Aquarium, Boston, Massachusetts, 15–23 June 1983*, edited by Robert L. Brownell, P. B. Best, John H. Prescott, the New England Aquarium Corporation, and the International Whaling Commission (Cambridge, Eng.: International Whaling Commission, 1986).

36. Ibid., 189.

37. Aguilar, "A Review of Old Basque Whaling and Its Effect on the Right Whales *(Eubalaena glacialis)* of the North Atlantic," 195.

stowed somewhat differently than barrels of oil. Whales taken per season would have totaled between 240 and 360 animals.[38] The Basques' Labrador whaling fishery seems to have sustained this level between 1530 and 1620. The estimated cumulative total catch would then have been 21,600 to 32,400 bowhead and right whales for that period.[39]

There is little doubt that New World whaling, which continued uninterrupted for such a long time, contributed substantial revenues to the economy of the Basque region. Even the humblest apprentices received 2 to 3 valuable barrels of whale oil—each worth twelve or more ducats in the late sixteenth century—when they returned from the year's expedition. Ratios varied according to individual agreements, but one common arrangement gave the whaling crew one-third of the proceeds from the oil; the owner of the ship, another third; and the outfitters who had financed and provided equipment and supplies, the final third. Moreover, the odds of whalers returning to their home port seem to have been no worse than for other mariners of the time. Casualties from the whale hunt were seemingly rare.

The outfitters or investors in each voyage retained profits from the whalebone brought back, which were not divided with the crew. A whaling galleon returning with whalebone and 1,000 barrels of oil in the late sixteenth century could realize six thousand to twelve thousand or more ducats depending on conditions that year. If we consider that the average amount of insurance taken out on each ship (limited to 90 percent of value) in that period was between two thousand and twenty-five hundred ducats, the potential for profit among all concerned was considerable.[40]

Demand for whale oil and whalebone remained high even as the price of a barrel of whale oil rose from six ducats in the 1560s to twelve to fifteen ducats in the 1590s.[41] Most captains sailed directly to their home ports and sold their cargoes immediately. For the northern, or French, Basque region, the primary oil markets were at Bayonne and Saint-Jean-de-Luz; for the southern or Spanish, they were San Sebastian and Bilbao. Foreign merchants kept agents permanently in residence in these towns.

After meeting local demand, buyers sold oil to wholesalers who dealt with retail apothecaries throughout France and Spain. Others sent whale oil to industrial centers such as the textile and soap factories of the Languedoc region. For example, in the winter of 1565–1566, two merchants, Geronimo de Salamanca Santa Cruz and Antonio de Salazar, shipped whale oil valued at

38. Aguilar suggests a figure of three hundred to five hundred whales taken per season.

39. Ibid., 196. Aguilar suggests that "an approximate cumulative catch for the period 1530 to 1610 would be between 25,00 to 40,000 whales." I have redone the calculation to extend the period to 1620 and have simply extended the barrels of oil per whale and per ship specified.

40. Proulx and the Canadian Parks Service, *Basque Whaling in Labrador in the Sixteenth Century*, 65–79.

41. Ibid., 78.

twenty-eight thousand ducats (thirty-five hundred barrels at a price of eight ducats per barrel) to northern Europe.[42]

After 1620, the numbers of Basque whaling ships coming to Terranova dropped to perhaps ten or twelve a year and the whaling grounds shifted westward to the Gulf of Saint Lawrence. It is very likely that whaling at this level of intensity had little impact on the numbers of either bowheads or right whales passing through the Strait of Belle Isle. After 1620, it was northern French Basques who remained active in the hunt and who benefited from the French colonial presence at Quebec. However, the Treaty of Utrecht in 1713 completely barred their entry to these waters and ended independent Basque whaling in Terranova.[43]

EXPLORATION IN NORTHERN WATERS

It was not until the early years of the seventeenth century that Europeans fully understood the potential richness of the bowhead whaling grounds to the north of Terranova, in the Arctic waters around Greenland. To hunt in these grounds, whalers first needed navigational and cartographic information about previously unexplored northern oceans. This knowledge was hard-won by decades of repeated voyages into ice-filled seas by a small group of determined mariners. Under varying forms of state and private commissions and financing, French, Dutch, English, and Danish ships probed the Arctic Ocean to find a direct northern sea route to China and Japan free of Spanish or Portuguese control.

One alternative, first proposed by Sebastian Cabot in 1548, was to seek a northeast passage to China by sailing north along North Cape of Norway into the White Sea, and then east into unknown northeast Arctic waters. Cabot's initial voyage, and several subsequent English voyages, reached the islands of Novaya Zemlya and Vaygach but could not penetrate the pack ice of the Kara Sea.

Dutch ventures were more fruitful. The Dutch led the way in exploring and charting Arctic waters.[44] Willem Barentsz and Jacob van Heemskerck, two extraordinarily gifted navigators and courageous leaders, conducted two Arctic voyages in search of the northeast passage in 1594 and 1596. These were sponsored and organized by private Dutch merchants, the Dutch States General, and the municipality of Amsterdam. The first expedition failed to get past Novaya Zemlya's west coast. In the second voyage, van Heemskerck

---

42. Ibid., 77.
43. Ibid.
44. Gunter Schilder, "Development and Achievements of Dutch Northern and Arctic Cartography in the Sixteenth and Seventeenth Centuries," *Arctic* 37, no. 4 (1984).

and Barentsz in one ship, and Jan Cornelisz Rijp as captain of the other, set a more northerly course than any before them.

On June 7, 1596, they first sighted Bear Island, located midway between Norway's North Cape and Spitsbergen (the Svalbard Archipelago) and then, proceeding north by northwest, reached the northwest tip of Spitsbergen (which they called the "sharp mountains"). The two ships parted in July. Rijp returned successfully from Spitsbergen. Barentsz set sail for the northern tip of Novaya Zemlya and reached it in late August, but was caught by ice and forced to go ashore with his crew for the winter of 1596–1597. Barentsz and van Heemskerck and their crew built two small, open boats. They set out in June 1597 on a fifteen-hundred-mile journey around the tip of Novaya Zemlya and down its west coast, and eventually reached the Kola Peninsula by the end of August. Barentsz and two other members of the fifteen-man crew died en route. Gerrit de Veer, a crew member, published his journal of the voyage in Dutch in 1598. Widely read, it was translated into French, German, Italian, and Latin by 1600 and English by 1609. Barentsz became a Dutch national hero in part because of the vividness and literary qualities of Veer's journal. Awareness of the Arctic burst upon European consciousness.[45]

Simultaneously, other mariners looked for a northwest passage to Cathay. English merchant speculators in London sent Martin Frobisher on three voyages north of Labrador into the Arctic in the 1570s. John Davis, who headed three expeditions in the 1580s, explored the eponymous Davis Strait off the west coast of Greenland as far as Upernavik.[46] Following on these voyages, a few British mariners sailed as far north as Bear Island and sighted numerous walrus herds. Other English ships sailing from Hull moved from their accustomed waters around Iceland to Greenland and began to hunt walruses for their ivory and oil. The Muscovy Company sent vessels in search of a northwest passage to China and Asia.

In 1604, Stephen Bennet, captain of the *Speed*, reached Bear Island, where he found a great walrus herd on the northeast shore of the island. According to his log:

> It seemed very strange to us to see such a multitude of monsters of the sea ley like hogges upon heapes: in the end we shot at them, not knowing whether they could runne swiftly or seize upon us or no. . . . Some, when they were wounded

45. Richard Vaughan, *The Arctic: A History* (Dover, N.H.: A. Sutton, 1994), 54–62. Also Felipe Fernández-Armesto, K. N. Chaudhuri, and Times Books, *The Times Atlas of World Exploration: Three Thousand Years of Exploring, Explorers, and Mapmaking* (New York: HarperCollins, 1991), 158–59; Gerrit de Veer, Charles T. Beke, and Laurens Reinhart Koolemans Beijnen, *The Three Voyages of William Barents to the Arctic Regions (1594, 1595, and 1596)* (New York: B. Franklin, 1964).

46. Vaughan, *The Arctic*, 64–74.

in the flesh, would but looke up and lye downe againe. Some were killed with the first shot; and some would goe into the sea with five or sixe shot; they are of such incredible strength. When all our shot and powder was spent, wee would . . . with our carpenter's axe cleave their heads. But for all we could doe, of above a thousand we killed but fifteene.[47]

On this voyage, Bennet and his crew only took the heads for tusks. On subsequent voyages in 1605 and 1606, they spent the summers killing walruses and boiling down their blubber for oil. They found that lances were more effective and cheaper than muskets in slaughtering large numbers of walruses. From the 1606 voyage, they returned with twenty-two metric tons of oil and three hogsheads of walrus tusks.[48]

In May 1607, the Muscovy Company sent the *Hopewell,* commanded by Henry Hudson, to make another attempt to find a northwest passage. On his 1607 voyage, Hudson, using Barentsz's charts, reached the Spitsbergen Archipelago. Hudson found the pack ice crowding much of Spitsbergen's coasts. Nevertheless, he reported that Kongsforden, a bay on the west coast of the archipelago, was teeming with bowhead whales. One bowhead even nudged his ship and made it list.[49] Another Muscovy Company voyage to Bear Island in 1608 resulted in the capture of a young walrus kept alive until the ship returned to London, "where the king and many honourable personages beheld it with admiration for the strangeness of the same, the like whereof had never before beene seene alive in England. Not long after[,] it fell sick and died. As the beast in shape is very strange, so is it of strange docilitie, and apt to be taught."[50]

In 1610, the Muscovy Company ordered Jonas Poole, commander of the *Amitie,* to make direct for Spitsbergen to hunt walruses. Poole found landing on the archipelago difficult, given the great amount of coastal ice and high winds, but when he did land, his crew reported the existence of unfrozen freshwater ponds. Poole and his crew were impressed by the abundance of animal life, including a "great store of whales" as well as polar bears, reindeer, walruses, and fowl. The *Amitie* returned with blubber, hides, and tusks from 120 walruses, hides and meat from 51 reindeer and 30 polar bears, and 3 bear cubs taken alive.[51]

---

47. William Martin Conway, *No Man's Land: A History of Spitsbergen from Its Discovery in 1596 to the Beginning of the Scientific Exploration of the Country* (Cambridge: Cambridge University Press, 1906), 21. Also William Martin Conway et al., *Early Dutch and English Voyages to Spitsbergen in the Seventeenth Century, Including Hessel Gerritsz. "Histoire du pays nommé Spitsberghe," 1613, Translated into English, for the First Time* (Nendeln, Liechtenstein: Kraus Reprint, 1967).

48. Conway, *No Man's Land,* 21.

49. Vaughan, *The Arctic,* 79; Conway, *No Man's Land,* 22–30.

50. Conway, *No Man's Land,* 30.

51. Ibid., 37.

EARLY COASTAL WHALING

Interest in possible profits to be made by Arctic whaling coalesced rapidly. Potential cargoes of oil from whaling promised to far outstrip the amount of oil gained from walruses. Colder climate conditions in the Arctic also seem to have favored Spitsbergen as a site for whaling. Winter pack ice solidified and extended farther southward than usual. Cooler summers meant that less drift ice was released in the grounds frequented by bowhead whales off the northeast coast of Greenland. Instead, the bowheads were forced toward the ice edge off Spitsbergen's bays and harbors. These conditions continued for the next several decades.[52]

In 1611, the entrepreneurs of the Muscovy Company sent two ships to Spitsbergen equipped to hunt whales; there were six Basque harpooners aboard. The expedition managed to kill one whale and five hundred walruses, and to render their fat into oil onshore, but both ships foundered. An English walrus-hunting ship out of Hull saved the crews and cargoes (for a fee). In 1612, spurred by shrinking numbers of whales off Labrador, a Basque whaling galleon from San Sebastian reached Spitsbergen and returned with a full cargo of whale oil.[53]

The next season, in 1613, strong market demand for oil sent at least twenty-six whaling ships to Spitsbergen's west coast. Most of the 1613 fleet were Basque whalers, including ten from San Sebastian and a giant 800-ton vessel from Saint-Jean-de-Luz captained by Miguel de Aristega. Two were Dutch whalers from Amsterdam and another two were Dutch vessels chartered by merchants from Dunkirk. Another seven were English: the Muscovy company commissioned seven English whalers with twenty-four Basque harpooners aboard. The 260-ton English flagship the *Tiger* was heavily armed, fitted with twenty-one cannons. When they arrived at Spitsbergen, the English ships sent out whaleboats to hunt whales in Forlandsundet Strait (between Prince Charles Island and the archipelago) and set up tryworks for the blubber on the shore.

The *Tiger* intercepted and boarded seventeen Basque, French, and Dutch whalers. The English admiral confiscated their catch and expelled the whalers from Spitsbergen waters. In several cases, such as that of Miguel de Aristega's great ship, the captain was permitted to stay and fish provided he hand over one-half the oil obtained.[54]

In January 1614, the Dutch whaling investors, stung by the English actions

52. Chr. Vibe, "Animals, Climate, Hunters, and Whalers," in *Proceedings of the International Symposium, Early European Exploitation of the Northern Atlantic, 800–1700,* edited by Rijksuniversiteit te Groningen, Noordelijk Centrum (Groningen, Netherlands: Arctic Centre, University of Groningen, 1981), 207.

53. Vaughan, *The Arctic,* 80–81.

54. Ibid., 81.

of the previous season, had organized themselves into a chartered trading company called the Noordsche Compagnie, with chambers formed in Amsterdam and the other leading towns in the Netherlands. Under a charter from the States General, they obtained a monopoly on whale hunting in Arctic waters off Greenland and Novaya Zemlya. The new Dutch company agreed on production quotas for whale oil, minimum prices, and maximum wages for seamen.[55] It also armed and equipped eleven ships for Spitsbergen and obtained an escort of three Dutch warships provided by the States General. At the whaling grounds, a standoff resulted: the Dutch whaled in the northwestern bays of the archipelago and maintained tryworks at Amsterdam Island, and the English remained in the bays of west Spitsbergen.

In the aftermath of these events, the territorial question of right of access to the whaling grounds came into sharp focus. Whose property rights were to prevail in the subsequent whaling seasons? Would the Muscovy Company dominate by force of arms? Would the Arctic waters fall under the control of one or more European states that claimed sovereignty? Would there be open access to this fishery, allowing participation by any whalers? In this dispute, the French and Spanish Basques obtained almost no early support from their respective rulers and were hampered by having less reliable and less copious investment capital. The principal claimants were the English, the Danes, and the Dutch. By the 1614 summer season, the Muscovy Company had obtained royal authority to annex Spitsbergen on behalf of King James I.

In the 1615 season, King Christian IV of Denmark and Norway sent a naval squadron to Spitsbergen that unsuccessfully tried to claim his old, established rights to Greenland and to rename Spitsbergen Christianbergen. The next year, Christian sent diplomatic representations to the courts of Europe to publicize his claim, but they failed to obtain support.

The Dutch view prevailed. Following their nation's general ideological position, the Dutch whalers articulated a doctrine of freedom of the seas (mare liberum) for the whale fishery and rejected the notion of a closed sea (mare clausum).[56] Stated firmly and backed by sufficient naval power, the Dutch view opened up the abundance of the Greenland fishery to any and all whalers. Rather than fight a costly war on the northern seas, the English and Danish kings acquiesced in the face of Dutch determination. There seemed to be enough whales for all.

The first shore-based phase of Arctic bowhead whaling established Dutch dominance over other European powers. The Dutch Noordsche Compagnie

55. C. De Jong, "The Hunt of the Greenland Whale: A Short History and Statistical Sources," in *Historical Whaling Records: Including the Proceedings of the International Workshop on Historical Whaling Records, Sharon, Massachusetts, September 12–16, 1977,* edited by Michael F. Tillman, Gregory P. Donovan, and the International Whaling Commission (Cambridge, Eng.: International Whaling Commission, 1983), 3:290.

56. Ibid., 3:2.

maintained its home monopoly until successful challenges from aspiring independent Dutch whalers and merchants led to its demise in 1642. From the very first, the whaling merchants in Amsterdam organized and financed a Europe-wide distribution network for whale oil and whalebone from that city. Although it never totally dominated the whale oil market, Amsterdam seems to have been the most efficient and reliable source for the oil throughout Europe. Dutch whalers, unlike their English counterparts, could count on ready sale of their product to a market far wider than that offered by the domestic market alone.

Every season, the Noordsche Compagnie sent between twenty and thirty whaling ships to the bays and fjords of Spitsbergen. Dutch whalers also hunted the well-stocked whaling grounds along the coasts of Jan Mayen Island to the south. Each whaling ship anchored in protected waters with ready access to the furnaces and cauldrons of the tryworks on shore. As the Basques had done before them in Labrador, the Dutch sent out boats—often commanded by Basque harpooners—in pursuit when bowheads entered the bays. The whalers harpooned and lanced the whales and towed their massive carcasses to shore. They tied them to the stern of the waiting whaling ship. Flensers pulled off long strips of blubber, cut them into pieces, and strung them on a line to be dragged ashore to the tryworks. Onshore, the blubber, minced into very small pieces, was boiled, strained, cooled, and poured into the wooden casks that would be loaded onto the whaling ship for the return voyage.

The principal Dutch shore station, called Smeerenberg (Blubbertown), located on the sandy beaches of the southeast corner of Amsterdam Island, was a scene of intense activity every summer season between 1619 and the 1660s. Each of the eight Dutch towns or chambers with a share in the Noordsche Compagnie had its own tryworks there and kept a shore crew of as many as forty men at work all season.[57] Smeerenberg probably processed 350 to 450 whales each year, and its competitors perhaps half that number.[58]

---

57. Louwrens Hacquebord, "The Rise and Fall of a Dutch Whaling-Settlement on the West Coast of Spitsbergen," in *Proceedings of the International Symposium, Early European Exploitation of the Northern Atlantic, 800–1700,* edited by Rijksuniversiteit te Groningen, Noordelijk Centrum (Groningen, Netherlands: Arctic Centre, University of Groningen, 1981); L. H. van Wijngaarden-Bakker and J. P. Pals, "Life and Work in Smeerenberg: The Bio-Archaeological Aspects," in *Proceedings of the International Symposium, Early European Exploitation of the Northern Atlantic, 800–1700,* edited by Rijksuniversiteit te Groningen, Noordelijk Centrum (Groningen, Netherlands: Arctic Centre, University of Groningen, 1981), 133–52; and G. J. R. Maat, "Human Remains at the Dutch Whaling Stations on Spitsbergen: A Physical Anthropological Study," in *Proceedings of the International Symposium, Early European Exploitation of the Northern Atlantic, 800–1700,* edited by Rijksuniversiteit te Groningen, Noordelijk Centrum (Groningen, Netherlands: Arctic Centre, University of Groningen, 1981), 153–202.

58. De Jong, "The Hunt of the Greenland Whale," 91. Occasionally, the total numbers of whales taken is listed with a fraction, e.g., 12 7/16. It is not entirely clear whether that fraction

The shore workers kept their ovens operating day and night. Each oven consisted of a brick ring, or fire screen, measuring 2.7 meters in diameter, surrounded by an insulating wall of stone with a sand layer in between them. A great copper kettle was set in the brick fire screen. The fire burnt in a funnel-shaped stoke hole located on one side of the brick fire screen, so that the heat circulated around the sides of the kettle. A chimney leading from the stoke hole discharged smoke. The heated whale oil drained in gutters to fill the barrels in which it was shipped.[59]

An archaeological expedition to Spitsbergen in 1980 from the University of Groningen found substantial numbers of artifacts from the settlement.[60] Dutch archaeologists have studied the material remains left at Smeerenberg and evidence of the layout of the original tent encampments and the later semipermanent wooden structures, as well as remnants of forges and try-works. They have found dozens of clay pipes, stoneware objects, bottles, more than one hundred leather shoes, and over one thousand pieces of cloth. Excavating the cemetery revealed 185 bodies, many with still-intact woolen clothing. A high percentage of the bones analyzed bear evidence of scurvy.

Soil samples and pollen analysis show that the settlement and tryworks heavily polluted the soil and vegetation of the area around Smeerenberg.[61] The men trampled the soil and it became very muddy. They carried with them alien cereals and pollens that were deposited in the soil as well. Decaying whale flesh and oil nourished the growth of closed grass vegetation in place of the original open moss cover. Gradually, more than a century after abandonment, the grass cover gave way again to open moss formations.

Pollen and other evidence obtained from stratified samples found in a peat section in a bird cliff four kilometers east of Smeerenberg permit reconstruction of local climate trends during the seventeenth century. These data reveal that the climate was cooling in 1615 and remained cool during the first half of the settlement period. Around 1645, the climate warmed

---

denotes a scavenged carcass, a whale divided between two ships, or a portion given up to a privateer. I have simply omitted the fractions in my calculations.

59. H. J. Zantkil, "Reconstructie van de behuizing op Smeerenburg," in *Walvisvaart in de gouden eeuw: Opgravingen op Spitsbergen,* edited by Louwrens Hacquebord and Wim Vroom (Amsterdam: De Bataafsche Leeuw, 1988). The article includes a black-and-white reproduction of a 1634 painting by Abraham Speeck, *Deens landstation aan de Noordelijke Ijszee* (The Land Station of the Northern Ice Sea), which depicts a Dutch tryworks (68).

60. Hacquebord, "The Rise and Fall of a Dutch Whaling-Settlement on the West Coast of Spitsbergen"; and Louwrens Hacquebord and Wim Vroom, *Walvisvaart in de gouden eeuw: Opgravingen op Spitsbergen* (Amsterdam: De Bataafsche Leeuw, 1988).

61. W. O. Van der Knaap, "De invloed van de landstations op hun directe omgeving; klimaatsverandering in de zeventiende eeuw," in *Walvisvaart in de gouden eeuw: Opgravingen op Spitsbergen,* edited by Louwrens Hacquebord and Wim Vroom (Amsterdam: De Bataafsche Leeuw, 1988).

somewhat during the last half of the settlement period, until 1660. After 1660, the climate cooled considerably, reaching a low point in 1670.[62] Chr. Vibe has suggested that the disappearance of bowhead whales from Spitsbergen and the abandonment of Smeerenberg resulted from a warming trend that permitted the whales to return to their normal summer grounds off the northeast coast of Greenland.[63] Since the climate by 1670 had become colder once again, this seems unlikely. That the whales who survived avoided the waters infested with whalers near Smeerenberg is a more likely scenario.

OPEN SEA AND DRIFT ICE WHALING

Between 1640 and 1670, all whalers were steadily forced away from sheltered coastal whaling into open waters. Whalers could no longer simply anchor offshore and send out their whaleboats to kill bowheads. The number of whales entering the bays of Spitsbergen and Jan Mayen Island dropped steadily as bowheads avoided areas where their fellows had been slaughtered. Pelagic whaling invariably led the whalers into the areas of drift ice favored by the bowhead. Whalers followed the borders of the drift ice west from Spitsbergen toward eastern Greenland. Aggressive pursuit of bowheads drew the whalers into difficult and risky navigation between giant ice floes and pack ice.

Whaling ships became more specialized and costly. The danger of collision with hidden ice formations forced redesign. The first special-purpose, fortified whaling ship was built in Amsterdam in 1660.[64] The new, more expensive ships had doubled planking on the hulls below the waterline and reinforced knees and ribs to withstand blows and pressure from ice. Every year, a few ships caught in the drift ice could not be freed and were abandoned by their crews. Generally, crew members moved onto the ice and waited in relative safety for rescue by fellow whalers. An elaborate set of rules quickly emerged that set out terms for proper treatment of such refugees.

At first, the open-sea whalers flensed their carcasses at sea and carried the blubber to be boiled on Spitsbergen and Jan Mayen Island. This expedient proved unsatisfactory as distances to the shore stations increased. The Dutch whalers then resorted to packing cut blubber into barrels and bringing it back for processing in their home ports. Amsterdam became a major processing and distribution center for whale oil. The tryworks at home were in-

62. Ibid., 145.

63. Vibe, "Animals, Climate, Hunters, and Whalers," 207.

64. C. De Jong, *Geschiedenis van de oude Nederlandse walvisvaart* (Pretoria: De Jong, 1972), 3:297.

dependent enterprises working on commission that processed other kinds of oil in the off-season.

The scale of Dutch whaling rose rapidly after the demise of the Noordsche Compagnie in 1642. With free entry into the industry, the number of whaling ships outfitted in the Netherlands more than doubled, to 70 in 1654, and doubled again, to 148 in 1670. In 1684, the Dutch Arctic whaling fleet reached its highest point. That year, 246 Dutch whalers sailed for Spitsbergen and captured 1,185 whales.[65]

Second to the Dutch were the Germans, whose interests closely converged with those of Dutch investors. As the Noordsche Compagnie dissolved, German shipowners from Hamburg, Bremen, and Emden began to outfit Arctic whalers, sometimes chartered Dutch vessels, and sent them out in considerable numbers. Hamburg developed tryworks to process bowhead blubber and distribution networks complementary to those of Amsterdam. From the 1640s, German whalers sailed to the Arctic nearly every season until the Napoleonic Wars. In the 1669 season, 37 whaling ships left Hamburg for the waters off Spitsbergen and returned with blubber from 260 whales.[66] In the peak year of 1684, German whalers brought 57 ships to the north, which killed 227 whales.

The Dutch also tolerated Danish whalers and permitted them to have a shore station on Spitsbergen. Christian IV of Denmark and Norway failed to sustain his claim to sovereignty over Spitsbergen, but Danish interest in extending whaling from Norway's North Cape continued. Between 1619 and 1622, Christian IV, acting as royal entrepreneur, sent several ships each year to Spitsbergen accompanied by a Danish warship. Christian IV did not use Danish ships but employed chartered Dutch ships and Basque whalers, and the proceeds were sold in Amsterdam. Thereafter, the Danish king issued licenses to Johan and Goddart Braem, two brothers who were Hamburg merchants, for a Danish monopoly on North Cape and Spitsbergen whaling.

Stiff Dutch opposition to these arrangements sharply curtailed Danish activities for a decade or more. Only after 1634 did the Danish company reach an accommodation with the Dutch Noordsche Compagnie and rebuild its shore stations at a new location on Danes Island called Copenhagen Bay. The Dutch and the Danes collaborated in sending armed naval vessels to drive French whalers from Spitsbergen. Even after the end of the Dutch monopoly in 1642, Goddart Braem kept the royal charter and monopoly for Danish whaling, until his death in 1655. By 1660, Danish investors had lost

65. Ibid.; De Jong, "The Hunt of the Greenland Whale," 91, table 1.

66. Harald Voigt, *Die Nordfriesen auf den Hamburger Wal- und Robbenfängern, 1669–1839, Studien zur Wirtschafts- und Sozialgeschichte Schleswig-Holsteins, Band 11* (Neumünster: K. Wachholtz, 1987), 25, 28.

enthusiasm, and dwindling profits brought closure to the Danish whaling effort. Throughout this period, Danish whaling voyages rarely exceeded five in a season and often numbered fewer than that.[67]

The Dutch and Germans were far more successful than the English and the French. After suffering considerable financial losses, the English Arctic whaling business declined precipitously in the 1620s. The Muscovy Company seems to have spent far more effort in fighting legal challenges from interloping English whalers at home than in developing its fleet. These problems were compounded by lessened demand for whale oil by English soap makers in London, who preferred oilseeds for their manufactures. Although occasionally English investors gambled on a whaling voyage, for the next century or more the English were a negligible presence in the hunt for bowheads.[68]

The French, despite Dutch hostility, remained active in Arctic whaling. In 1629, Cardinal Richelieu obtained a royal charter for a French company headed by the Basque whaler Jean Vrolicq, who commanded whalers sailing from French ports. The Dutch did not permit the French to set up shore stations on Spitsbergen and forced them into open-water whaling very early. The French also resorted to hunting for right whales near Iceland and Norway's North Cape. Lack of shore stations forced them to devise methods for trying whale oil on board ship.[69] Although little has been published about the French chartered company, it seems likely that it never operated more than a few whalers each year. The company survived until 1665, when its monopoly was ended.[70]

Freedom to engage in the industry did not attract many French investors and entrepreneurs in spite of the pool of expertise offered by the Basque port towns. Most French whalers sailed from Le Havre and Honfleur, not the Basque ports, and these were relatively few. Between 1668 and 1689, fifty-seven whalers returned to Le Havre and thirty-two whalers to Honfleur, for an average of only 4.2 voyages per year for the two ports.[71] Together, Le

67. Sune Dalgård, *Dansk-norsk hvalfangst, 1615–1660: En studie over Danmark-Norges stilling I europaeisk merkantil expansion* (København: G. E. C. Gad, 1962). An English summary is appended on pp. 419–29.

68. G. Jackson, "The Rise and Fall of English Whaling in the Seventeenth Century," in *Proceedings of the International Symposium, Early European Exploitation of the Northern Atlantic, 800–1700*, edited by Rijksuniversiteit te Groningen, Noordelijk Centrum (Groningen, Netherlands: Arctic Centre, University of Groningen, 1981). See also a description of an unsuccessful English voyage in 1656 in J. C. Appleby, "A 'Voyage to Greenland for the Catching of Whales.' "

69. Thierry Vincent and Nicolas-Victor Fromentin, *Le "Groënlandais": Trois-mats baleinier des mers polaires: Journal de bord du Capitaine Fromentin* (Luneray: Editions Bertout, 1994), 36.

70. Ibid., 57–58.

71. J. Thierry Du Pasquier, "The Whalers of Honfleur in the Seventeenth Century," *Arctic* 37, no. 4 (1984): 535.

Havre and Honfleur offered a much better market and distribution system for whale oil than did the Basque ports to the north.

French whalers tended to take larger catches than the Dutch. In seventeen voyages for which catch data exist, the total kill was 226 bowheads and right whales, with an average of 13.3 per ship—a much higher figure than for Dutch or German ships.[72] These higher totals primarily resulted from the Basque practice of boiling the blubber and storing it in casks on board ship before returning to port. This practice meant that they had room to store more whales. The French also stopped off in Iceland and hunted right whales more consistently than did the Dutch. In common with other European whalers, the French suffered remarkably few human casualties. Logbook notations for thirty-two voyages from Honfleur record that, among about thirteen hundred crewmen, only one man had been killed by a whale, three men had drowned, one man had been killed in a collision, and two men had died of illness.[73]

Beginning in 1661 in the Netherlands and 1669 in Germany, private individuals compiled detailed annual whaling statistics for the Greenland fishery. Each season as the whalers returned to Amsterdam, Hamburg, and other whaling ports, merchants, investors, and other interested parties recorded the particulars for each: the name and size of the ship; its commander; number of whales caught; output of blubber, whale oil, and baleen; and current prices. So popular was the practice that local printers even made up booklets with lists and columns to be filled in.[74] Those records preserved in archives permit a detailed reconstruction of the industry.

Arctic whaling became firmly emplaced in the consciousness of citizens of the Dutch Republic during its golden age. As we have seen, whaling was an important industry. Many Dutchmen had a direct economic interest in the industry either as investors or workers. However, what caught the popular imagination was the exotic appeal of dangerous voyages to the ice-filled seas of the far north to pursue marine animals as large as bowhead whales. Depicting northern whaling became a minor genre for Dutch painters and engravers. Examples of some of these paintings include *The Whaler "Prince William" on the River Maas, near Rotterdam,* by Lieve [Pietersz.] Verschuier (1630–1686), showing a whaler's safe return from the northern ice seas.[75] *Whaling in a Northern Ice Sea,* by Abraham van Salm (1660–1720), portrays eleven ships of a whaling fleet operating in an ice-filled northern sea. His

72. Ibid., 537, table 3.
73. Ibid., 534, table 1.
74. De Jong, "The Hunt of the Greenland Whale," 83.
75. George S. Keyes, Minneapolis Institute of Arts, Toledo Museum of Art, and Los Angeles County Museum of Art, *Mirror of Empire: Dutch Marine Art of Seventeenth Century* (Minneapolis: Minneapolis Institute of Arts; Cambridge: Cambridge University Press, 1990), 182–84.

painting shows the tails of two sounding whales pursued by men in boats and a ship caught in the ice and in the process of being abandoned by its crew.[76]

Despite increased costs and greater risks, open-water whale hunting in the drift ice between Greenland and Spitsbergen was successful and profitable. Dutch and German investors built and sent a rising number of specially designed ships to the Arctic. Between 1661 and 1719, the peak period for drift ice whaling in this region, Dutch and German whalers made 10,610 trips to the Arctic, averaging 176 voyages per year. Over the same period, 548 ships (5.2 percent) were lost in the ice or to privateers. Whales killed totaled 49,973, or an average of 832 bowheads per year. Whale blubber totaled just over 2 million tuns at an average of 40.3 tuns (1,145.3 liters per tun) per whale. Whale oil produced for the six decades was 4.9 million quarters *(kardels)*, or barrels, at 232.8 liters per unit.[77] The average yearly output was 82,822 quarters or 19.2 million liters of oil. To this figure, we must add a modest contribution from the French, essentially Basque, whalers and a few others. Cornelis De Jong's estimate that Dutch and German whalers caught 95 to 98 percent of the Greenland bowheads in this period is probably accurate.[78]

FREDERICK MARTENS

We possess a detailed firsthand account of a late-seventeenth-century Greenland whaling voyage, compiled and later published by Frederick Martens, a native of Hamburg. His text, although relatively brief, illustrates the matter-of-fact experience of European whalers engaged in what had become a routine extractive enterprise in the ice-filled northern oceans. In addition, Martens was an intellectual who participated in European scientific reporting about distant regions. Following his narrative of the voyage, Martens's account contains a lengthy set of responses to a list of questions about Spitsbergen's weather, land, flora, and fauna posed by Henry Oldenburg, secretary of the Royal Society in London.[79]

76. Ibid., 144–46.
77. Calculated by De Jong, "The Hunt of the Greenland Whale," 98, table 9, n. 2.
78. Ibid., 91.
79. Adam White et al., *A Collection of Documents on Spitzbergen [sic] and Greenland* (London: Hakluyt Society, 1855), iii–v. Another firsthand account is to be found in the memoirs of Johann Dietz, also a German and a surgeon and barber. In a Hamburg tavern in the late 1680s, three Dutch mariners recruited Dietz from his post as a surgeon-barber to serve as ship's surgeon for the *Hoffnung*, a whaler from Rotterdam, at a wage of twelve thalers per month and rations. The *Hoffnung*, a well-armed Dutch whaler with twenty-six guns, sailed for Spitsbergen with a forty-five man crew. The *Hoffnung* had good fortune and killed nine bowhead whales and one right whale (in Dutch, a Nordkaper) in a relatively short time. This catch "was a remarkable success. It meant also a great deal of money for the ship, for one fish may richly repay all the expenses and still leave something over." Johann Dietz, Bernard Miall, and Ernst Consentius, *Master Jo-*

During the whaling season of 1671, Martens sailed as a ship's surgeon on the *Jonas im Walfisch,* captained by Peter Peterson of Friesland. The ship left the Elbe River at noon on April 15, heading north by northeast. By April 27, the ship had reached pack ice at the seventy-first parallel, turned back, and arrived within ten miles of Jan Mayen Island. Over the next ten days, it traced the ice border heading for Spitsbergen. Martens notes that, two days out from the archipelago, "we saw daily many ships, sailing about the ice: I observed that as they passed by one another, they hailed one another, crying Holla and asked each other how many fish they had caught. . . . When they have their full fraight of whales, they put up their great flag as a sign thereof: then if any hath a message to be sent, he delivers it to them." They had arrived in a region where the frost was constant, despite the summer sun that did not set, and where "their teeth chatter in their heads commonly, and the appetite is greater than in any other countreys."[80]

The *Jonas im Walfisch* did not put in to land when it reached Spitsbergen on May 7, but joined other whalers at sea to hunt for bowhead. On May 14, in sunny, calm weather, states Martens, "we told twenty ships about us" at "seventy-five degrees and twenty-two minutes." That same day, they spotted a whale and sent four boats after the animal, but lost it when it dived. On May 21, the *Jonas* sailed into the ice along with another Hamburg ship, the *Lepeler,* where both whalers fixed their ice hooks to "a large ice-field" and joined another thirty whaling ships in a "harbour or haven" in the ice-pack. On May 30, the captain of the *Jonas* sent out his "great sloop" further into the ice, where the party heard a whale blow and succeeded in killing it—their first catch of the season. They brought the whale back to the ship, where it yielded seventy barrels of fat. That same night, another captain lost his ship when it was crushed between two sheets of ice.[81]

On June 4, they missed yet another whale that dove precipitously, for there were so many ships in the vicinity that "one hunted the whales to the other, so they were frighted and became very shy." By June 13, they were sailing "somewhat easterly towards Spitzbergen," when "that night we saw more than twenty whales, that run one after another towards the ice; out of them we got our second fish, which was a male one; and this fish, when they

hann Dietz, Surgeon in the Army of the Great Elector and Barber to the Royal Court: From the Old Manuscript in the Royal Library of Berlin (London: Allen and Unwin; New York: Dutton, 1923), 122. With this success, the captain and crew, including Dietz, were able to go ashore at Spitsbergen and indulge in such diversions as a reindeer hunt. This good fortune extended to the return voyage, when the *Hoffnung* narrowly escaped being seized by a French raider. On Dietz's second voyage with the *Hoffnung* the next season, the catch was only five whales due to a near disaster in the northern ice that forced an early return. Dietz's account, somewhat more entertaining, agrees with Martens in nearly every detail.

80. Ibid., 4, 38.
81. Ibid., 5–6.

wounded him with lances, bled very much, so that the sea was tinged by it where he swam."[82]

The *Jonas* reached Spitsbergen on June 14 and anchored in South Bay. Here, they flensed the whale taken the day before, which yielded sixty-five barrels of fat. That night they sent out three boats into the English bay where they harpooned and lanced a whale but lost it under the ice. They did come across "two great sea-horses" (walruses) asleep on a sheet of ice, which they lanced and killed. On June 22, still at Spitsbergen, the men of the *Jonas* killed their third whale from among six that were sighted: "This fish was killed by one man, who flung the harpoon into him; and killed him also, while the other boats were busy in pursuing or hunting another whale. This fish run [*sic*] to the ice, and before he died beat about with his tail; the ice settled about him, so that the other boats could not come to this boat to assist him, till the ice separated again that they might row, when they tied one boat to another, and so towed the whale to the great ship." The carcass gave up forty-five barrels of blubber.

On June 29, they scavenged "a great quantity of the fat of a whale, three vessels [boats] full" that had been left by a whaler caught in the ice. On July 1, a *Jonas* boat crew harpooned a female bowhead who was "beating about with her tail and fins, so that we durst not come near to lance her." The stricken whale struck one harpooner with her tail "over his back so vehemently, that he had much ado to recover his breath again." The whale overturned another boat that approached her, "so that, the harpoonier was forced to dive for it, and hide his head under the water; the rest did the same; they thought it very long before they came out, for it was cold, so that they came quaking to the ship again." This seems to have been the fourth whale taken.[83] The same day they just missed one whale and lost another to a Dutch whaler that succeeded in harpooning him first.

In rapid succession, they took, on July 2, the fifth, a male bowhead, and two days later the sixth, another male. The latter filled forty-five barrels. During these days, notes Martens, "we saw more whales than we did in all our voyage."[84] On July 5, they struck another whale, which broke the harpoon line against a rock and escaped, but then the same day they killed the seventh whale, a female that yielded forty-five barrels.

In a brief respite, the *Jonas* dropped anchor in a sheltered Spitsbergen bay to cut up and put in barrels large pieces of blubber from two whales that had simply been flung in the hold in the press of the hunt. Cruising again on July 9, they took their eighth bowhead and "filled with him fifty-four kardels of fat." On July 12, they killed three polar bears swimming in the water and then

82. Ibid., 7.
83. Ibid., 9.
84. Ibid., 10.

rowed up to a herd of walruses resting on the ice and killed ten of them, but not without protest. The remaining walruses "came all about our boat, and beat holes through the sides of the boat, so that we took in an abundance of water; were forced at length to row away. . . . They pursued us as long as we could see them, very furiously."[85]

The *Jonas* continued to sail up and down the Spitsbergen coast, among drifting ice, but bowheads were becoming scarce in these waters. On July 15 the *Jonas im Walfisch* entered South Harbor, where twenty-eight whalers—eight German and twenty Dutch—lay at anchor.

A week later, on July 22, the *Jonas im Walfisch* left South Harbor for the un-eventful voyage home. On August 20, the ship took on a Hamburg munici-pal pilot near Heligoland, and on August 29, it anchored in the Elbe River after a four-and-a-half-month absence. The hold was filled with at least four hundred sixty-four-gallon barrels of fat from the eight bowhead whales killed. Another two bowheads had been hit and wounded by harpoons and lances but not taken. The fat was processed into whale oil at Hamburg for sale in European markets. The whalebone, carefully extracted from each car-cass, "doth only belong to the owners of the ship and the others that run their hazard, whether they catch few or many whales. The rest [i.e., the officers and crew], which take their pay by the month, receive their money when they come home whether they have caught many or none, and the loss or gain falls upon the merchants."[86]

THE EXPANDED EIGHTEENTH-CENTURY HUNT

During the first half of the seventeenth century, the Noordsche Compagnie had sent several expeditions to the west of Greenland in a futile search for a northwest passage to Asia or, failing that, valuable minerals, whales, seals, or other opportunities. In tandem with these exploratory ventures, Dutch traders, mostly from the North Sea island of Terschelling, began a modest barter trade with the Inuits of Greenland's west coast. They organized and equipped smaller vessels of fifty to one hundred tons, assembled ten- to fifteen-man crews, and stocked European consumption goods and tools as trade goods. Departing early in February or March, they made the long voy-age to Greenland's west coast, where the Inuits bartered whale and seal blub-ber, whalebone, walrus and narwhale tusks, and furs for European products. The trading vessels also carried two whaleboats and equipment to hunt whales if the opportunity arose. In 1720, a Terschelling Island captain, Lourens Feykes Haan, codified the accumulated knowledge of western

85. Ibid., 11.
86. Ibid., 129.

Greenland by publishing in Amsterdam a detailed description of the lands and people of the strait.[87]

By the 1720s, Dutch-Inuit trade was steadily declining as Denmark sent settlers and assumed formal colonial powers in Greenland. Official disapproval by Danish authorities increased risks and reduced returns to the Dutch traders. Danish authorities, who wanted to reserve trading profits for their own nationals, argued that the barter trade "was morally prejudicial to the Inuit."[88] Largely in response to this pressure, the Terschelling Island trading captains switched to open-water whaling in the Davis Strait. News of abundant stocks of bowheads in this region filtered out to other whaling captains and investors whose catches off eastern Greenland and Spitsbergen were in a temporary slump.

In 1719, unofficial whaling statistics began to record voyages and whales taken in the Davis Strait as a separate category. The western whaling grounds became an important addition to the Greenland fishery but never fully replaced or even equaled the eastern grounds. During the 1720s, Dutch whaling voyages to the Davis Strait averaged 148 per year, compared to 258 per year made to the eastern whaling grounds. In the 1730s, the numbers were nearly equal; and in the 1740s, the balance had shifted heavily again, with an average 246 voyages per year to the eastern whaling grounds and only 64 to the west.[89]

With the additional catch afforded by the Davis Strait whaling grounds, Dutch and German whalers brought back profitable cargoes of whale blubber to Amsterdam and Hamburg for the rest of the century. No technical or business innovations occurred; the whaling fleets followed long-standing routes and long-established procedures. Between 1720 and 1800, Dutch and German whalers averaged 169 voyages per year to both eastern and western Greenland, for a total of 13,501 trips. In an average year, they killed 498 whales, whose carcasses produced 24,819 barrels of oil. The aggregate catch was 39,833 bowhead and right whales, for a total of 2 million barrels of whale oil placed on European markets.

In the 1780s, both Dutch and German whaling went into rapid decline. By the 1790s, only one-fifth the previous number of Dutch whalers sailed to the Arctic and no German voyages are recorded. The total catch declined accordingly. By this time, new competition from British and Scandinavian whalers began to press hard against the Dutch. The British, Danish, and Swedish governments put up handsome subsidies to encourage their own whaling fleets, and they heavily taxed imports of foreign whale oil.

British blockades and seizures put an end to voyages during the

---

87. De Jong, *Geschiedenis van de oude Nederlandse walvisvaart*, 3:303.
88. Ibid.
89. De Jong, "The Hunt of the Greenland Whale," 92, table 2.

Napoleonic Wars as the Royal Navy blockaded the French-held Netherlands from 1795 to 1813. In 1798, when thirty-one Dutch whalers tried to sail under neutral flags, the British seized twenty-nine of the vessels. Neither Dutch nor German whaling recovered, even after the liberation of the Netherlands in 1814 and restoration of peace in Europe.

BRITISH WHALING AND THE FINAL DEMISE OF THE GREENLAND BOWHEAD

Between the mid–seventeenth and mid–eighteenth centuries, various attempts to organize British whaling companies and make them profitable ended in failure. Britain's poor showing in northern whaling became a matter of injured national pride. If the Dutch could succeed in this lucrative endeavor, why could not British mariners and investors? One of the most vocal proponents of restored Greenland whaling was Henry Elking, who published in 1722 his *A View of the Greenland Trade and Whale Fishery, with the National and Private Advantages Thereof*, in which he argued forcefully that the Dutch, Germans, French, and Spaniards "are made rich" from whaling.[90] Even if the domestic British market was presently well supplied with whale oil, "we know how many other parts of Europe want the train oil, and the soap boiled of the same," which could be efficiently and cheaply supplied by British enterprise.[91]

Finally, in 1724, Elking received approval for a Greenland venture. Armed with a massive amount of capital, Elking commissioned new ships, docks, and warehouses and hired whaling specialists. In the course of eight years and 172 whaling voyages, his whalers brought back only 160 whales—far from enough to pay start-up expenses. In 1731, Elking ended the experiment.

This failure convinced Parliament that greater encouragement from the state was needed. In 1733, Parliament offered an annual subsidy or bounty of twenty shillings per ton for each British whaler exceeding two hundred tons capacity equipped and sent to the Arctic. When this did not work, the official rate increased to thirty shillings per ton in 1740 and finally to forty shillings in 1749.[92] At that threshold, investors' risk was much reduced and a boom in Arctic whaling began. From an average of four British voyages to

90. Quoted in G. Jackson, *The British Whaling Trade* (Hamden, Conn.: Archon Books, 1978), 42. See Henry Elking, *A View of the Greenland Trade and Whale Fishery, with the National and Private Advantages Thereof.* In *A Select Collection of Scarce and Valuable Economical Tracts, from the Originals of Defoe, Elking, Franklin, Turgot, Anderson, Schomberg, Townsend, Burke, Bell, and Others; with a Preface, Notes, and Index*, edited by J. R. McCulloch (London: n.p., 1859); William Scoresby, *An Account of the Arctic Regions, with a History and Description of the Northern Whale-Fishery*, reprint of the 1st ed. (Newton Abbot: David and Charles, 1969), 2:98–109.

91. Jackson, *The British Whaling Trade*, 43.

92. Scoresby, *An Account of the Arctic Regions, with a History and Description of the Northern Whale-Fishery*, 2:109.

Greenland each year, for the next quarter century (1750–1776) the average jumped to 57 voyages per year and, despite a slow decrease in the rate of subsidy, voyages more than tripled, to an average of 171 by the early 1790s.[93]

British northern whaling was once again competitive with the Dutch and German industry. Although London continued to fit out the greater number of whalers, a number of new ports formed private whaling companies. Liverpool, Whitby, Hull, and other English northern ports had a decided advantage in terms of location. This was even truer of Aberdeen and other Scottish ports, from which the round-trip distance to Greenland waters was much shorter.[94]

Between 1733 and 1800, British whalers made 4,006 voyages to the ice fields, killed approximately twelve thousand whales, and produced 1.4 million hectoliters (608,447 quarters or 123,688 English tuns) of whale oil and 5,303 metric tons of whalebone.[95] By the end of the century, the British exchequer had paid 1.98 million pounds sterling in subsidies to whalers.

During the Napoleonic Wars, the bowhead whale gained a respite. Whaling ventures during the two decades between 1795 and 1815 were intermittent and much reduced. When peace returned, however, the avid hunt for whales resumed. British, rather than Dutch or German, whalers dominated the final phase of Arctic whaling. Within thirty years, by midcentury, British whalers had exterminated the last remaining bowhead whales—the Spitsbergen stocks—to be found in the Atlantic.[96]

As postwar whaling renewed, reduced numbers of increasingly wary whale stocks forced British whalers into new grounds. By 1817, they entered the

93. Jackson, *The British Whaling Trade*, 264, appendix 3.

94. W. R. H. Duncan, "Aberdeen and the Early Development of the Whaling Industry, 1750–1800," *Northern Scotland* 3 (1977–1978).

95. Jackson, *The British Whaling Trade*, 264, appendix 3. English tuns of whale oil have been converted to the older quarter, or barrel, at 4.92 to the tun. These are volume measures. (Based on De Jong, "The Hunt of the Greenland Whale," 98, n. 2, in which a quarter is equal to 232.8 liters and a tun to 1,145.3 liters.) Historians of British whaling have not compiled the actual number of whales killed in the eighteenth century, although those data are available in logbooks and other primary sources. The number for whales killed is calculated by a ratio of 10.2 English tuns of oil, or 50.2 barrels of oil, per whale taken from the aggregate Dutch and German figures above for the same period.

96. The western Arctic stocks of bowhead whales in the Bering, Chukchi, and Beaufort Seas were left relatively undisturbed until American whalers found their way into that region in the 1840s. The estimated population of twenty thousand to forty thousand bowheads declined steadily until the industry collapsed in the early twentieth century. John R. Bockstoce and Daniel B. Botkin, "The Historical Status and Reduction of the Western Arctic Bowhead Whale *(Balaena mysticetus)* Population by the Pelagic Whaling Industry, 1848–1914," in *Historical Whaling Records: Including the Proceedings of the International Workshop on Historical Whaling Records, Sharon, Massachusetts, September 12–16, 1977*, edited by Michael F. Tillman, Gregory P. Donovan, and the International Whaling Commission (Cambridge, Eng.: International Whaling Commission, 1983).

dangerous waters of Baffin Bay and pressed on to the Canadian archipelago. British whalers sailed earlier in the season to intercept the earliest bowhead migrants, largely the nursing and immature animals, before they reached the dense drift ice in the north. Between 1815 and 1842, British whalers made 2,634 voyages, during which they killed 21,548 bowhead whales. From this northern fishery (as distinguished from the pursuit of the sperm whale in southern oceans), their efforts generated 2.8 million hectoliters (1.2 million quarters or 238,460 tuns) of whale oil and 12,249 metric tons of whalebone.[97] The whale oil became especially useful as a cheap fuel to light municipal street lamps, which, for the first time, were being introduced in British and European cities.

THE ANCILLARY HUNT FOR WALRUSES

Throughout the whaling grounds around Spitsbergen and the Davis Strait, whalers continually encountered large assemblages of walruses. They treated them with caution because the animals, when affronted, attacked small boats, using their bulk and swimming speed of up to thirty-five kilometers per hour to great effect. However, Eskimo, and later European, hunters found that walruses which had hauled out of the water onto pack ice or beaches were vulnerable. Hunters could thrust sharp iron lances or whaling harpoons through the tough hides of the walruses into their chest cavities and kill them. If their lances were long enough—up to three meters—this could be done by surprise with little danger to the hunter.

During the walrus summer breeding season, which, after 1600, coincided with the summer whaling voyages, whalers who reached Spitsbergen and other islands nearby found large numbers of walruses hauled out of the water. The walruses favored sandy, flat bays in well-protected fjords that were easy to reach at flood tide.[98] Since each walrus carcass produced about two hundred kilograms of blubber that could be boiled down to about a standard barrel of oil and pass for whale oil, whalers had some incentive to kill walruses if easily done. This might be a matter of killing a few animals simply to round out a load of whale blubber. Alternatively, it might mean on occasion a wholesale slaughter to take on nearly a full cargo of walrus blubber instead of whales. Whalers also took walrus tusks and sold them when they returned home.

Early in the seventeenth century, English whalers drove the annual walrus breeding herds away from their usual sandy beaches on Bear Island. In July 1604, an English whaling ship that landed on Bear Island found over

97. Totals calculated from Jackson, *The British Whaling Trade,* 270, appendix 9.
98. Nils Stora, "Russian Walrus Hunting in Spitsbergen," *Études/Inuit/Studies* 11, no. 2 (1987): 117–38.

1,000 walruses pulled out on the beaches. They killed 100 of them. The next year, in July 1605, the same ship was back to kill between 700 to 800 walruses. Three years later, the same ship returned in summer 1608 to slaughter 900 animals in only seven hours. In the 1610 season, English whalers killed another 800 walruses. Thereafter, walruses did not return to Bear Island to breed for many years.[99] Despite this and other similar assaults, however, it was more cost-effective to kill whales than to pursue walruses for their blubber.

The most avid walrus hunters on Spitsbergen and the other islands of the Svalbard Archipelago were the Russians, who did not participate in commercial whaling. Since at least as early as the tenth century, hunters from the region of Pomor on the White Sea had killed walruses for the European market. They sold hides and tusks to Norsemen and other medieval European seafarers who found their way around the North Cape to buy ivory and tusks, probably at the mouth of the Dvina River.[100] Walrus ivory from northern Russia—with tusks that could reach half a meter in length and weigh five or more kilograms—was used for knife, sword, and dagger handles and other carved durable objects. Walrus hides, cut into strips, made extremely strong cart straps and durable harnesses and ships' rigging. By the early sixteenth century, English traders from the Muscovy Company were buying these products at Archangel on the Dvina River.

As late as the sixteenth century, walruses still could be obtained in and around the White Sea, especially at the mouth of the Pechora River and along Kostin Sound. However, Russian walrus hunters had begun to sail north to Spitsbergen to hunt the far more numerous walruses in the Svalbard Archipelago. By the seventeenth century, walruses were so depleted in the White Sea region that the entire Russian effort shifted north. Moscow's efforts to centralize all Siberian trade at the capital prevented hunting in Siberian waters. In 1620, the Russian tsar issued an edict that forbade inhabitants of the Dvina and Pechora River areas from sailing east to the Kara Sea and entering Siberia by that route.

Instead, throughout the period from about 1600 to as late as 1830, Russian hunters sailed every year to the Svalbard Archipelago. Some Russian hunters who stayed only during the summer season were financed by peasant villages. Those more expensive expeditions that wintered year-round required funds from traders. Several Old Believer orthodox monasteries, most notably the island monastery of Solovetsk, funded and organized regular hunting expeditions, manning them with monks and lay adherents.

The annual fleet was composed of 60- to 160-ton sailing and rowing vessels (*lodya*) capable of bringing back substantial loads. Each carried teams of fifteen to twenty-five hunters led by a master hunter. The ships set out on the

99. Ibid., 131.
100. Ibid., 120–21.

voyage to Spitsbergen in June or July, arriving up to fifty days later. Those who did not winter returned with their catch at the end of September. Those who stayed over returned in October of the following year, some fifteen months after their departure. During the summer, the hunters relied on finding walruses on the beaches, where they could kill great numbers of them while they were sleeping. Generally, Russian hunters only took the heads with the tusks and skins, which filled their small boats, and left the walrus blubber.

Those hunters who stayed over took shelter at about ten or so established main camps, using either prefabricated huts brought on the boats or occupying huts still standing. They used stone or brick stoves fed by driftwood. They actively hunted walruses in small boats, moving among the ice floes to find them where they had hauled out on the ice. The hunting teams also sought out and killed seals and beluga whales *(Delphinapterus leucas)* for oil and skins and eiders *(Somateria mollissima)* for down. All these activities began in February, when daylight returned, and continued until November and the onset of the polar night. By that time, the ice on the fjords, snow blizzards, and darkness made it impossible to hunt on the water. Instead, the Russians turned their attention to trapping and killing polar bears and arctic foxes for their fur.[101]

Around the end of the eighteenth century, observers counted about 270 ships with twenty-two hundred Russian hunters gathered during the summer season at Spitsbergen.[102] What their annual catch might have amounted to is impossible to estimate. We do have figures from one Russian hunting party that wintered on Spitsbergen in 1784–1785. When they returned, they had tusks and hides from 300 walruses as well as oil and skins from 230 seals, 150 polar bear skins, and 1,000 fox skins. They carried 300 kilograms of eiderdown. They also had killed 100 beluga whales and 1 larger whale, presumably a bowhead.[103] If this level of efficiency were typical, then it is surprising that walruses and other prey animals persisted in the Svalbard Archipelago as long as they did. It was not until about 1850 that walruses were extinct in these marine ecosystems.

ECONOMIC BENEFITS

Europe received large material benefits from its slaughter of the Greenland whale. The massive living biomass of the bowhead whale was a resource free for the taking. Whaling was an industry that extracted from the flesh of wild

101. Mark E. Jasinski, "Russian Hunters on Svalbard and the Polar Winter," *Arctic* 44, no. 2 (1991).

102. Stora, "Russian Walrus Hunting in Spitsbergen," 126.

103. Ibid., 119.

animals a needed industrial commodity. Whales provided an extraordinary energy link between the smallest phytoplankton swarms of the northern oceans and humans. The whaler's costs were those of the hunter, not those of the pastoralist. The demand for oil suitable for use in lamps, for soap making, for curing leather, and for lubrication of machinery grew steadily.

Arctic whaling displayed the characteristic pattern of commercially driven resource extraction. No allowance was made for any sort of conservation or sustainable use of these stocks. The Arctic bowhead herds became an open-access resource without any discernible management or restraint on the part of the users. From the early sixteenth century to the mid–nineteenth, as bowheads were killed off, the whalers shifted to more and more distant, difficult, and dangerous regions. To move from shore whaling off Labrador to drift ice hunting in Baffin Bay challenged the skill and daring of whalers, who routinely sailed where no one had ever sailed ships of that size before.

Over the entire period, and in each phase of the hunt, there was a slow reduction in productivity as the number and size of whales caught declined. For example, in the 1670s, each Dutch whaling ship took an average each year of 6.4 whales and brought home on average 279.5 metric tons of blubber. One hundred years later, in the 1770s, the annual average catch per ship was only 2.2 animals that yielded 100.7 tons of blubber.[104] Whaling became more costly and uncertain but remained profitable until the final years of each phase.

Despite productivity trends, supplies of whale oil proved to be reliably available and consistently price-competitive with vegetable and other sources for oils in the early modern market. From 1661 to 1800, Dutch and German whalers brought back to Europe blubber sufficient to produce 5 million barrels of whale oil (11.6 million hectoliters). Replacing the whale oil consumed in the European economy every year with vegetable oil would have placed heavy demands on agriculture. Thousands of hectares of land would have been devoted to growing rape and other oilseeds in addition to or at the expense of growing food grains or other edibles. The thousands of tons of whalebone that landed in European ports became a consumption material that had no real equal in flexibility, strength, and versatility until the arrival of plastics in the late nineteenth century.

By any of the standard economic measures, whaling was more than a niche or specialty enterprise. The industry made a substantial contribution to the economy of early modern Europe. Chartering, insuring, provisioning, and supplying equipment to the combined Dutch and German whaling fleets each year demanded a heavy investment. By one estimate contempo-

104. De Jong, "The Hunt of the Greenland Whale," 99, table 11B.

rary to the time, preparing the typical Dutch whaler of the early eighteenth century to make the voyage cost 12,500 guilders: 6,500 Dutch guilders for casks, provisions, whaleboats, and gear; 3,000 guilders for the hire of the ship and insurance; and 3,000 guilders for payment of the forty-two-man crew.[105] If in an average year 175 ships sailed to the Arctic from Dutch and German ports, the initial investment needed was about 2 million guilders. This was a considerable sum if we consider that total private capital in the Netherlands in 1650 is estimated at 500 to 550 million guilders.[106]

Employment generated by whaling remained consistently high. Direct employment of seamen averaged around eighty-five hundred men per whaling season for the combined Dutch and German fleets in the seventeenth and eighteenth centuries.[107] Indirect employment of coopers, smiths, warehousemen, blubber boilers, shipyard workers, ships' chandlers, traders, and others was probably equal to that figure. Demand for whale oil and whalebone rose steadily. The price of whale oil, amid fluctuations, doubled from 35 guilders per quarter in the 1660s to 62 in the 1770s; whalebone nearly tripled, from 48 to 120 guilders per hundredweight in the same period.[108] Dozens of whale oil refineries and soap factories grew up along the Zaan River opposite Amsterdam and in Rotterdam. France imported by far the greatest share of Dutch refined whale-oil exports.[109]

Was Arctic whaling profitable for the nation? Certainly, contemporaries and near-contemporaries thought so. Early modern European states repeatedly sent warships to escort their whaling vessels, waived customs duties on incoming whale blubber, offered royal monopolies to whaling entrepreneurs, organized state-run whaling companies, and even offered subsidies to

105. Scoresby, *An Account of the Arctic Regions, with a History and Description of the Northern Whale-Fishery*, 2:150. Scoresby, a British whaling captain himself, relied on the statistical work of the Dutch whaling historian Cornelis Zorgdrager, who published his results in the eighteenth century. Cornelis Gijsbertsz Zorgdrager and Georg Peter Monath, *Beschreibung des groenlaendischen Wallfischfangs und Fischerey, nebst einer gründlichen Nachricht von dem Bakkeljau- und Stockfischfang bey Terreneuf und einer kurzen Abhandlung von Groenland, Island, Spitzbergen, Nova Zembla, Jan Mayen Eiland, der Strasse Davids u. a.* (Nuernberg: G. P. Monath, 1750). In his own calculations, Scoresby used the lower figure of 10,000 guilders suggested by another eighteenth-century Dutch student of whaling.

106. Jan Luiten Van Zanden, "Economic Growth in the Golden Age: The Development of the Economy of Holland, 1500–1650," in *The Dutch Economy in the Golden Age*, edited by Karel Davids and L. Noordegraaf (Amsterdam: Nederlandsch Economisch-Historisch Archief, 1993), 23, table 10.

107. Calculated at an average of forty-two men per crew for recorded sailings in the period 1670–1770. See De Jong, "The Hunt of the Greenland Whale," 91, table 1.

108. Scoresby, *An Account of the Arctic Regions, with a History and Description of the Northern Whale-Fishery*, 2:156.

109. Jonathan I. Israel, *Dutch Primacy in World Trade, 1585–1740* (Oxford: Clarendon Press; New York: Oxford University Press, 1990), 115, 268, 285–86.

encourage the industry. The Dutch were much envied and admired for their skill and profits.

William Scoresby, using Dutch statistical data, calculated for the period 1669–1778 that Dutch whalers received 274.8 million guilders for whale oil and whalebone at prevailing prices. Their expenses—including allowance for lost ships—totaled 218.6 million guilders, leaving a gross profit of 56.2 million guilders. This works out to an average of 525,523 guilders average profit per year on expenditures of slightly over 2 million guilders, or 26.2 percent.[110] This figure is probably high, as Scoresby admits, because his figure of 10,000 guilders per ship for expenditures is on the low side. If he had allowed a higher figure for construction and ownership of the vessels, the profit margin "would have been reduced to near one-half" or 12 to 13 percent.[111]

Obviously, as later historians have commented, this kind of all-encompassing calculation disguises short-term fluctuations and losses. Nevertheless, year after year, European investors put large sums of capital into building or renting, fitting out, manning, and sailing whalers to the Arctic. At the end of the day, the biomass of the Arctic translated into energy and profits for Europeans.

CONCLUSION

What were the environmental effects of three centuries of mayhem inflicted by European hunters on the walrus and the Greenland bowhead whale? (See table 16.1.) Human predation killed off both species in that region. From an original herd size estimated at 25,000 animals, the Atlantic walrus disappeared completely from the marine ecosystem around Spitsbergen by 1870.[112] No estimate for average or annual kills is really possible, but descriptive evidence implies incessant hunting, especially by Russian hunters, as well as ongoing kills by whalers seeking to round out their cargoes of whale oil.

Removal of 36,000 bowhead and 25,000 walruses from the marine ecosys-

110. Scoresby, *An Account of the Arctic Regions, with a History and Description of the Northern Whale-Fishery,* 2:157. I have combined the totals for the Greenland and Davis Straits fisheries that Scoresby separated out.
111. Ibid.
112. Louwrens Hacquebord, "Three Centuries of Whaling and Walrus Hunting in Svalbard and Its Impact on the Arctic Ecosystem," *Environment and History* 7 (2001): 176–77. Hacquebord offers the larger figure of 46,000 as the preexploitation herd size for bowhead whales, but assumes a lower annual food consumption figure of 76 metric tons per animal to arrive at 3.5 million tons of zooplankton consumed yearly.

TABLE 3   Greenland Whales Killed, 1500–1800

	Dutch	Germans	English	French	Basques	Danes	Total
1530–1607	—	—	—	—	25,000	—	25,000
1607–1661	24,000	—	2,000	2,000	2,000	1,000	31,000
1661–1719	31,000	11,000	—	3,000	2,000	—	47,000
1719–1800	34,500	5,500	—	1,000	1,000	—	42,000
1800–1850	1,000	—	16,500	—	—	—	17,500
TOTAL	90,500	16,500	18,500	6,000	30,000	1,000	162,500

tem made some 4 million metric tons of additional food available each year for other organisms. Bowhead whales feeding on tiny crustaceans or zooplankton consume about one hundred metric tons per animal per year. The beneficiaries of the whales' disappearance were polar cod *(Boreogadus saida)* and capelin *(Mallotus villosus)* as well as planktonivorous seabirds like little auks *(Alle alle)*. When cod and capelin increased, the numbers of fish-eating seabirds such as Brunnich's guillemots *(Uria lomvia)* and common guillemots *(Cepphus grylle)* must have risen. The same is true of the cod-eating populations of Greenland seals *(Phoca groenlandica)* and minke whales *(Balaenoptera acutorostrata).*[113] Walruses feed on bivalves and decapod crustaceans, annually consuming, on average, around 20 metric tons per year per animal.[114] Their disappearance freed up food for bearded seals *(Erignathus barbatus)* and diving ducks such as eiders.

From a herd in the eastern Arctic originally made up of about 36,000 large animals that live forty years or more, Europeans killed between 150,000 and 200,000 bowhead whales. Logbook data from whalers suggest that between 15 and 20 percent of the whales struck were lost.[115] Of these many, if not most, were presumed to have died of their wounds. Year after year, several hundred whales were slaughtered in a harrying that surely disrupted and reduced their slow reproductive cycles. (See table 16.2.)

For animals that had few natural predators and few mortal dangers to overcome in the course of their long lives, human predation must have been

113. Ibid., 178.
114. Hacquebord, "Three Centuries of Whaling and Walrus Hunting in Svalbard and Its Impact on the Arctic Ecosystem," 176.
115. Woodby and Botkin, "Stock Sizes Prior to Commercial Whaling," 393.

TABLE 4 Peak Dutch and German Whaling, 1661–1800 (by Dates Ships Sailed)

| | 1661–1719 | | | | | | | |
| | Dates Ships Sailed | | | | | | | |
	1661–1669	1670–1679	1680–1689	1690–1699	1700–1709	1710–1719	Totals	Annual Averages
Number of ships								
German	0	561	553	492	544	573	2,723	45
Dutch	970	985	1,922	944	1,631	1,435	7,887	131
TOTAL	970	1,546	2,475	1,436	2,175	2,008	10,610	177
Ships lost								
German	0	19	26	36	44	15	140	2
Dutch	19	80	114	79	61	55	408	7
TOTAL	19	99	140	115	105	70	548	9
Whales caught								
German	0	3,747	2,376	1,129	2,343	1,431	11,026	184
Dutch	4,815	6,325	9,529	5,474	7,982	4,822	38,947	649
TOTAL	4,815	10,072	11,905	6,603	10,325	6,253	49,973	833
Tuns of blubber								
German	0	186,084	101,295	48,569	81,164	54,175	471,287	7,855
Dutch	231,565	275,304	370,190	209,982	279,439	176,274	1,542,754	25,713
TOTAL	231,565	461,388	471,485	258,551	360,603	230,449	2,014,041	33,567
Tuns of blubber per whale	48	46	40	39	35	37	40	
Whale oil (in quarters)								
German	0	279,126	151,943	72,854	121,746	78,263	703,932	11,732
Dutch	347,348	412,956	555,285	314,973	419,159	264,411	2,314,132	38,569
TOTAL	347,348	692,082	707,228	387,827	540,905	342,674	3,018,064	50,301

1720–1800

| | Dates Ships Sailed | | | | | | | | | Annual |
---	1720–1729	1730–1739	1740–1749	1750–1759	1760–1769	1770–1779	1780–1789	1790–1799	Totals	Averages
Number of ships										
German	427	401	222	215	273	302	376	0	2,216	28
Dutch	2,239	1,847	1,712	1,677	1,620	1,289	541	360	11,285	141
TOTAL	2,666	2,248	1,934	1,892	1,893	1,591	917	360	13,501	169
Ships lost										
German	17	10	3	9	3	10	6	0	58	1
Dutch	57	34	28	36	26	37	5	31	254	4
TOTAL	74	44	31	45	29	47	11	31	312	5
Whales caught										
German	1,077	544	563	503	589	889	1,306	0	5,471	91
Dutch	4,762	4,386	8,011	5,336	4,500	3,878	2,697	792	34,362	573
TOTAL	5,839	4,930	8,574	5,839	5,089	4,767	4,003	792	39,833	664
Tuns of blubber										
German	44,179	25,792	24,598	16,573	21,862	46,584	46,805	0	226,393	2,830
Dutch	207,427	216,834	256,851	160,909	144,501	129,776	63,779	22,489	1,202,566	15,032
TOTAL	251,606	242,626	281,449	177,482	166,363	176,360	110,584	22,489	1,428,959	17,862
Tuns of blubber per whale	43	49	33	30	33	37	28	28	36	
Whale oil (in quarters)										
German	67,079	38,688	36,897	24,860	32,793	65,376	70,208	0	335,901	4,199
Dutch	311,141	325,251	385,277	241,364	216,752	194,664	95,668	34,274	1,804,391	22,555
TOTAL	378,220	363,939	422,174	266,224	249,545	260,040	165,876	34,274	2,140,292	26,754

SOURCE: De Jong, *Geschiedenis van de oude Nederlandse walvisvaart*. Calculated from tables in vol. 3.

especially trauma inducing. The extent of collective and individual trauma inflicted by the whalers on the survivors—highly intelligent, highly sociable animals—can only be surmised. By mid–nineteenth century, of the once prolific herds of bowheads in Greenland waters, only a few animals remained.

INDEX

Page numbers in italics refer to illustrations.

voles, 71
volosts (Russian tax districts), 69–70
Vrolicq, Jean, 136
Vulpes species, 9

Wallerstein, Immanuel, xiv
walleyes, 22
walruses, 61, 63, 67, 113–14, 118, 119, 141;
   commercial hunting of, xi, xv–xvi, xviii,
   113, 128–30, 140–41, 145–47; declining
   populations of, xii, 147, 150
wars, 24, 27, 79, 119, 46, 93, 95; of American
   Indians, 2, 17, 24–27, 36, 40, 54;
   American Revolution, 39, 100, 102;
   Napoleonic, 102, 135, 143, 144; of Siberian indigenous peoples, 63, 80
weasels, 71, 82
West Indies, 86, 95, 97, 98, 100, 121
Westos, 33
whalebone, xv, 112–14, 121, 123, 141,
   148–50; markets for, 126, 132, 149; tonnage produced, 144, 145, 148
whale oil, 113, 121, 122, 124–27, 130–38,
   141–45, 148–50
*Whaler "Prince William" on the River Maas, near
   Rotterdam, The* (Verschuier). 137
whales, xvii, 113–18; beluga, 147; bowhead,
   xv, xviii, 107, 114–17, 119–20, 123,
   125–27, 129–48, 150–51, 154; gray, 114;
   hunting (*see* whaling); killer, 116; mink,

151; right, xi, xv, xviii, 107, 114, 117–18,
   122, 125–27, 136–37, 138*n*, 142; sperm,
   114, 145
whaling, xv–xvi, 112–54, *117, 151–53. See
   also* whales; by Basques, 122–27; British,
   and demise of Greenland bowheads,
   143–45; coastal, 130–34; economic benefits of, 147–50; eighteenth-century
   expansion of, 141–43; and exploration in
   northern waters, 127–29; by indigenous
   peoples, 118–22; Martens's account of,
   138–41; open sea and drift ice, 134–38;
   products of (*see* whalebone; whale oil);
   walrus hunting ancillary to, 145–47
Whaling in a Northern Ice Sea (Salm), 137–38
Whitburne, Richard, 102
whitefish, 22
white suckers, 21, 22
Wisconsin, University of, xii
wolverines, 9, 32, 51, 52, 75, 78, 82
wolves, 22, 34, 51–52, 82
world-systems theory, xiv
Woronocos, 18

Yakuts, 64–66, 76–78
Yandins, 67
York Factory, 31
Yukagirs, 67, 76

zooplankton, 87, 107–108, 115, 150*n*, 151